The Philippines

and the

United States:

Problems of Partnership

The Philippines
and the
United States:
Problems of Partnership

by GEORGE E. TAYLOR

Published for the
Council on Foreign Relations
by
Frederick A. Praeger, *Publisher*
New York · London

Frederick A. Praeger, Publisher
64 University Place, New York 3, N.Y., U.S.A.
77-79 Charlotte Street, London W.1, England

Published in the United States of America in 1964
by Frederick A. Praeger, Inc., Publisher

Published in the United Kingdom in 1964
by Frederick A. Praeger, Inc., Publisher

THE PHILIPPINES AND THE UNITED STATES: PROBLEMS OF PARTNERSHIP

For information, address Council on Foreign Relations,
58 East 68th Street, New York 21

FIRST EDITION

Library of Congress catalog card number: 64-12080
Printed in the United States of America
by Quinn & Boden Company, Inc., Rahway, N.J.

Council on Foreign Relations

The Council on Foreign Relations is a non-profit institution devoted to study of the international aspects of American political, economic and strategic problems. It takes no stand, expressed or implied, on American policy.

The authors of books published under the auspices of the Council are responsible for their statements of fact and expressions of opinion. The Council is responsible only for determining that they should be presented to the public.

For a list of Council publications see pages 324 and 325.

Preface

This book is a study of the relations between the United States and the Republic of the Philippines from the point of view of the United States. Its purpose is to clarify the alternatives that are open to the United States in the very special relationship that exists between the two countries. The emphasis is on the present and the future, but I have had to take into account the living past because the quality of the relationship is determined as much by memories of history as by hopes for the future. If something is said of the past, it is of those things that have bearing on the present and the future.

The book has grown rather slowly. In the fall of 1957 the Council on Foreign Relations organized a study group on United States policy and the Philippines. In a series of meetings we discussed most of the issues that are here presented. The extraordinary range of experience represented in this group led to stimulating discussion and the expression of a wide variety of opinion. Our chairman, former Ambassador Myron M. Cowen, brought to our meetings a vigorous leadership and a fine sense of practical politics. It is a pleasure to acknowledge the invaluable assistance not only of the chairman but also of every member of the group, whose enthusiasm and commitment to the task were of decisive importance to the author. The members were: Alexander D. Calhoun, John C. Campbell, Melvin Conant, Myron M. Cowen, Michael J. Deutch, William Diebold, Jr., Julius C. C. Edelstein, John Exter, Charles B. Fahs, Donn V. Hart, William Henderson, Maj. Gen. Leland Hobbs, Alpheus W. Jessup, Lt. Col. Amos Jordan, John Kerry King, Col. Edward G. Lansdale, Paul M. A. Linebarger, Donald H. McLean, Jr., Philip E. Mosely, J. Morden Murphy, Horry F. Prioleau, Albert Ravenholt, Richard W. Reuter, Hon. Edwin F. Stanton, Albert F. Tegen, Merle D. Thompson, Frank N. Trager, and Gordon

B. Tweedey. Reuben H. Gross, Jr., served as rapporteur. Among the guests who were invited on occasion to contribute their special knowledge were: Frank M. Golay, Lt. Col. Hartwell C. Lancaster, Raymond Moyer, and David Warfel.

In the Philippines there were many members of the various U.S. missions and of the business world who were very helpful in securing material and making suggestions. It was a very special privilege to have the opportunity to talk with Ambassador William S. Stevenson. I profited from many conversations with Filipinos from all walks of life. As it is most helpful in any effort to understand another people not only to like them but also to work with them, I owe a great deal to the University of the Philippines and the time I spent there both as a professor and as a consultant to the men who established an Institute of Asian Studies in 1955.

It is important to state that my indebtedness to the study group and to the Americans and Filipinos in the field does not imply any responsibility on their part for the facts and opinions expressed in this book.

My interest in U.S. policy in the Philippines goes back to 1928 when I came to the United States to write a book on that subject but was diverted into the study of China. It revived in a practical way during the war when I was engaged in psychological warfare under Elmer Davis. I became involved more seriously in the study of Philippine affairs as a result of my session at the University of the Philippines 1955-1956. To Philip E. Mosely I owe the suggestion that this book be written; I am most grateful to him for his constant encouragement, advice, and assistance. The very cooperative staff of the Council makes all tasks easier to complete. It is a pleasure to acknowledge the help of my colleague, Karl A. Wittfogel, who read the manuscript, and of my research assistant, Thomas Pasion, a Filipino student of political science, and of Alice C. Russell who prepared the manuscript and attended to innumerable details.

GEORGE E. TAYLOR

Seattle
September 1963

Contents

The Philippines
and the
United States:
Problems of Partnership

Introduction

U.S. Policy, the Philippines, and Asia

In 1934, when the U.S. Congress promised the Filipinos their independence, it expected the Philippines would take its place in dignity and peace as a Christian, democratic, and modern state. No one could have anticipated that the first decade of independence would begin at the close of a world war, with a devastated country, a ruined economy, a corrupted social order, and a people torn by divided loyalties. Least of all could it be foreseen that the American and Filipino peoples would be forced into close alliance as partners in a system of collective security. Practically every assumption about the future development of the Philippines and its relations with the United States has had to be modified, and both sides have been slow to adjust, first to the full implications of Philippine independence and then to the new developments in American policy that were so soon to follow.

It is not generally understood that U.S. policies in Southeast Asia today depend in great measure on a political and military partnership with the Republic of the Philippines, a partnership that began on July 4, 1946, the day the United States restored to the Filipinos the independence they had wrested from Spain in 1898. The major concern of U.S. policy is now to maintain and develop this peculiarly intimate, complex and dynamic relationship. Without it the U.S. position in Southeast Asia would be extremely difficult. Properly handled, it can become a creative instrument of great benefit to both countries and of enormous influence in Asia.

3

The success of the partnership, however, can no longer be taken for granted. In view of the likelihood that the efforts of the Communist bloc to take over Southeast Asia will mount in intensity and of the certainty that the Philippines has entered a period of turbulent domestic growth, marked by strong nationalistic drives, the task will not be easy. It is essential, therefore, that U.S. policy be directed in fact and in theory to the task of imaginative participation in the political and economic development of the Philippines. The fact that the Philippines now enjoys political independence does not necessarily make the task more difficult than it was in the colonial period, since nationalism provides the political dynamism that can change social values and institutions. It may even be easier.

The first condition for successful participation is a purposive evaluation of Philippine affairs based, as much as possible, on a scientific analysis of the problem of economic growth and the nature of the political process. The second condition, which is harder to meet, is to focus the purposes and practices of those institutions that implement U.S. policy—the separate diplomatic, military and economic aid missions—on the main objective of realizing the full potentialities of the partnership between the United States and the Philippines. This calls for a measure of integration that is not now common.

The stakes are high. The Philippine Republic is an essential member of the system of mutual security pacts and of U.S. regional security arrangements for Southeast Asia, as well as a prominent member of the United Nations. The Philippines is a staging area for operations in Southeast Asia, a center for U.S. air forces, a site for naval bases. The Philippines is also of continuing economic importance as a source of raw materials, a market for American products, and a field for American investment. The viability of its economy is a matter of both political and economic concern to the United States.

Most significant of all, however, is the political issue. This has two aspects. At a time when the United States is trying to bolster the political institutions and the economies of the independent countries of Southeast Asia while protecting them from Communist aggression, it is politically essential that these objectives

In a general sense this series of propositions about our economic relations with the underdeveloped part of the world describes the adjustment of the industrially advanced powers to the political emancipation of the colonial world. The imperial powers have come to terms with the passing of imperialism. The United States played an important part in this adjustment and bears the brunt of the counterattack. Since 1954 the Communists have embarked upon a program of foreign aid through barter agreements, technical assistance, and long-term credits, a not inconsiderable effort which has the political objectives of infiltration, subversion, and the discrediting of all foreign aid from non-Communist sources.

Very few former colonies have refused aid of some sort from the industrialized states, most of whom were imperial powers not too long ago. But with very few exceptions, the Philippines for one, most Asian countries are led by men who have spent a good deal of their lives fighting for independence in the belief that imperialism is a manifestation of the highest stage of capitalism and that all capitalism is bad. Nor should we underestimate the appeal to Asian leaders of a thesis which suggests that the problems of the present are due to the ineluctable forces of the past. What appears to Americans as a perfectly natural reaction to a present danger and a realization that our society and prosperity cannot be separated from that of other nations, appears to others as a device by which the United States brings them into the cold war in order to help fight its own battles. Comparatively few Asian countries—Japan, South Korea, South Viet-Nam, Formosa, Thailand, the Philippines, Pakistan—have been willing to accept military missions, formal commitments, and American bases. But those are more than enough to make any generalization about Asian attitudes very speculative. Among the neutralist countries there is good reason to suppose that there is uncertainty about the capacity of the United States to defend them, even with their own assistance, in a time of crisis. These countries also find it hard to identify the "mutual interests" of a powerful capitalist country and a weak, ex-colonial, socialist country situated close to the borders of the Soviet bloc.

Part of the problem lies in the official explanation of U.S. policies. What does "mutual" mean? It is not always easy to persuade even Americans that the United States needs allies, must retain access to vital raw materials and markets, and can ill afford to allow the uncommitted nations to fall into the hands of the Communists. Some $60 billion have been spent since the war in economic aid and mutual security. All too often the explanation of this massive effort is that the security of the United States depends upon our collective security system, which, in turn, depends upon our military assistance program. This is true, as far as it goes. But as a formula it is too simple, limited, and negative. It does not do justice to our policy, and it helps not at all in persuading other countries that the word "mutual" has meaning for them.

Mutual confidence is hard to establish, for most of the countries of Southeast Asia have been colonies for varying lengths of time and their nationalist movements have a history of anti-Western and often anticapitalist feeling. In most of the countries the population is too large in relation to existing methods and levels of production, and capital is both insufficient and misapplied. For these countries to use domestic or foreign capital constructively to modernize their economies, their levels of technology must rise and their value systems must change. In the language of United Nations experts, "Ancient philosophies have to be scrapped; old social institutions have to disintegrate; bonds of cast, creed and race have to be burst." [2] Great courage and skill are required of leaders who would bring these changes about.

It is also true of Asia in general that men who have led successful independence movements often find them disintegrating into rival groups after the achievement of independence. They may lead the struggle against traditional values but offer nothing attractive to put in their place. Sometimes in the aftermath of independence there are only two institutions with the discipline and organization to take over power: the army and the Communist party. The compelling need for national unity in the face of tremendous difficulties may override the individual and national commitment to democratic methods. The leaders who achieved freedom often find themselves poorly equipped to handle the problems of administration, and often the new generation

[2] Brown and Opie, cited, p. 386.

of leaders have other values and different objectives. It is unlikely that there will be continuity of leadership, or widespread agreement on the priorities that must be followed in order to achieve orderly growth, or on which model to adopt.

The leaders of the new countries must thread their way through the intricacies of domestic and international politics. The Communists in the meantime prepare native leaders for this task by training them in the techniques of acquiring and maintaining power, and they provide guidance from the experience of Soviet Russia and Communist China. For many years Americans have thought well of their Philippine experiment because they compared it, rather complacently, with the colonial policies of the other imperial powers. That day, with all its illusions, has long since departed. It is in comparison with Communist models and policies in Asia, not those of Western imperialism, that the words and deeds of the United States are now evaluated.

The United States-Philippine Partnership

The steps that the United States has taken to meet the cold war in Asia have been bold, costly, and moderately successful. Forty-eight hours after the North Korean forces attacked South Korea on June 25, 1950, President Truman issued a policy statement directing that Formosa be neutralized; that military assistance be extended to the Philippine government, to French forces in Indochina, and to the Nationalist Government of China; and that U.S. forces in the Philippines be strengthened. At the same time the President ordered economic assistance to these areas and sent the Bell Mission to the Philippines to draw up a program of economic and administrative reform as a basis for further aid.

The same considerations led to the hastening of negotiations to bring about a change in the status of Japan, the base for United Nations operations in Korea. The treaty of peace with Japan, signed in 1951 and effective in April 1952, permitted the conclusion of a U.S.-Japanese Mutual Security Pact, and under this pact Japan accepted the stationing of American troops as allies on Japanese soil. The United States moved rapidly into the construction of a system of mutual defense treaties, including one with Australia and New Zealand (the ANZUS Pact), and a new defense agreement with the Philippines. It later added a separate defense pact with the Nationalist Government of China and promoted the Southeast Asia Treaty Organization (SEATO), which included the Philippines, Thailand, and Pakistan, together with Britain, France, Australia, and New Zealand. This system of bases and alliances made it possible for the United States to control the Western Pacific.

Changes of this magnitude had serious consequences for the Philippines. It became a very important link in the chain of off-shore bases and a pivotal member of Southeast Asia alliances, but its relative position was not the same. Japan was no longer an occupied and defeated enemy, but an ally of America, one whose industrial capacity was to be strengthened rather than despoiled and whose bargaining position in regard to reparations had improved. The Filipinos looked with suspicion on Japan as an ally of the United States and with jealousy at the amount of economic and military aid extended to it; the Philippine image of Japan as the brutal conquerer could not easily be changed.

The process of readjustment was all the harder for the Filipinos because they felt that the United States had restored their independence under onerous conditions. At a time when they were still struggling with an internal threat from the Communist-led Hukbalahaps, the Bell Mission drew attention to widespread corruption in government, the obstacles to economic development, and the need for land reform. Japan, by contrast, had achieved land reform, adjusted to new political institutions, and started on what was to be one of the most remarkable examples of industrial growth in the world. Which was going to receive the most help and attention—the loyal ally which had fought side by side with the United States throughout the war, or the defeated enemy? The issue was not one that Filipinos wished to have raised, because the contest was uneven. Their strategic and political importance had increased in absolute but not in relative terms, for they were now dealing with a United States that had global responsibilities and commitments. The relatively secure international status enjoyed by the Philippines during the long period when American-Japanese relations were strained, China impotent, and U.S. interests in the rest of Southeast Asia of no great consequence, had come to an end. The rise of a new and hostile power-group in China, the changed position of Japan, and the disappearance of the colonial powers in Southeast Asia, combined with the enormous growth of U.S. involvements in Asia, seemed to many Filipinos to reduce their status, their bargaining power, and their opportunities for leadership in Southeast Asia.

The Filipinos, however, went along with all the major developments of U.S. policy in Asia. They accepted both economic and military aid, refused to recognize Communist China, allowed American forces to remain on Philippine soil, sent troops to fight in Korea, sponsored the Manila Charter, joined SEATO, spoke up for democratic ideals and hopes at Bandung, and in general stood firmly by their former guardian and present ally.

The Philippines did all this at the price of serious differences with Burma and Indonesia, both of which followed a neutral line and refused to accept military aid or join in regional arrangements for collective security. The Philippines was one of the very few Asian countries to reject neutralism, a decision that identified it all the more with the United States and opened it to further charges of being a puppet. No other former colony had behaved in this way and with such enthusiasm. In the face of this evidence it is difficult, at first glance, to argue that any real tensions exist between the Philippines and the United States, if by tensions we mean fundamental and permanent differences in outlook, policy, and national objectives. The commonly held view is that there is no conflict between the two nations on fundamental objectives and that every issue can be accommodated with the help of a little good will on both sides. But good will is not the real point at issue. The problem is one of diverging interests and changing values. The most serious shifts in attitude are not likely to come up for negotiation or attract publicity, and changes can go on unobserved until they suddenly express themselves in totally unexpected forms.

Nationalism, the greatest force for change, has already helped to bring about a shift in the attitudes and aspirations of Filipinos to which the United States has adjusted in a hesitant and awkward manner. But we are only at the beginning of the changes that the new nationalism of the Philippines is going to make, and alternative courses of action now are possible that would have been unthinkable in the first decade of independence. Nationalism is the only force that can provide the dynamism to make a modern society in the Philippines and give to Philippine foreign policy the dignity and independence that will compel the respect of others. It is the task of U.S. policy to ally itself with Philippine nationalism and make it a positive force in the partnership between the two countries.

The spirit of nationalism is a sense of tradition, of common purpose and common values, a sense of community for which men are willing to make great sacrifices. If this is strong, a nation can survive even if the other desirable conditions, such as a well-defined geographical area, a common language, homogeneity of race and religion, are not completely satisfactory. Those who write history can influence tradition; if their image of the past is accepted, they can help to determine the future. In this sense the story of the revolt against Spain and the struggle with the United States is very important, and it is no accident, therefore, that Filipino revisionists are actively attempting to present their history in such a way as to make it a guide to thought and action today. The Filipino people are in a stage of development when books may well make history; the simplicities of anti-Japanese resistance are over and the Filipino nationalism of today is much harder to define or to predict.

For this reason U.S. policy is as much concerned with the creation as with the preservation of the new nation. We are inevitably involved in the internal problems of the new Philippines, even including the intimate task of fabricating the very spirit of nationalism. The United States cannot limit itself in dealing with existing governments to observing the legalities of international law or showing respect for the sensitivities of Asian leaders. The problems of the new nation are all inter-related and participation in their solution is no simple matter. To do it successfully requires, in fact, the coordination of U.S. political, economic, cultural, and military policies for a common purpose.

This takes more than the will to cooperate. The problem is rather a conceptual one of arriving at a common view of U.S. objectives and of the way in which they can be achieved in view of the particular conditions of the country concerned. In the realm of policy we have to clarify the objectives in order to co-ordinate the means. The various arms of policy must be seen as different, not competitive or independent, means by which those objectives can be achieved. The danger is that if there is no agreement on objectives, the economic program may hinder as much as help the political and military. Military and economic missions are in control of such vast amounts of money and materials that they tend to accumulate political influence and objectives of their own and even to overshadow the diplomatic representation.

The economic mission may be endeavoring to assist in the raising of living standards, the application of science to agriculture, the development of a labor force for light and heavy industry, the training of management, social reorganization in the villages, modern banking and credit facilities—in other words, in the re-making of the economic structure of society. Old values are discarded and ancient ways destroyed in the process; new social groupings emerge and find themselves in conflict with the old. In order to succeed, the economic program is bound to bring about social and political dislocation and a great deal of domestic stress and strain. On the other hand, a military mission has to deal with those in power; it is interested in a stable political situation. In some cases, though not in all, the price of political stability is support of groups that are averse to the changes necessary for the success of the economic program. It is quite possible, therefore, for one mission with one set of objectives to undermine another mission with another set of objectives. Some of the problems in our relations with the Philippines have arisen from factors such as these; from the failure, in other words, to coordinate American policy within the framework of overriding political objectives.

If the military, economic, and political missions all had the same concept of American purposes in the Philippines, half the battle would be won; but there remains the second question of how to achieve these purposes. This is a problem of understanding the nature of the forces at work in the Philippines and of taking them into account when devising policy. This is not easy to do if slogans such as "the Philippines is the show window of democracy" are substituted for a carefully coordinated program based on an orderly evaluation of the social and political forces at work in the country. Because our relations with the Philippines have been so intimate, the need for careful analysis of our objectives and of the way in which they can be achieved is so great. There is, to be sure, a large measure of overt agreement between Americans and Filipinos on such fundamental matters as democracy, free enterprise, communism, civil liberties, freedom of the press, and collective security. There is no denying that many Americans and Filipinos share a common view of the good society and even of the good life, but there are also important differences which lie concealed beneath the surface and which are all the more difficult to identify because of the very real area of agreement.

Despite fifty years of colonial administration, it is amazing how little we know of the Filipino. If our understanding of Filipino values rarely rises above the pragmatic level, this is partly the consequence of earlier assumptions that it hardly mattered what Filipino values might be, as they were soon to be replaced with American ones. The assumption that the introduction of science and the idea of progress, combined with access to the world market, would make all people alike was based on the fallacies that Asian societies were merely at an earlier stage in the unilinear development of all societies, and that the values and institutions of Western civilization, once introduced into Asian societies, would grow and flourish by virtue of their own intrinsic merit.

It is clear today that in spite of its debts to Spain and the United States, Philippine society has distinguishing features of its own; that institutions with familiar names do not have the same content; and that men using the same symbols do not always give them the same meaning. It is clear that there is a unique Philippine society that is neither a little America nor a little Asia, and that the first condition of our understanding it is to accept Philippine cultural distinctness and political independence in fact as well as in name. That this is difficult for the small number of Americans who cannot get rid of the "little brown brother" attitude, or for the few Filipinos who continue to behave as colonials, is not important. The main fact is that in order to formulate an effective policy for the Philippines we shall certainly have to understand the character and ideological content of Filipino nationalism. For fifty years the United States imposed upon the Filipino people its own concept of what a nation should be, and large elements in this concept have been accepted. But today the Filipinos themselves are deciding who they are and where they are going, and it is with this issue that they are more and more engaged. It is the theme of much of their art and literature, of their religious life, and of all discussions of educational policy, domestic politics, and foreign relations. It nags at the Filipino in his endless conflicts over the national language, and it confronts him at every national election; it haunts him, especially in Asia, when he travels abroad. The search for national identity is the basic problem of the Filipino, and therefore of United States relations with the Philippines.

Part I

Emergence of the Issues

Chapter 1

The People and Their Land

The Specter of Overpopulation

The Republic of the Philippines is unique in its combination of Asian and Western cultures, but it shares with most of its Asian neighbors the problems of overpopulation, mass poverty, and unfulfilled nationalism. This raises the question of whether or not the Philippines can win the race between the rate of economic growth and the rate of population increase.

It is a very difficult race to win. The annual increase of population in the Philippines is 3.25 per cent, one of the highest in the world. There were 7.5 million Filipinos in 1902, 11 million in 1922, 17 million in 1942, and 29 million in 1962. If this rate of growth continues, in 1982 there will be 55 million, and twenty years after that, 105 million. The increase in the rate is due largely to improved public health measures which have lowered infant mortality, increased life expectancy, and eliminated most of the contagious diseases that formerly kept the population down. The sad irony is that the millions who now survive to swell the population are not very well nourished or healthy, and they lack stamina and initiative. Yet it is they who must help to solve the problem of economic survival.

President Macapagal raised the population question in his State of the Nation address of 1962. According to him, merely to maintain present consumption levels—which already are below nutritional standards—the Philippines will have to increase rice production by 1.56 million cavans (about 3.3 million bushels) per year, meat by 14 million kilos, and milk and dairy products by 11 million pounds, a not inconsiderable task. Fifty years hence,

122 million Filipinos will be crowded into 297,410 square kilometers (some 115,000 square miles), which is about 800 square meters per person. Yet the Philippines, which cannot feed its present population, has made no national effort to reduce the fantastic rate of population increase. In its issue of March 3, 1962, the *Philippine Free Press,* a national weekly that has been publicizing the population problem, carried a statement on birth control by a Catholic theologian to the effect that the Church agreed with the objectives of birth control but was against methods other than natural ones. Catholics are not urged to beget as many children as possible; on the contrary, Pope Pius XII has said that it is possible to be exempt from the obligation of bearing children if there are medical, eugenic, economic, or social "indications," such as ability to provide for children and the degree of population density of a country. It would seem that something could be built on this statement in the Philippines, a strongly Roman Catholic country, but success would depend on the enthusiastic backing of the Church.[1]

Large families were necessary in countries where agriculture depended on the application of human capital to the land and where the death rate was kept high by disease, lack of medical knowledge or facilities, violence, and natural disasters. Children represented capital, insurance, and old-age compensation; and in the Philippines they still do. The trouble is that law and order and public health measures have outdistanced the social and institutional changes that reduce the incentives to produce more children, such as an increase in the application of capital to the land and a general modernization of the economy. This is likely to be a frantic race even if the country is fully determined to succeed.

Poverty is not new to most Asians. What is new is the consciousness of relative poverty due to the economic advances of the West, and the discovery that poverty is not simply a natural condition of man. Filipinos make no effort to conceal the grinding poverty of the poor or the ostentation of the rich. In his mes-

[1] Edward Kiunisala, "Too Many Filipinos," *Philippine Free Press,* March 3, 1962 (Manila: Philippine Free Press, Inc.), pp. 10-11, 30, 50. (Hereafter cited as *Free Press.*)

sage to the National Assembly, October 18, 1937, President Manuel Quezon made some remarks on "social justice" that are often recalled in the Philippines today:

The rich can live in extravagant luxury. Some of their offspring grow up in an atmosphere of ease, with an outlook on life which gives paramount importance to society affairs, vanities, trivialities and material possessions devoid of discipline, love for work or human sympathy. The middle class have attained a higher standard of living as compared with that prevailing during the Spanish regime. The comforts of present-day civilization are within their reach and they are enjoying them. Their sons and daughters are better fed, better clothed, better educated—thousands upon thousands of them are now receiving the benefits of higher instruction.

Sad to tell, but it is none the less true, the same cannot be said of our laboring population. The men and women who till the soil or work in the factories are hardly better off now than they were during the Spanish regime . . .

The Filipino laborer now knows that the Father of mankind loves him as much as every other human being, and, therefore, that the world has not been made for the benefit of a few, but for the happiness of all.

Still more: The Filipino workingman has heard, if he is not able to read, of the equality before the law of the poor and the rich. He has heard of democracy, liberty and justice, since every candidate for an elective office discourses on these topics, painting to him in glowing terms the meaning of those words.

And yet, what does he actually see? How do these doctrines that he has heard propounded from the platform affect his every day life. His hopes have been broadened, and his outlook has been painted in bright colors. But thirty-five years of American regime has brought him only disappointments and, sometimes, despair . . .[2]

The annual per capita income of the Filipino, according to United Nations figures, is $200 (as compared with $50 in Laos and Burma, $60 in Indonesia, India and Pakistan, $150 in South Korea and South Viet-Nam, $350 in Malaya, and $400 in Singapore. Allowing for the fact that many grow their own food and spend little on heat, housing, and clothes, this is still grinding poverty. Filipinos are asking themselves what can be done.

[2] Theodore Friend, "What Kind of Nationalist was Manuel L. Quezon?" *Manila Sunday Times Magazine*, August 17, 1958, p. 13.

More than half of the four million families in the Philippines receive less than ₱80, or about $20 a month. About six million persons can be counted as being on a starvation diet. According to the Social Welfare Administration, there are more than three million physically handicapped persons dependent on others for a livelihood.[3] According to the 1958 Survey of Households, more than one-half of all wage and salary workers earn about ₱2, or a little over fifty cents a day. Out of eleven million who have to earn a living, said Vice-President Emmanuel Pelaez, about 730,000 have no source of livelihood whatsoever. With a labor force growing at the rate of 3.4 per cent a year it is possible that within fifteen years there will be six million unemployed and underemployed, and three-fourths of these will be in the rural areas. The gap between the living standards of the urban and the rural areas is probably going to get wider as time goes on. President Macapagal, who promised to find a job for everyone, has a stupendous task ahead of him and the administration is thinking frantically about the problem.[4] The Congress passed his ₱100 million employment bill because many Filipinos know that if unemployment is not drastically reduced, there will be a social explosion. But this was only a beginning.

Natural Resources

The Philippine environment, it is usually assumed, provides all that is necessary to produce a good living for its inhabitants. Actually the Filipinos have only just begun to explore their natural resources, and there is not, today, a basic inventory of either the human or the natural resources of the country.[5] From what is known, however, a close look at the climate, soils, minerals, and topography does not fully support the popular view that all tropical lands are lush and productive, that everything grows

[3] Teodoro M. Locsin, "The Challenge of Poverty," *Free Press,* April 21, 1962, pp. 2-3, 94.

[4] Edward Kiunisala, "The Hungry Millions," *Free Press,* April 28, 1962, pp. 20-21; Edward Kiunisala, "Wanted: Two Million Jobs," *Free Press,* June 2, 1962, pp. 2-3, 33, 36, 49-50.

[5] Human Relations Area Files, *Area Handbook on the Philippines,* v. 1 (New Haven: Author, under Sub-contract HRAF-1, Chi-1, 1956), p. 23.

and nature is bountiful.[6] Some of the assets, however, are clearly observable. While the climate is not attractive to those brought up in the temperate zone, it is adequate for agriculture. There are areas where the soils are good and agriculture can be highly productive, as some enterprising farmers have shown. Soils and climate are good for the growing of rice, corn, sugar, abacá, coconuts, rubber, pineapple, tobacco, and spices. Cotton and ramie also can be grown. Dairy farming is possible in certain areas.

There are great possibilities for hydroelectric power, some of which are being developed. There are adequate deposits of iron ore, gold, copper, silver, and chrome. The waters surrounding the seven-thousand-odd islands of the Philippines can provide enough fish for the needs of the population. The forest growth is plentiful and includes many hardwoods and other valuable species, including some very fast-growing bamboos. There are those who would also count among the assets of the Philippines its beautiful scenery, on which could be based a sizable tourist industry.

But there are shortcomings, such as the lack of significant supplies of coal and petroleum, although exploration for the latter still continues and valuable resources may yet be found. In the event that solar energy could be economically harnessed, the Philippines would be in an advantageous position.

Although the physical base could be better, it is certainly adequate, if properly used, to provide a higher living standard for the present population, and possibly for more. But it will require substantial changes in attitude and approach to take full advantage of what nature has provided.

Whatever the quality of their natural heritage the Filipinos have not used it to the greatest advantage. While there may be enough land for everyone if it is divided equally among the people, the problem of soils depleted by poor cultivation methods still remains. There is serious soil erosion on 75 per cent of the land.[7] One of the most effective ways of depleting soils and erod-

[6] Benjamin Higgins, *Economic Development* (New York: W. W. Norton and Co., 1959), pp. 267 ff.

[7] J. E. Spencer, *Land and People in the Philippines* (Berkeley: University of California Press, 1954), p. 49.

ing hillsides is to practice what the Filipinos call "caingin cultivation," or shifting agriculture, which still proceeds on a large
scale. It can be practiced without too much damage if nature
is given plenty of time to restore the resources taken out of the
soil by the short-term cultivators, but that margin has long since
been passed in the Philippines. There is a strong likelihood that
more arable land is ruined every year through misuse than is
newly brought under cultivation. Nor has the settled agriculturist
used much fertilizer or paid much attention to the application of
science to the land.[8] Even the limited knowledge we have of the
soils of the Philippines makes it obvious that there is an urgent
need for soil conservation, restriction of caingin agriculture, pre-
vention of erosion, and protection of the now all too rapidly exploited forests.

In this lush and fruitful land most of the population lives on
a monotonous diet of rice and fish, in neither of which, however, is the Philippines self-sufficient. Of the twenty-four countries that produce rice in quantity, the Philippines, which produces an average of 26 cavans of rice per hectare compared with
92 for Japan, is almost at the bottom of the list. Yet it would
take only a modest improvement in agricultural techniques and
the use of capital, combined with the removal of certain political
obstacles, to produce a surplus of rice. The same is true of fish,
one of the main sources of protein in the diet of the Filipinos
as it is of the Japanese. Fishing is actually more of a sideline to
agriculture than an independent industry. The methods used are
very simple, involve little capital investment, and are not highly
productive. The extensive use of dynamite in fishing destroys
fish at the source, and it is estimated that not more than 10 per
cent of those killed are actually brought in. The Philippines imports canned fish; yet if commercial fishing were improved and a
canning industry developed, there would be no difficulty in
producing more than enough fish for the needs of the country
and for export.

President Macapagal has pointed out on various occasions
that it is preposterous for the Philippines to be unable to produce enough rice, fish, and other staples to feed its own people

[8] Same, p. 53.

for the islands are better endowed than many countries in the resources necessary for life. It will require a new attitude toward the use of those resources, however, if the Philippines is going to improve the livelihood of its people. The task is difficult. The Filipinos have yet to solve the most fundamental problems of all, those of food, shelter, and social justice.

The Human Resources

The common man, or *tao,* as he is called in the national tongue, comprises possibly 70 to 80 per cent of the population and lives in barrios of 500 to 1,000 persons, in relative isolation from other barrios and without roads, electricity, or public services. The typical dwelling is a nipa hut which is usually built off the ground on poles and is as unsanitary as it is picturesque. By Western standards such housing costs very little to construct or maintain, but for men who live from day to day it represents a considerable capital investment. The tao lives without privacy, a whole family in one room. The tao wears short cotton pants, a straw hat, and carries a bolo; he seldom owns a pair of shoes. He cannot afford enough to eat; he has no money to get professional attention for his teeth or general health, or to buy more than a few of the necessities of life. If he can read or write he is one of the lucky ones. It is he and his like who make the statistic that 70 per cent of all Filipinos have tuberculosis at some stage or other.

The tao also gives some substance to the statistic that the Philippines is a Catholic country, but his practice is probably animism, a belief that the spirits in the rocks and trees are very real forces that have to be treated with respect. He gives his mite to the Church for the ceremonies of birth, marriage, and death, but he pays his respects to the spirits by appeasing or avoiding them in his daily routine. His outlook is circumscribed—far beyond the comprehension of the educated urbanite even in the Philippines. He knows who his enemies are, and they are within easy reach, except for the absentee landlord living in the provincial town or in Manila.

President Magsaysay, who did not come from a very poor family, glamorized the tao and rode to victory on his votes. Diosdado

Macapagal, who also was not a tao though he went barefoot to school, secured an education with the help of a sponsor and rose to be president. No barriers of race, caste, or creed block the way of the lowest from rising to the position of the highest in the land. But the bulk of the common people do not find this fact of any great importance as their condition is no better today, according to such studies as we have, than it was under Spanish rule.

The common man is not even a hero in Philippine literature; in fact, he is almost forgotten except as background material. Writing at the height of the Huk rebellion, José Y. Ortega called for something more significant in literature, in words that would be equally appropriate today:

Let our writers turn to the peasant and write of him in terms of the brutal narrowness, emptiness and misery of his life, and not treat him as a rather quaint character in a folk tale. . . . Let our writers begin to depict the sterile horror that is life in a provincial town, with its cultural waste, its rigid caste system, its ruthless gossip. . . . Let our writers turn to the Tondo slum and etch the spectacle of filth, despair, privation and degradation that makes the very act of remaining alive a triumph. Let us have the labor leader, the peasant leader, the dissident and revolutionist, spoken of with candor along with the large truths that bring them into being. Where in our literature is the honest portrait of an hacendero, a wealthy business man, a politician, a collaborator, a querida, a corrupt official? [9]

As far as literature is concerned the common man is still much more of a statistic than a person.

The tao has no reserves of capital, energy, or initiative. He can take no risks even if he knew what should be done to improve his lot; and although he knows something about rising levels of expectation, he does not know very much about the concept of a Philippine Republic. In some areas, such as Central Luzon, the center of agrarian unrest, he takes his lot with sullen resignation, breaking out into sadistic violence against landlords and moneylenders when the limits of frustration have been reached. In other areas, where the situation is less tense, the tao is cheerful if not op-

[9] Jose G. Ortega, "For a Significant Filipino Literature," *Literary Apprentice*, v. 14, no. 2, March 1950 (Quezon City: University of the Philippines), pp. 54-55.

timistic, but violence is always close to the surface and often takes the form of "running amok," a custom to which society has long been resigned.

Only recently has the tao attracted the attentions of the historians, for he took no recognized part in the making of history. Teodoro A. Agoncillo and Oscar M. Alfonso, however, bring the tao in for some remarkably frank treatment in their textbook *A Short History of the Filipino People*.

[The *tao*] has been, since Spanish times, the object of ridicule, contempt, and, at best, pity. He has been the victim of injustices, brutality, and all sorts of unnameable barbarism, but, like the carabao that symbolizes him, he suffers all those with abundant patience and amiable tolerance. In all difficult undertakings, as in the Spanish pacification campaigns and expeditions to foreign lands, in the American campaigns against the Muslims, and in the Filipino participation in World War II, he has been a beast of burden. The backbone of the nation, his voice has nevertheless been unheard in all matters that pertain to the national welfare. He has unlimited duties, but his rights have been circumscribed either by property qualifications or by literacy requirements. During election time, his role has been passive: during the Spanish period, he had no vote but paid burdensome taxes nevertheless; during the American and the Filipino periods, he raised—and still raises—food for the nation but has been ignored by those in authority. Nobody has seemed to think of him; the life he leads has been the life his ancestors led. There has been, since the American occupation, a little change in his earning capacity but his purchasing power has remained the same, comparatively speaking, so that actually there has been negligible change for the better in his way of life.

For almost four hundred years he had lived the life of the dumb beast of burden. His grievances accumulated and when a leader came around to remind him of his destitution he unburdened himself by grasping anything within reach and shedding his blood for his redemption. Those in power have looked upon this resort to arms as an aberration, a pure lunacy, and an attempt to seize the authority of the state by illegal means. No one in the government ever thought of honestly examining the causes of his discontent; it was enough that he took up arms against those in power to condemn him as dissident, bandit, and highway robber. Invariably, swift punishment is meted out to him to teach him a lesson in social cohesion, which means conformity in all respects with what the upper classes decide. The result of such a policy has been the degradation of the *tao* and his acquisition of habits of thought that spell negligence, indolence, and *bahala na* attitude, a fatalism augmented by ignorance and religious fanaticism.[10]

During the presidency of Ramón Magsaysay the tao, for the first time in his history, was given a small but glamorous place in the sun. The President took the unprecedented step of inviting everyone to visit Malacañang, the presidential palace, and many poor, common people accepted the invitation, much to the horror of officials and legislators who preferred not to be so close to the masses. An invitation to send telegrams, free of charge, to the President about any matters of complaint produced nearly 60,000 telegrams in one year. On one occasion the President held a cabinet meeting in a barrio.

Magsaysay was dramatizing, apparently with some success, the concern of the government for the welfare of the common man. He has been criticized, probably with some justice, as not dramatizing the corollary that the common man must do things for himself if the government is going to be able to give him effective assistance. But this criticism is as nothing when measured against Magsaysay's main contribution: the projection of self-respect and dignity into the outlook of the peasantry. His concern for the tao was genuine, spontaneous, and consistent. For this he was hated by the elite, to whom the masses are beneath contempt, and dismissed as something of a simple-minded buffoon. The elite finds it as difficult to conceive of the tao having anything whatsoever to offer society as the tao finds it difficult to believe that the government has any interest in him other than work and taxes. The blindness of the one is matched by the blindness of the other.

Magsaysay, however, seems to have had a permanent effect on the outlook of the common people. His personal warmth is legendary; his support of barrio autonomy, of cooperatives, rural banks, and reform of tenure and land titles has become a point of reference for later reformers. The aristocratic concern of Quezon followed by the humanitarian approach of Magsaysay may have been necessary steps toward the present hope, otherwise unthinkable, that rural leadership might come from the rural areas rather

[10] Teodoro A. Agoncillo and Oscar M. Alfonso, *A Short History of the Filipino People* (Quezon City: University of the Philippines, 1960), pp. 532-533.

than from Manila. If that should happen, the tao can help to make democracy possible in the Philippines; if it should not, then antidemocratic forces will organize the peasantry in other ways and for other purposes.

It may be no exaggeration to say that unless the Filipinos can immediately reduce their birthrate, any hopes they may have of improving their material conditions will be vain. Even if they can slow down the increase in population, which is doubtful, they must, as they themselves recognise, carry out an ambitious social and economic program over a long period of time with skill and resolution. To do this requires a high level of leadership and a dedicated group of men who can stay in power, which means that they must get themselves elected. There must also be other men outside government, other leaders, who promote the objectives of the program in their own way and in their own sector of society. This combination of men and circumstances came one step closer to realization in 1961 with the election of Macapagal to the presidency. If history is any guide, the Philippines will not fail because of any lack of leaders of the quality that the situation demands. Not all Americans are aware that the Filipinos have produced leaders who compare with those of any other country in talent, vision, and courage.

Today there are enough Filipinos trained in the professions and in government to construct a modern state with democratic institutions. And the social basis of leadership is broad enough to make it possible for a man to rise from the very poor, as did President Macapagal. The Philippine Republic certainly has the human resources to solve its problems, and it has the political dynamism of nationalism. Nationalism can remain narrowly based, or it can broaden its base to include the tao. If the leaders of the Philippines should decide to include him in the nationalist movement, there are no difficulties that cannot be overcome.

Chapter 2

The Beginnings of Nationalism

The quality of Philippine nationalism is the single most important concern of U.S. policy in the Philippines today. National consciousness, a composite of many different attitudes and values, is the one essential ingredient in the making of a nation. Without it there can be no effective nationalism, and without effective nationalism there cannot be a successful Philippine Republic. It is no easy task to determine the nature of nationalism in the Philippines, for the national consciousness of the Filipinos took shape under conditions without parallel in the modern world. The results are unique: rarely has history bequeathed to a people so mixed and contradictory a heritage. But the Filipino cannot change his past; he has to take his history as it happened and use it to discover himself and clarify his national memory. The influence of Philippine history on the character of Philippine nationalism is therefore determined, to some extent, by the way in which it is being interpreted today.

The story of the Philippines before independence falls naturally into three main periods: the pre-Spanish, the Spanish, and the American. Until recently the small band of Filipino writers interested in the past has been very much influenced by Spanish and American writers, who have naturally tended to emphasize the part that their respective countries have played in the Philippines. The present generation of Filipino writers and historians somewhat self-consciously takes the point of view of the Filipinos and changes the perspective and the analysis accordingly.

The Pre-Spanish Period

In their efforts to identify the unique traditions and achievements of their people, Filipino scholars are examining as never
before two periods of their history. One is the pre-Spanish period,
which they describe, with good reason, in much more attractive
terms than has been customary; the other is the revolution against
Spain at the end of the nineteenth century. For both periods
there is a new interpretation. In the Philippines, as in other parts
of the world, the Spaniards certainly did their best to destroy
what there was in the way of an indigenous culture and to implant, quite successfully, a sense of inferiority among the Filipinos about their own past. It is not surprising, then, that the
Filipinos today do not always do justice to the Spanish record
and tend to romanticize the pre-Spanish period.

In a typical example of this reaction, one author argues that
before the coming of the Spaniards the Philippines was well-pop-
ulated, and the people industrious and commercially active with
all neighboring countries. "Morga, Chirino, Colin, Argensola,
Gaspar de San Augustin of the earlier colonial period, and observers two hundred fifty years later, were unanimous, according
to Rizal, that Filipinos in spite of the climate were not the in-
dolent creatures of a latter-day epoch, their ethics and mode of
life not what later were attributed to them." [1] It was the Spaniards, he claims, who reduced the size of the population with
their military adventures and economic practices and destroyed
the incentives to work. Colonialism is therefore the cause of Philippine poverty, indolence, and corruption, and what the Spaniards started the Americans continued.

There is increasing evidence, especially from the work of
American scholars such as Otley Beyer and Ralph Fox, that the
pre-Spanish period was richer in cultural and material achievements and in contacts with the rest of the world than Spanish
historians would have us think. Furthermore, according to John
Leddy Phelan, the American historian, "Pre-conquest society

[1] Frederico Mangahas, "The Economics of Philippine Culture," *Comment*,
no. 5, First Quarter, 1958 (Manila: Regal Printing Co., Inc.), pp. 64-75.

was not swept away by the advent of the Spanish regime . . . significant elements of the old culture blended into the new society emerging under Spanish auspices, and in many cases took forms contrary to the wishes of the new regime. . . . Although partially Hispanized, they never lost the Malaysian stratum which to this day remains the foundation of their culture." [2] Unquestionably, much of the pre-Spanish culture survived the conquest, but when the Spaniards came, there was neither a nation nor a state.[3] There were isolated heroes such as Lapu-Lapu, who killed Magellan, but the Spaniards eventually conquered the Philippines with only a few hundred men. Yet their superior firepower would not have sufficed if Filipinos had not been willing to fight Filipinos. Even such a self-conscious nationalist historian as Teodoro Agoncillo makes no claims for national unity before the nineteenth century. In short, the pre-Spanish period provides the nationalist not with the glories, say, of ancient China but with a memory of which there is no need to be ashamed.

The Legacy of Spain

Spain gave to the Filipinos one of the first essentials of nationhood, a national entity. Under Spanish rule the Philippines could be identified in geographical, political, and international terms. But because the Filipinos had little or nothing to do with the achievement of what most nations have fought and bled for, this most elementary condition of all is no source of national pride.[4]

[2] John Leddy Phelan, *The Hispanization of the Philippines* (Madison: University of Wisconsin Press, 1959), pp. 8, 26.

[3] Robert B. Fox, "The Pre-Historic Filipino Village," *Progress Magazine 1960* (Manila: Manila Times Publishing Co., 1960), pp. 162-166.

[4] The authors of a textbook on Philippine history for freshmen at the University of the Philippines are quite frank to say that they dismiss the Spanish period in three chapters because most of the documents before 1872 deal with the history of Spain in the Philippines, not with the history of the Filipinos. For the same reason they deal briefly with Philippine "representation" in the Spanish Cortes because the representative was chosen from among the Spaniards born in the Philippines, or *insulares* (who were actually called "Filipinos" by European-born Spaniards), while the true native Filipinos, or *indios,* had nothing to do with the selection. To the authors, Philippine history before 1872 is a lost history; the real story begins with the revolt against Spain.

It was the Spaniards, not the Filipinos, who decided that these 7,000 islands, strung out between Formosa to the north and Borneo and Indonesia to the south, should be a political unit under a central administration linked to the Spanish throne.

The centralization of political, ecclesiastical, and economic power in Manila strongly influenced the character of that Philippine nationalism which Spain successfully held in check for two centuries. In handling the many different ethnic and linguistic groups of the Philippines, the Spanish administration employed the old technique of divide and rule, and even denied to the Filipinos the unifying influence of access to the language of the conqueror. Having conquered the Philippines cheaply because the inhabitants were disunited, the Spaniards certainly had no intention of encouraging the growth of a national consciousness. But the Spaniards did not leave the regional ethnic and linguistic groups as they found them. They took away from the regional groups their local political autonomy; they permitted regionalism to continue as an expression not of the strength but of the weakness of local government. Their rule was marked by a lack of participation by the majority of the population in the process of government and, what is worse, by the absence of any expectation of participation. The decisions were made in Manila; they still are. In the general population, the Spaniards left behind them habits of submission and obedience and an inability to take political initiative and responsibility—habits which are deadly enemies of democracy and which are very slow to change even when democratic institutions have been substituted for centralized autocracy.

The special relationship between church and state under Spanish rule was based on a denial of political or ideological pluralism. It was as much through the church as through the Civil Guards that Spain administered the island. The imposition of Roman Catholicism and the extension of political power went hand-in-hand: those inhabitants who were not converted to the Roman Catholic persuasion and brought "within sound of the bells," the mountain tribes and the Moslems, were only nominally under Spanish rule. The authority of church and state was coterminous. The officials of both spoke Spanish, the language of the ruling class, and no one else was expected to be literate in any language. (And for this reason the demand that all should be permitted to learn Spanish was one of the first objectives of Philippine nationalists.) The centralization of political and ecclesiastical power imposed a structural unity on the population of the Philippine Islands that had never been known before and inevitably suggested the possibility of a Philippine nation state.

The Roman Catholic Church trained Filipinos in the articles of the faith, but for loyalty to the international church it depended upon foreign priests. In most of the Philippines the Spanish clergy faced no opposition from large-scale political or religious organizations. Where they did meet organized resistance, as with the Moslems, the clergy had very little success. Where they succeeded, primarily in the lowlands and coastal areas, it was because they came to terms with the existing Filipino loyalties which are based on kinship.

Anthropologists believe that the two basic units of Philippine society today, the elementary family of father, mother, and children and the bilateral extended family with its network of primary relationships that include all relatives of the mother and father, were also characteristic of the pre-Spanish Filipino communities. There were no clans or similar unilateral groupings, for each person reckoned his relationship, as now, with both the paternal and maternal kin-groups.[5] The main conflict was that between rival kinship groups, and there is still much of that today. The social problem of dealing with nonmembers of the kin group was handled through elaborate rules of hospitality and a highly structured language of courtesy. Decision-making was mainly in the hands of the older generation, and respect for the older generation is still an important factor in interpersonal relationships in the Philippines.

It would seem that the basic values of Philippine life have continued from pre-Spanish times, and while they have been adapted to Spanish and American influences, there has always been something very significant that can be identified as Philip-

[5] Human Relations Area Files, *Area Handbook on the Philippines,* v. 1 (New Haven: Author, under Sub-contract HRAF-1, Chi-1, 1956), p. 415. (Hereafter cited as *HRAF Handbook.*)

pine. According to modern scholarship this quality in Philippine society, the adaptive character of the bilateral type of Philippine social structure, which is not unlike structures found in the highly urbanized and industrialized societies of America and Europe, has always been potentially dynamic because it did not develop rigid and embracing institutions.[6] Indeed, it is arguable that during the Spanish period the Philippine family system, providing as it did an acceptable base for an authoritarian ecclesiastical and political system, was strengthened rather than weakened. For one thing, the church civilized and honored the family by providing orderly ceremonies and ritual for all family affairs. The state protected the authority patterns of the family structure with the power and prestige of the Civil Code, which strongly supported the authority of the father over the children and transferred to the teacher, who was usually a priest, powers equivalent to those of the parent. Nor did economic developments do anything to undermine the family system, for those economic activities which might have led to stresses and strains were undertaken by Spaniards and Chinese. What the Spaniards did, in effect, was to compensate for the mutual antagonisms of kin groups, the main fault of the Philippine kinship structure, by relating all kin groups to church and state, thus making it possible for the Filipinos to become accustomed to a sense of community and, eventually, of nationalism.

Nationalism also owed much to the economic developments under Spanish rule. When the Spaniards came to the islands in the sixteenth century, they found scattered settlements based on sedentary agriculture and some fishing, with barter exchange and no market mechanism. The level of technology was low even in comparison with neighboring Asian countries. The economy was constricted, apparently, by the limitations of the social and political system and by the small kinship groups in which economic functions were related more to social status than to the needs of a free market. Such economic relationships as there were with the outside world were dominated mainly by foreigners, the Moslems, who had trading settlements in Manila and Cebu.

6 Same, p. 203.

The Spaniards modified the social and political organization in the direction of a unified theocratic system, and this, combined with considerable technological advances in agriculture and industry, laid the foundations of a national economy. Through the Spaniards the Filipinos acquired many new plants (notably tobacco, American corn, and cassava), new techniques like the use of stone for construction of government buildings and churches, and methods of organizing large labor forces. If these changes had led to the destruction of the small local economic and social units, there would have been serious implications for the family structure; but they did not do so. The Spaniards took some payments in kind, but they took much more in labor service for the construction of churches, government buildings, and galleons. Apart from draining off the agricultural surplus and using *corvée* labor, the Spaniards left the existing settlements as they found them and had no further economic plans for the Philippines, once it was clear that spices and minerals were not abundant. The one major exception was the development of Manila as an entrepôt for the China trade—really a trade between the silver-rich New Spain and China—a trade that led to further development of Manila and to the neglect of the economy of the Philippines.

Not until the nineteenth century was the colony, including the hinterland, opened to world trade. Following this fundamental change in policy, Chinese and Westerners poured into the Philippines to take advantage of the new opportunities for domestic commerce. The former came principally as retailers; the latter, as merchants, bankers, shippers, and technicians. Production for the world market came to be organized not by the old chieftains of the kin-affiliated settlements but by a new class of landlords drawn mainly from the chiefs but also from Chinese who intermarried with Filipinos and dropped their Chinese connections. (Many of the most important men in recent Philippine history are partly of Chinese lineage, for example, Rizal, Quirino, Quezon.)

On his hacienda the landlord tended to take over the powers that the chieftain had, and as there was no one in the provinces to dispute the authority that he had arrogated to himself, land-lordism emerged as a new socio-economic phenomenon of great importance. So much is said about the evils of landlordism in the Philippines that it is well to remind ourselves that the unscrupulous land-grabbing and extra-legal powers of the new class made possible important economic developments that might not otherwise have come about. The landlords collected rent instead of tribute and introduced new crops and grew old ones for market. They took the leadership in bringing the hinterland into contact with the outside world and in changing the old subsistence economy. They were the Filipino elite at the time the Spanish occupation came to an end, the class that produced the *ilustrados*,[7] the leaders of the Commonwealth period, and the big family empires that until recently dominated Philippine politics —the Cuencos, Osmeñas, Laurels. They have been the main bearers of Philippine culture even though they have shared control of the economy with two other important groups, the Spaniards and the Chinese.

By the end of the Spanish period social, political, and economic power and prestige were combined to a remarkable degree in the hands of this one class of mixed Malay, Chinese, and Spanish blood. Its economic base was in land ownership, and it exercised over the other class, the peasantry, complete social and political as well as economic control. The widespread landlord-tenant relationship was much more than a contractual one; in return for acknowledgement of his wealth and authority the landlord was expected to help the tenant at times of crisis or religious celebration. But the contrast between the small upper class and the rest of the population in wealth, education, justice, political participation, and human comforts was one of the most extreme in Asia. It still is, at least economically. There was little if any

[7] Luisa H. A. Linsangan, "Our Changing Leisure Class," *Progress Magazine 1959* (Manila: Manila Times Publishing Co., 1959), p. 163. The term *ilustrado* meant more than mere intellectual superiority. The word suggested a whole way of life: a well-appointed home in the city, a large estate in the province, sojourns in Europe, a knowledge of the arts, and an awareness of political and economic trends across the seas. Obviously this was the ideal type, and the term was used more loosely to include men of less wealth; but intellectual superiority was always the essential element.

social mobility upwards. To all intents and purposes the Spaniards left behind them a two-class system.

The opening up of the Philippines to world contacts also resulted in students going to various countries of Asia and Europe. There they became aware of the revolutionary movements of nationalism and liberalism that were spreading even to Spain. Among those who took advantage of study abroad were the mestizos, the product of interbreeding between Spaniards, Chinese, and Filipinos, who were looking for doctrines that would aid them in improving their position in the Philippines, for they considered themselves superior to the Malay stock, yet were not fully accepted by the pure-blooded Spaniards.

Revolt Against Spain

Nationalism in the Philippines came into its own with the revolutionary period of the second half of the nineteenth century. National pride in this period is shown by the fact that of the 36 commemorations listed in the school calendars, 22 occurred between 1872 and 1899 or are the birthdays of patriots active at that time.[8] One item dates from April 27, 1521, when Lapu-Lapu killed Magellan. In 1962 President Macapagal issued an order changing the date for the celebration of Philippine Independence from July 4 to June 12 in order to commemorate the occasion on which General Emilio Aguinaldo proclaimed the independence of the Philippines from Spain. For the Filipinos July 4 is the date on which the occupying power agreed to give up its control and can be compared, in their view, to November 30, 1782, when the British acknowledged the independence of the United States of America. But on June 12, 1898, Aguinaldo, now the only living leader of the revolutionary period, proclaimed the independence of the Philippines from Spain by hoisting the Philippine national flag, introducing a national anthem, and ordering the public reading of the Act of Declaration of Independence by its author, Ambrosio Rianzares Bautista.

The revolt against Spain was preceded by long intellectual

[8] Conrado Benitez, *History of the Philippines,* rev. ed. (Manila: Ginn & Company, 1954), pp. 521-522.

preparation lasting over a quarter of a century. Beginning as an effort to win for Filipinos equality of status within the Spanish dominion, it ended as a violent attack on Spanish rule and virtually complete success in destroying the ecclesiastical and temporal power of Spain in the Philippines. Filipinos like to take the year 1872 as the beginning of the struggle. In that year the Spaniards used the occasion of an easily suppressed mutiny at the Cavite naval arsenal as an excuse to execute three Filipino priests whom they accused of participation in a movement for separation of the Philippines from Spain. Actually, the priests had nothing to do with the mutiny, which had been sparked by the arbitrary cancellation of privileges on the base. It appears that the execution was undertaken at the instigation of the Spanish friars, who had no intention of surrendering their control of the parishes to the Filipino priests, among whom these three were particularly active, or to the Archbishop who preferred seculars (nonmembers of religious orders) to friars because the friars refused to accept his authority. The execution of the priests was a costly mistake that did much to encourage the movement for separation from Spain.

The struggle was taken up first in Spain, where the sons of wealthy Filipinos went to study. There they started what has been called the Propaganda Movement for the purpose of bringing about reforms in Spanish colonial administration. Among the more important of these young men were Graciano López-Jaena, Marcelo H. del Pilar, and José Rizal, who for ten years brought the plight of the Filipinos to the attention of Spain, Europe, and their own countrymen. February 15, 1889, the date of the first issue of *La Solidaridad,* one of their best-known publications, is on the school list of days of commemoration. This Propaganda Movement called for neither revolution nor independence, but rather for equality before the law for Spaniards and Filipinos, the status of a province for the Philippines, representation in the Spanish Cortes, the appointment of Filipino diocesan priests to Philippine parishes, and the same freedom for the Philippines as for the mother country.

Many Filipinos who took part in this movement are duly remembered in the mausoleum of the Veterans of the Philippine

Revolution at Manila. The two that concern us most are José Rizal and Andres Bonifacio. Rizal, a very gifted man—physician, scholar, poet, novelist, and sculptor—is a national hero, and his statue stands in many towns. His novels, *Noli me tangere* (1887) and *El Filibusterismo* (1891), are known to every literate Filipino. After ten years abroad Rizal returned to the Philippines in 1892 and founded a society called La Liga Filipina, which had as its aims the unification of all Filipinos, mutual protection, defense against injustice, and the encouragement of education, agriculture, and commerce. The Spanish authorities quickly suppressed the League and exiled Rizal to Dapitan on Mindanao. This gave the signal to Andres Bonifacio to organize a secret revolutionary society, the Katipunan, drawn largely from the lower classes of the Tagalog-speaking areas. Unlike Rizal, Bonifacio was not an intellectual, though he had some education; he knew Spanish and had come under the influence of Masonic ideas. After the conspiracy was discovered in August 1896, members of the Katipunan openly revolted against Spain at a spot called Balintawak, near Manila. The Spaniards dispersed Bonifacio's forces, but troops under the command of another revolutionary leader, General Emilio Aguinaldo, achieved remarkable successes. Aguinaldo set up his own provisional government and when Bonifacio refused to accept it, had him executed for treason.

The Spaniards won all the battles in which they had organized forces available, but they were not numerous or strong enough to suppress the revolution; neither were the revolutionary forces strong enough to evict the Spaniards. After long negotiations both sides agreed to a truce. Aguinaldo was exiled to Hong Kong, and the Spaniards agreed to pay indemnities, undertake certain reforms, and declare a general amnesty. As part of the agreement Aguinaldo and some thirty other leaders went to Hong Kong, carrying with them $400,000, part of the indemnity promised by Spain, which they kept intact for future operations. The refusal of Spain to honor most of the amnesty terms led to the renewal of hostilities in March 1898, several weeks before the battle of Manila Bay. After the war broke out between Spain and the United States, the American consul in Singapore approached

Aguinaldo, who was then in that city, to secure his assistance in a joint attack on Spain in the Philippines. Admiral Dewey cabled Aguinaldo, inviting him to confer with him in Hong Kong, but left for Manila before the Filipino leader arrived. Aguinaldo reached Manila more than two weeks after the battle. After conferring with Dewey about cooperation against the Spaniards, he was put ashore at Cavite, where his forces were already in control.

Admiral Dewey asserted that no promises were made about the future of the Philippines; but in his recent book, *A Second Look at America*, Aguinaldo is still reluctant to give up the claim that Dewey promised him help in establishing an independent Philippines.[9] The misunderstanding was serious, yet it is easy to see how it might have arisen. The United States had not yet decided what to do about the Philippines, although it had declared itself in favor of Cuban independence. And Dewey, according to his dispatches, thought the Filipinos far more capable of self-government than were the Cubans. Whatever passed between Dewey and Aguinaldo, the State Department made it very clear that there were to be no alliances with the Filipino insurgents and no commitments for the future.

Within a very short time the Filipinos were in control of the island of Luzon, except for Manila, and on June 12, 1898, they declared the Philippines independent. The provisional government adopted a liberal and democratic constitution. As the United States refused to recognize the new government and had occupied Manila without its help, conflict was difficult to avoid. On February 4, 1899, fighting broke out between Philippine troops besieging Manila and the American forces that held the city. It did not end until Aguinaldo surrendered on March 23, 1901, and took the oath of allegiance to the United States. The last remnants of resistance were put down in 1904, after a bloody struggle.

The "insurgents," as the United States called the forces of General Aguinaldo, had to fight their battles without foreign assistance, although two efforts to help are on record. Many American army officers believed that the Anti-Imperialist Society of

---

[9] Emilio Aguinaldo and Vicente Albano Pacis, *A Second Look at America* (New York: Robert Speller & Sons, 1957), pp. 49-66.

Boston, founded in 1899, which included among its members Andrew Carnegie, Samuel Gompers, David Starr Jordan, and Charles F. Adams, was providing the "insurgents" with money and arms. No proof has ever been established of military assistance to the Filipinos, but there is evidence that the publications of the Society gave encouragement to the "insurgents" and that Aguinaldo was in touch with sympathetic Americans. The Aguinaldo regime hoped, it is claimed, that guerrilla resistance would influence the presidential election of November 1900 and that an America, tired of war, would elect William Jennings Bryan to office and give independence to the Philippines.[10]

The Chinese nationalist leader, Sun Yat-sen, made the other effort to help the newly created Philippine republic in its fight for existence against the Americans. He secretly arranged for a shipload of arms from Japan and for some Japanese officers to assist in the campaign. The officers arrived, but the shipload of arms was lost at sea, and with it went all hope of continuing effective military operations against the United States forces.[11]

What was the character of the Philippine republic under Aguinaldo? Its leaders, except for Bonifacio, who was a marginal case, came from the elite. Its mass support came mostly from the tenants of church lands and was particularly strong in Cavite province and central Luzon. The backbone of the revolutionary movement was the Tagalog-speaking group; in fact, American commanders were surprised when resistance continued after suppression of what they called the "Tagalog revolt."

The Tagalog-speaking area practically surrounds Manila Bay, whence it stretches north into the central Luzon plain and south to the Ragay Gulf. This key economic and strategic area, the "waist" of Luzon, had had the greatest contact with other countries and the strongest infusion of foreign blood. Here was the great port of Manila, the center of political, ecclesiastical, and economic power, the military and naval base of the occupying power, and the intellectual center of the Philippines. Within

[10] William T. Sexton, "Soldiers in the Philippines," *The Infantry Journal* (Washington: GPO, 1944), pp. 217-219.

[11] Marius Jansen, *The Japanese and Sun Yat-sen* (Cambridge: Harvard University Press, 1954), pp. 68-74.

this Tagalog-speaking area were some of the most pronounced contrasts in wealth in the Philippines. Thus, where the might and power of Spain were greatest, the resentments against its rule were the more articulate. No wonder that the revolt began in the Manila area, or that Tagalog is the national language of the Philippine Republic.

The revolt against Spain was more than a political demand for independence; it was the expression of a social, intellectual and economic revolution. When the Filipino nationalist looks back to the men and events of the last century, he can draw upon a rich heritage of liberal and democratic ideas and a choice of methods of bringing about change; the Propagandists tried peaceful persuasion and the Katipunans tried force. Above all, the nationalist can take pride in the extraordinary degree of unity among Filipinos in the struggle against Spain and the long and bitter resistance to American arms. With 126,468 officers and men, in addition to the navy, which guaranteed complete command of the sea, it took the Americans over two years to conquer the Philippines. The United States lost 4,234 dead, 2,818 wounded, and inflicted 16,000 casualties on Filipino troops. It is estimated that some 100,000 Filipinos died of famine and disease. The war cost the United States about $600 million.[12]

A combination of three classes—the native clergy, the *ilustrados,* and the caciques—led the revolution against Spain. Each one, for different reasons, wanted to reduce or eliminate the influence of the friars and if necessary to bring Spanish rule to an end. The friars, in fact, became the symbol and object of all that the Filipino nationalists feared and detested. Since the antifriar movement has left such an indelible impression on Filipino nationalism, affecting current discussion of the relations between church and state, it is important to understand its origins and significance.

The division of powers between church and state was never very clearly defined in Spanish times, but as Spain always considered the Philippines as primarily missionary territory, the church was expected to play an important role. High officials of the church served on all the advisory bodies to the governor-gen-

[12] Sexton, cited, p. 3.

eral. Within the ecclesiastic hierarchy the monastic orders came close to assuming an autonomous role, refusing, for example, to accept visitations from the Archbishop. In the provinces they exercised so much control over local affairs that they could, on occasion, bring sufficient pressure to bear in Madrid to force the recall of a governor-general if they disagreed with his policies.

Except for the Civil Guards, the friar was the main contact that the Filipino had with Spain. The principal civil duties of the parish priest were inspector of primary schools, president of the boards of health and charities, inspector of taxation, and president of the board of public works. For purposes of taxation he certified the correctness of the *cedulas,* seeing that they conformed to the entries in the parish books. Under Spanish law every man had to be furnished with these certificates of character, which were worthless without the priest's stamp. By law the parish priest had to be present when there were elections for municipal offices, and he passed on the municipal budget. He was censor of plays in the local dialect; he was president of the prison board; he was a member of the board for partitioning crown lands.[13]

In short, with control of the parishes went control of the municipalities. The friars were obviously powerful men; nothing could happen without their knowing about it, and nothing could be done without their approval. As they stayed in office permanently, they had a great advantage over the civil and military officials who rarely stayed for more than four years. Since the authority of the friars depended upon a monopoly on learning and on the power and prestige of Spain, the friars naturally opposed the secularization of the parishes, the extension of educational facilities, and popular participation in government. They were particularly averse to highly educated Filipinos who knew Spanish, had been abroad, or had written about the abuses of the friars. The native secular clergy wanted appointments to the parishes but were blocked by the monastic orders, which have been rightly described as being practically a state within a state. It is estimated that only one-seventh of the total Catholic

[13] Cesar Adib Majul, *The Political and Constitutional Ideas of the Philippine Revolution* (Quezon City: University of the Philippines, 1957), p. 101.

population of some six and a half million in 1898 were entrusted to secular clergy, the majority of whom were Filipinos.[14]

The case against the friars is an essential part of the ideology of the nationalist movement. Charging that the friars were not upholding Spanish rule but were actually endangering it, the policy of the propagandists was to make themselves indispensable by promising the government to save it from a rebellious people. Part of the purpose of Rizal in *Noli Me Tangere* was to establish the charge that the friars used the church as an instrument of domination, multiplying its services and ceremonies as a source of wealth. Rizal also expressed the widely held view that the friars, who controlled education, deliberately kept the Filipinos ignorant, pouring contempt and ridicule on those who tried to educate themselves. The hostility of practically all classes toward the friars, who were held responsible for every imaginable evil, came to be directed towards the Spanish government, which supported them.[15]

Except for the Franciscans, the religious orders were also large holders of agricultural estates; the enemies they did not make by their political and administrative functions they made as landlords. Three-quarters of the land holdings of the religious orders were in the Tagalog area around Manila. The Filipinos felt that the friars had come by their land holdings through fraud and deceit and that they administered them with ruthless greed. Rizal himself became involved in a dispute between tenants and landlord friars in 1887 when he drew up a petition to present to the government, listing the grievances of the tenants of the town of Calamba. The Spanish authorities drove the tenants out of town, burned down the houses, and exiled the leading citizens, including Rizal's family. It was from circumstances such as this that the resolve of the revolutionaries arose to have all friar lands re-

---

[14] The population was divided up among the clergy as follows:

Augustinians	2,082,131	Dominicans	699,851
Recollects	1,175,156	Jesuits	213,065 (as of 1895)
Franciscans	1,010,753	Secular clergy	967,294 (as of 1896)

Same, p. 102.

[15] Same, pp. 108, 120. But see also Pedro S. deAchutequi, S. J., and Miguel S. Bernad, S.J., *Religious Revolution in the Philippines* (Manila: Ateneo de Manila, 1960), p. 36.

stored to their former owners, turned over to the state, or sold in small lots. This did not include church properties other than land.

According to the Treaty of Paris that ended the Spanish-American War, the property of the church was to be restored. The authorities, moreover, made no statements to the effect that the land problem would be ameliorated by the new sovereign power. The Filipinos, assuming that the Americans would restore the friars to their lands, quickly transferred to the United States the hostility that they had formerly directed against Spain. There is plenty of evidence to support the view that the Filipinos were not, by and large, against the Roman Catholic Church as such; they wished to Filipinize but not to eliminate their religious life and institutions.[16] The delegates who wrote the Constitution of the Philippine Republic at Malolos, for example, voted in favor of the separation of church and state by a majority of only one.[17]

Another group of great importance, the *ilustrados,* led the movement for reform and provided leadership for the Propagandist movement. Some of these *ilustrados* were sons of wealthy Filipino families, others were well-to-do mestizos of Spanish, Chinese, and Filipino blood whose opportunities for education, professional advancement, government service, and social recognition were denied by the Spaniards. Some even came up from the peasantry. Those who went to Spain suddenly realized the dismal plight of the Filipino people, particularly their own class.

It was the *ilustrados* who brought to their country the revolutionary ideas that had provided the philosophical basis of the French and American revolutions. As the isolation of the Philip-

16 Majul, cited, Chap. VI.

17 This period, however, did see the birth of what came to be known as the Philippine Independent Church, more often called the Aglipayan Church after Bishop Gregorio Aglipay, Military Vicar-General to Aguinaldo. Aglipay called on the Filipino clergy to take over the parishes and support the revolution, thus bringing down on himself a decree of excommunication. All efforts to avoid a schism having failed, Aglipay became in 1902 the Supreme Bishop of an Independent Church. According to one Filipino historian this was the only tangible result of religious revolution; see Teodoro A. Agoncillo and Oscar M. Alfonso, *A Short History of the Filipino People* (Quezon City: University of the Philippines, 1960), p. 279.

pines came to an end, the ideas of the Age of Reason captured the imagination of the men who guided the revolution and the short-lived Republic. Of particular appeal was the view of John Locke, that government is for the protection of the natural rights of the people and that if a government fails to protect these rights, then the people have the right to overthrow it. Jean Jacques Rousseau's *Social Contract* also provided the Propagandists with the intoxicating doctrines that men are born free and can protect their natural rights by choosing their own government.

The third group that played a decisive role in the revolt against Spain was the cacique class, the powerful landowning "bosses" of the provinces. The caciques contributed importantly to the organization of military forces during the struggles with Spain and the United States. They were the bridge between the *ilustrados,* the revolutionary leaders, and the so-called "masses." Many of them felt the appeal of nationalism because they stood to gain economically and politically by limiting the power of the friars and eliminating that of Spain. Doctrines of social equality and popular sovereignty meant, to them, the promotion of their own personal and class interests against the Spaniards rather than a humanitarian interest in the peasantry. Rizal, in fact, opposed violent revolution partly because he foresaw that if the Spaniards were to be overthrown before the Filipinos were spiritually prepared through education and self-discipline, the tyranny of Filipinos over Filipinos (*caciquismo*) might be just as bad as, if not worse than, that of the Spaniards. Yet without the cooperation of the caciques there could not have been any "mass" support of the revolution or, in other words, any peasants to be soldiers.[18]

Aguinaldo and the caciques, however, realized that they had to have the support of the *ilustrados* if they were going to replace the Spaniards and make a success of the republic. The *ilustrados* were the "vanguard" of the revolution, an elite group that was persuaded that it knew best what was good for the Philippines and had no intention of consulting the people or being "governed by the leaders of the masses." According to Professor Majul, the Philippine revolution was begun by the masses (that

[18] Majul, cited, pp. 60-61.

is, the Katipunan), but the *ilustrados* took the leadership away from them. It is his feeling that if the Americans had not destroyed the Republic, republican and democratic tendencies would have continued to gain in strength because of the propaganda of the *ilustrados* and the concessions to the democratic mood that they had already made.[19] Be that as it may, there is no doubt that the Malolos Constitution was designed to give power to an "intellectual oligarchy," an oligarchy that assumed it could count on the support of the military and the caciques.

The revolution did not achieve many of its social aims. The expulsion or at least secularization of religious orders was, as we have seen, one of the earliest demands of the revolutionaries. They expelled the friars and took over their lands. But it is thought by some that the revolutionists soft-pedalled the idea of the redistribution of land because there were too many wealthy landowners in the revolutionary Congress at Malolos, which passed a constitution limiting to some extent the powers assumed by Aguinaldo. This is probably a correct interpretation, in that the revolutionaries were more concerned with civil rights than with land tenure, with Spanish tyranny than with Spanish exploitation. The Malolos Constitution, which probably expressed the aims of the revolution most fully, was liberal and democratic. It provided for the protection of the rights of the individual and for improving the conditions for the mass of the people. It gave the president far fewer powers than does the American Constitution. Against the advice of his friend, Apolinario Mabini, Aguinaldo accepted the limitations imposed on his powers by the landowning elite. Even so, most of the elite did not stand by him after the American forces drove him into the hills. They preferred to come to terms with the conqueror, exacting from him promises and concessions in return for their assistance in restoring civil government—a pattern to be repeated in 1941 when the Japanese invaded the Philippines.

Three centuries of Spanish rule familiarized the Filipinos with Western forms of government and permitted a few Filipinos to gain practical experience in local administration. Though

[19] Same, p. 184.

corrupt in practice, "in theory and profession the colonial system of Spain was fine and uplifting. Spaniards and Filipinos may have failed always to maintain high standards, but those standards were ever before them in the laws and precepts of both the state and the church. There could be no better evidence that these standards did make an impression upon the Filipino mind than the rebellion of the Filipinos against Spanish rule." [20] The Filipinos fought and died for political ideas they had learned from the West, although the Spaniards had not put into practice what they taught the Filipinos. The leaders of the revolution were not a band of armed peasants; they were cultivated and able men with wealth and influential connections. Given protection against outside aggression, it is quite possible that they would have provided the Philippines with a workable government.

Among Filipinos the story of the revolutionary struggle is very much in the foreground of attention today, a story rich and varied enough to provide material for many an analysis. During the period of American colonial rule Rizal, the peaceful reformer, was honored as the outstanding national hero despite strong clerical opposition to the many anticlerical ideas in his works. Filipinos feel that the Americans overemphasized Rizal because he did not advocate violent revolution, and by the same token neglected the activists. Today special attention is devoted to Bonifacio, the active leader of the Katipunan in the armed revolt against Spain, especially by the historical revisionists who seemingly wish to build up the image of a "proletarian" leader who understood and organized the "masses." Aguinaldo is strangely underplayed by the revisionists. And those Filipinos who collaborated with the Americans in the campaigns of 1899-1902 are now described as a "dark blot in the annals of Filipino nationalism." [21] Filipino nationalists draw what they need from this one great revolutionary period, which, in consequence, looms so importantly in Philippine and United States relations.

[20] Joseph R. Hayden, *The Philippines: A Study in National Development* (New York: Macmillan, 1942), pp. 29-30.

[21] Romeo V. Cruz, "The Filipino Collaboration with the Americans," *Comment*, no. 10, First Quarter, 1960 (Manila: Regal Printing Co., Inc.), p. 10.

The Acquisition of an American Colony

What Filipinos and Americans say and think about the United States as a colonial power in large measure establishes the character of the dialogue between the two countries. This in turn affects their political relations. It is difficult to determine what measure of agreement there is on the meaning of the record because there has been remarkably little mutual discussion; the Americans have stated their case, and the Filipinos have stated theirs. One school of thought in the Philippines must be taken seriously, for it limits discussion of the American period entirely to the question of American "imperialism" and hopes to change the intellectual climate in such a way as to endanger the present partnership. Hence the need for a frank discussion of American imperialism and an examination of the credentials of this school of thought.

The conquest of the Philippines is often represented as an aberration from the main stream of American thought and practice. In some highly important ways it was this. The general tenor of American policy during the nineteenth century was certainly anti-imperialist, partly because of the manner in which the thirteen colonies had won their freedom and partly because the chief danger to the new republic came from the old empires, particularly, it was thought, the British. But the conquest of the Philippines differed from other imperialist adventures of the period not so much in character as in style. The important considerations are not that American imperialism lasted only a short time, involved little territory, and affected relatively few people, but that almost from the very beginning it was seen as a self-liquidating enterprise, an ambitious experiment in controlled and planned political growth. The story of the Philippine adventure is a composite of some of the worst and some of the best features of American society. At its worst it subordinated national responsibility to special interests. At its best it anticipated the reconstruction of a defeated Japan as well as U.S. policies toward the underdeveloped parts of the world.

How did it come about? First, throughout the second half of

the nineteenth century an influential school of thought in the United States had been in favor of acquiring naval bases in the Pacific. If the navy and its political supporters had had their way, the American flag would have been flying in Hawaii, the Bonins, Formosa, and other places in the Pacific long before the end of the century. The reasons are not hard to find. From the earliest days of the republic the navy played a necessary role in promoting and protecting American commerce. The original colonies had to trade to live, and this trade had to be conducted in an unfriendly world where naval and commercial power were closely related in theory and in practice. By the middle of the nineteenth century U.S. navy doctrine, reflecting the ideas of the British, the most important competitor, stressed the importance of acquiring not colonies but naval bases, particularly in the Pacific Ocean. The navy doctrine was eloquently expressed by that ardent Anglophobe, Commodore Matthew C. Perry, both in his correspondence and in his famous instructions for the mission to Japan. The American navy wanted bases in the Pacific in preparation for an expected naval struggle with the British and other empires, and hoped for a friendly Japan to fall back on for refuelling and repairs. It is not usually realized how deft or how dangerous was the naval diplomacy that succeeded, if not in securing bases, at least in neutralizing Japan. The same sort of considerations that led to the opening of Japan also moved Secretary of State Seward to the purchase of Alaska.

Two developments after the Civil War explain, at least in part, the strength the expansionist forces had acquired by the end of the century. One was the growth in industrial and commercial strength that increased the pressures for foreign trade and investment, particularly in the Caribbean; the other was Captain Alfred T. Mahan's formulation of navy doctrine in terms of a national strategy. The international situation also began to look as ominous as it had in the early days of the republic. Imperialist competition, stepped up by the arrival of Germany, France, Russia, and other powers on the scene, seemed to threaten U.S. economic interests in the western Pacific and China to such an extent that having military power available in that area seemed to be the only way in which to protect those interests.

By the time of the Spanish-American War, therefore, the case for expansion had grown more persuasive; its exponents had a concept of national strategy to inspire them, and the commercial and financial interests that supported expansion were stronger. It was now possible to compete on more equal terms with those political and economic interests that opposed imperial adventures. Furthermore, in addition to the teachings of Mahan, the harsh doctrines of social Darwinism justified, in the minds of the new industrial and financial giants of America, the ruthless struggle for survival both at home and abroad. If Spain could not maintain law and order in Cuba and protect American economic interests, and if the Filipinos were not capable of governing themselves or protecting themselves from German or other imperialism, then it was the duty of the United States to intervene, to assume the "white man's burden." Ancient customs, pre-industrial societies, decaying imperialisms could not forever stand in the way of science and progress.

The justifications of the time sound quaint today, and most of them are deservedly out of fashion, especially the racial theories and the assumption that civilization was limited to the Western world, particularly to the Anglo-Saxons. But nothing could have stopped the expansion of a rapidly industrializing Europe and America.[22] There were no practical alternatives at the time to the political device of colonization as a method of expanding the world market and organizing its resources. At a different time and under different conditions, the United States had offered an alternative solution in the opening of Japan, which was thus enabled to adjust itself to the modern world with very few restrictions on its sovereignty. But in 1898 the wonder was not that the United States took the Philippines, but that it did not take more. Compared with the behavior of the other powers toward Africa and the Far East, the actions of the United States in 1898 still represent a deviant pattern. The U.S. failure to

[22] Karl A. Wittfogel, *Oriental Despotism* (New Haven: Yale University Press, 1957), p. 423, for the views of John Stuart Mill and Karl Marx on this subject.

annex Cuba and the willingness to promise eventual independence to the Philippines were not the typical actions of a great power; they reflected the special balance of forces in the United States at that time.

The men who wanted the "larger policy"—Henry Cabot Lodge, Theodore Roosevelt, Admiral Mahan—saw in the war with Spain, which they helped to force at a time when Spain had agreed to all reasonable demands, the opportunity to seize in the Pacific some of the positions that many Americans had coveted for half a century. President McKinley was not uninclined to go along with the imperialists, as the "larger policy" men can properly be called, but he had to watch public opinion. When the war with Cuba began, Congress passed the Teller Resolution, which disclaimed any disposition on the part of the United States to exercise sovereignty, jurisdiction, and control over Cuba except for the purposes of pacification. Although Puerto Rico and the Philippine Islands were not included in the scope of the resolution, it gave hope to the Filipinos that the United States would also support their independence from Spain. Events proved otherwise. Due mainly to the forehandedness of the Assistant Secretary of the Navy, Theodore Roosevelt, Commodore Dewey was ready on the declaration of war to attack the Spanish fleet in Manila Bay, which he did on May 1, 1898. At the same time the United States annexed Hawaii and Guam. By August the war with Spain was over. In the protocol of August 12, Spain agreed to Cuban independence, ceded Puerto Rico and an island in the Ladrones to the United States, and accepted the condition that the Philippines should remain under American authority pending a final settlement. By the Treaty of Paris, signed December 10, 1898, Spain ceded the Philippines to the United States in return for the payment of $20,000,000 and the admission of Spanish ships and merchandise to the Philippines for a ten-year period on the same terms as U.S. ships and merchandise.

The conquest of foreign peoples without the intention of bringing them into the Union was certainly a departure from the general practice and philosophy of the American people, as President McKinley himself indicated only a few months before the war in his message of December 1897: ". . . forcible

annexation . . . cannot be thought of, [and] by our code . . .
would be criminal aggression." [23] It took several Supreme Court
decisions, known as the Insular Cases, to clarify the legal status
of the unincorporated territories. By a five-to-four decision the
Supreme Court decided that the Philippine Islands were not
foreign territory within the meaning of the Constitution and that
congressional action would therefore be necessary to prevent
duty-free shipment of goods from these insular territories. By
another decision Congress was allowed to legislate on formal
rights, such as trial by jury, American citizenship, and the right
to bear arms. As Mr. Dooley put it, ". . . whether the Constitution followed the flag or not, the Supreme Court followed th'
'illiction returns," [24] for the election of 1900 carried McKinley
back to power with a sizable majority, and to some extent it can
be considered a mandate for the actions of 1898-99.

At the same time it would be a misreading of the ambitions of
the "larger policy" school and of the doctrines of Mahan, or of
Perry before him, to suppose that the acquisition of large alien
populations was their main objective. The navy's interest was
in bases, preferably with little or no responsibilities for the governing of native peoples. If it had been possible to hold Manila
Bay without taking the rest of the Philippines, this would have
been more desirable; in fact, the Philippines had no place in
Mahan's orginal plans for the Pacific. But it was quite clear
that no naval base in the Philippines would be of any value
unless the whole island group was kept out of the hands of other
powers. This in itself was good enough reason for acquiring the
islands, assuming that the United States had to have a naval base.
But the doctrine of naval bases was bound up with other considerations: the promotion and protection of commerce and the
national security.

The advocates of imperialist expansion got their way as a result of the coming together of a variety of forces. Even so, the
Treaty of Paris was approved in the Senate with a margin of only

[23] Charles A. Beard and Mary R. Beard, *The Rise of American Civilization*
(New York: Macmillan, 1930), p. 374.
[24] Garel A. Grunder and William E. Livezey, *The Philippines and the
United States* (Norman: University of Oklahoma Press, 1951), p. 79.

one vote beyond the two-thirds majority required. Support for the conquest of the Philippines came from the Protestant churches, which half a century earlier had denounced the British for the Opium War on China but were now taken up with the spirit of the times, the civilizing mission of the white man—the duty, as President McKinley put it, ". . . to educate the Filipinos, and uplift and civilize and Christianize them, and by God's grace do the very best we could by them as our fellowmen for whom Christ also died." [25] That most of the Filipinos were already Roman Catholics was apparently beside the point. It is difficult to fathom all the motives that moved William Jennings Bryan, but without his support the treaty would not have been ratified in the lame duck session of the Fifty-second Congress. The next Congress, with its stronger Republican majority, would probably have ratified the treaty in any case. By then the public had seemingly shown its approval of expansion. How close was the division of opinion in Congress is also shown by the vote of 29 to 29 on the Bacon Amendment to disclaim any intention to exercise permanent sovereignty over the Philippines and to turn over the government and control of the islands to their own people. The deciding vote of Vice-President Garret Hobart was against the amendment, and thus the United States forfeited the renown of being the first great power to assist an Asian people to gain its independence. So uncertain was President McKinley of public reaction that it took him five months to decide that the whole of the Philippines must be occupied.

Opposition cut across party lines, but the arguments were predictable. Congressman Hoar, an influential Republican from Massachusetts, opposed imperialist expansion because it violated the Constitution and because the American people had no right to impose the Declaration of Independence and the Constitution on an unwilling people; Americans ". . . wore with ill grace the cast-off clothing of pinch-back emperors and pewter kings." [26] Senator Caffery of Louisiana warned that Philippine products and labor would compete with agriculture and labor

[25] Thomas A. Bailey, *A Diplomatic History of the American People* (New York: F. S. Crofts & Co., 1942), p. 530.

[26] Same, p. 538.

at home, that tropical countries export more than they import, and that therefore the prospects of trade were not as rosy as some people thought. Others were afraid that the Philippine connection would involve the United States in Far Eastern politics and wars. Mark Twain poured his contempt on those who wanted to civilize and Christianize natives by the use of guns and the water cure. There is much evidence that the Senate ratified the treaty only because the administration resorted to extraordinary pressures.

The term colonialism is in such bad repute today that it is difficult to recall the seriousness with which the civilizing and Christianizing mission was regarded at the turn of the century. Imperialism is an extremely complex phenomenon. It cannot be understood if it is reduced to so-called economic factors any more than if it is explained solely in terms of the "white man's burden." The taking of the Philippines could hardly have come about without the extraordinary combination of different factors: the accident of the war with Spain; the presence in high position of three or four strong advocates of expansion; the victory at Manila Bay; the enthusiasm of the Protestant churches; the international situation; the unexpected behavior of William Jennings Bryan; the special balance of agrarian, industrial, and financial interests; the conflict between American and Filipino troops; and the widespread belief that civilization was a condition achieved by the Western powers and that they must inevitably carry it to the far corners of the earth. There was nothing new about the concepts that the United States government should further the interests of commerce and that the churches had a duty to spread the gospel, or about the professional interests of the navy or the need to compete with the other empires. What was new was that all these views and interests came together for a brief period and thus made action possible.

Chapter 3

The Political Legacy
of the United States

The Continuing Revolution

A half century of American rule in the Philippines was devoted to the self-imposed task of mothering the national revolution of another people. When the United States granted the Filipinos their independence in 1946, it turned over to them a revolution which they themselves had started and no one else could finish.

While denying to the Filipinos for almost fifty years the main objective of their revolution—political independence—the United States strongly supported other objectives. It imposed the doctrine and practice of the separation of Church and State, insisted on the secularization of education, took away from the friars their local administrative and political power, opened up all careers to Filipinos, improved public health, stimulated the development of the economy, and above all, eventually provided for a constitution based on the same philosophical concepts of natural rights that had inspired the writers of the Malolos Constitution. The Propagandists had demanded that all Filipinos should be permitted to learn Spanish; the Americans insisted that English should be the language of instruction. Instead of representation in the Spanish Cortes, Filipinos were to send delegates to the American Congress. Freedom of the press and other rights, at first denied until American sovereignty was accepted, were soon to be firmly established.

The parallel between measures taken by the United States in

57

the Philippines and the objectives of the Filipino nationalists is not surprising in view of the fact that the Propagandists drew their ideas from the same sources as had the Americans a century before, but the program that the United States carried out was actually more revolutionary than that of the most extreme nationalists. It carried to its logical conclusion the idea of popular sovereignty, which the Propagandists had used more as a stick with which to beat the Spanish administration than as an appeal to the masses. It developed compulsory education for all far beyond anything the Propagandists had in mind. While it did not take away all the friar lands or banish the religious orders as some of the nationalists wished, it began to lay the foundations of a new land title system which was not at all to the liking of some who had supported the revolution. The United States, in a word, tried to shift the internal balance of forces away from oligarchy and in favor of political and social democracy.

Filipinos are still in the process of evaluating the changes that took place under the Americans and of finding out what happened to their nationalism and which direction, now that they are in control again, the national revolution should take. After the establishment of U.S. sovereignty there was something of a partnership between Filipinos and Americans in carrying out important social and political changes that led to the growth of real bonds of mutual respect between the two peoples. Except for the humiliation of having had to accept foreign rule, the Filipino nationalists acknowledge the fact that the Americans helped them achieve many of the things that they wanted for themselves. But partnership in revolution can exist side by side with a good deal of hostility and political antagonism. This is quite apparent in Teodoro Agoncillo's treatment of the American Occupation:

In consonance with President McKinley's "Benevolent Assimilation" Proclamation, the United States introduced in the Philippines a regime of democratic partnership under which the Filipinos played the role of junior partner. The policy, while not satisfactory enough from the point of view of the Filipino nationalist, was nevertheless a decided improvement over that of Spain. Universal education was stressed; public health and welfare was carried to the remote barrios; commerce, industry, and trade were given impetus; basic individual freedoms were respected; means of communication and transportation were greatly improved; and political consciousness was developed through the introduction of American political institutions and practices. Side by side with these positive results of the American Occupation were the negative results: the general economic dependence on the United States, the partial loss of the racial heritage, the continuance of the colonial mentality, and a distorted sense of values.[1]

Mr. Agoncillo's statement represents the views of one large group of Filipino nationalists who are sufficiently honest and objecttive to see the picture in colors other than black and white.

It is because the program of the American administration was more revolutionary than that of the leaders of the revolt against Spain that so many Filipinos accepted American rule. Some elements of the elite resisted, not unsuccessfully, certain aspects of the American-style revolution, which from their point of view were far too extreme. And for others, the Americans did not go far enough. But for all Filipino nationalists today there is no escaping the fact that it was a foreign power that carried out their revolution for them, and this fact alone affected the quality of Filipino nationalism.[2] No matter which way the Filipino turns for inspiration, for examples, or for concepts about himself, his country, and his future, he has to come to terms with the record of the United States of America in the Philippines.

Growth of a Policy

It was a political fact of the first order that a great power surrendered sovereignty over a colony on its own initiative and not under effective pressure from the colony itself. But so much is made of the granting of independence to the Philippines that it is necessary to put it in the perspective of the American view of colonial responsibilities.

Colonial responsibility began at a time when the United States had no colonial policy and no tradition. Even Charles A. Beard has said that the McKinley school did not openly "adopt the

[1] Teodoro A. Agoncillo and Oscar W. Alfonso, *A Short History of the Filipino People* (Quezon City: University of the Philippines, 1960), p. 435.
[2] Same, pp. 293 ff.

imperialist dogma in the British, French, and German style, although the deed implied the word" and that McKinley took advantage of the popular enthusiasm of the moment over the war with Spain to push his policies. "Yet as the course of events subsequently showed," according to Beard, "the program of the school had not become a national creed rooted in the unshakeable affections of the whole people." [3] The tradition that emerged was thoroughly American in character. The pacification of the islands was not a pleasant undertaking as the Filipinos did not welcome the Americans and fought hard to resist them; some ugly methods were used by both sides. Although civil government began in the pacified areas in July 1901, it was not until July 4, 1902, that the U.S. considered the situation sufficiently well in hand to terminate military government throughout the islands. Pockets of resistance continued to hold out for several more years.

The first recommendations on how to govern came from a commission sent to the Philippines in March 1899 under the chairmanship of President Jacob G. Schurman of Cornell University. While in Manila, Schurman stated that the United States intended to accustom the Filipinos to an ever-increasing measure of self-government, and to encourage them in democratic aspirations, sentiments, and ideals. The commission later suggested a government comprising a U.S.-appointed governor-general with an absolute veto, a cabinet of his own choosing, a general advisory council chosen on a limited suffrage, and an independent judiciary. These suggestions had a great deal to do with the decision of important leaders among the Filipinos to come to terms with the United States. Though it thought immediate self-government impractical, the commission made it clear that only by understanding the Filipinos and sympathizing with their aspirations and ideals could the United States govern them well. The commission recommended that the customs duties, the whole taxation system, and all Philippine finances should be separate from those of the United States and the government should be self-supporting. Most of these recommendations were accepted and

[3] Charles A. Beard and Mary R. Beard, *The Rise of American Civilization* (New York: Macmillan, 1930), p. 374.

formed the basis of the instructions to the second commission, sent to the Philippines under the chairmanship of William Howard Taft, who, like Schurman, had not been in favor of their acquisition.

The instructions to the Taft commission, drafted by Elihu Root, were issued in April 1900. Although the occupation began with assurances to the Filipinos that they were to be given a large measure of self-government, it was made clear that this was to be within the confines of a policy of "benevolent assimilation"; neither McKinley nor Taft was in favor of independence. Taft did not exclude the possibility of independence but thought it highly unwise to make premature promises when, in his view, the Filipinos still had so far to go before they could govern themselves. All legislative power was to be transferred to the commission on September 1, 1900, and civil government was to be established with elected officers and with municipal and provincial governments. McKinley instructed the commission to respect the main body of Philippine law and custom but to impose American concepts of the division of power, strong local government, due process, respect for private property, and public education. On June 21, 1901, President McKinley appointed Taft civil governor of the islands, and the system of governors-general continued until the coming of the Commonwealth in 1935. Three Filipinos were added to the commission within a year of its assumption of legislative power, and Filipinos were employed in the whole administrative system. In large measure the United States stayed clear of the temptation to establish a huge, centralized bureaucracy of Americans to run its colony.

After rejecting a bill to promise independence, Congress passed the Cooper bill, the first Philippine Organic Act, in July 1902. This act legalized the organization and functions of the Taft commission and recognized the islands as an unincorporated territory. All persons who were Spanish subjects became citizens of the Philippine Islands if they so wished, and as such they were entitled to the protection of the United States and the Bill of Rights. An elected Philippine lower house (the commission was the upper house) would send two resident commissioners to the United States, and under certain conditions appeals could be made from the Philippine Supreme Court to that of the United States. In other words, the United States appointed the chief executive, the governor-general, and a commission that had both legislative and administrative functions; and the Filipinos elected a lower house, which could block an increase in appropriations but not the continuation of the budget of the previous year. Until 1916 the Filipinos had little positive influence, though they did have a considerable negative one, on the governing of the islands.

The Filipinos acquired even more power over their own affairs as a result of the Jones Act of 1916 and the rapid "Filipinization" policy during the eight years of the Democratic administration. The Republicans in the 1920s tried to undo some of the damage, as they saw it, that had been done to the public services by the steady attrition of American authority and administration, but it was imposible to turn the clock back. Hopes for independence had been raised, but it was not until the early 1930s, when powerful economic pressure groups helped to bring about the passage in 1934 of the Tydings-McDuffie Act, did independence become practical politics in the United States Congress.[4] The act set a definite date for independence; it was to be ten years after the establishment of a Commonwealth Government. With the establishment of this government in 1935, the U.S. Governor-General became High Commissioner. During the Commonwealth period certain duty-free quotas were fixed on Philippine imports into the United States, but after independence, all Philippine products were to be subject to the full U.S. tariff rates on foreign goods. The act limited Filipino immigration into the United States but set no limits on American immigration to the Philippines.

The United States retained the right to maintain military bases in the Philippines after independence. Thus, the strategic considerations that played so large a part in the acquisition of the Philippines were not sacrificed to the economic interests which hoped to gain by cutting off the Philippines from free trade with the United States. The Filipinos wanted their independence so

[4] Grayson Kirk, *Philippine Independence* (New York: Farrar & Rinehart, Inc., 1936), pp. 100-101.

badly that they were willing to pay the price, but the price was high; at the time it looked like economic ruin, bringing in its train political chaos. Writing at the time, Grayson Kirk charged the U.S. government with the betrayal of a national trust, for which, however, no single person or group could be held responsible. "It means, rather, that a great ideal was traduced, less by individual or group malevolence than by the sheer force of circumstances bearing inexorably in a depression-ridden democracy upon harrassed and none too farsighted public servants." [5] About this event, Charles A. Beard wrote that the neutrality legislation of 1935, coupled with the granting of independence to the Philippines, signified, at least temporarily, "the steep decline of the imperialism sponsored by McKinley, Mahan, Lodge, Hay, and Theodore Roosevelt, and also punctured the universal philanthropy expounded by Woodrow Wilson." [6] From the worst features of the Tydings-McDuffie Act the United States and the Philippines were saved by the cruel accident of Japanese occupation during World War II, but even in the entirely changed circumstances of the postwar world the United States made arrangements with the Philippines of which it has little reason to be proud. It did, however, accept the moral obligation to grant independence, and on July 4, 1946, the Filipinos celebrated their independence amid the ruins of war.

Criteria for Independence

The concept of a self-liquidating colony inevitably raised the question of what conditions would have to be met in order to achieve independence. American colonial experience produced more thought on the criteria by which to judge the capacity of a people to govern itself than on any other aspect of colonial government. Contributing to this debate were the Americans who had kept alive the independence movement in the United States, the Filipino nationalists, who argued their case in Washington and Manila, and American officials and members of Con-

[5] Same, p. 208.
[6] Charles A. Beard, *America in Mid-Passage*, v. 1 (New York: Macmillan, 1939), p. 433.

gress. The discussion of criteria was important for several reasons. In the first place, it set the tone in the relations between ruler and ruled and thus probably had something to do with the absence of any violent Filipino efforts to secure independence. In the second place, the discussion made it possible for the Tydings-McDuffie bill to become law in 1934 because all parties to the debate took for granted the eventual granting of independence. It was because the mood of the country in 1934 was for independence that powerful economic interests which wanted to cut the Philippines loose succeeded in getting their way. It is perhaps necessary to make this point because the view is often advanced that the United States deserves no credit for promising independence to the Philippines in the 1930s as the enabling legislation was passed at the bidding of sordid economic interests. Those who hold this view usually charge that President McKinley took the Philippines because of tinsel dreams of empire, of popular support for "manifest destiny," and the missionary enthusiasm of the Protestant churches. Third, the discussion comes back to haunt us as we struggle with the unfriendly charge that legal sovereignty coupled with military and economic dependence is meaningless, that the United States is still an imperialist power and the Philippines a colony. The granting of independence is not, of and by itself, the ultimate political weapon.

The criteria for independence were not objective standards whose achievement could be measured quantitatively, and by the nature of the situation, the United States was judge and jury in its own case. When the decision to grant independence was actually made, many of the arguments used only a few years before to prove that the Philippines was not ready were brushed aside in the rush to protect American agricultural interests by ending free trade between the two countries. Very few of the criteria had been satisfactorily met when independence came in 1946, except possibly the most important one of all: the will of a people to fight and suffer for its right to a separate national existence.

The most important criteria were: the political maturity of the Filipino people, including the level of popular participation in government and the will to be independent; the stability of the political process and of public administration; the viability of the economy; the treatment of minority groups; and the capacity of the Philippines to protect itself. The range of opinion on these criteria was wide indeed, and a few voices were even raised in favor of permanent occupation. Even those who wished to delay independence for the Philippines accepted the assumption that some day, at some time, it would have to be granted. This distinguishing feature of American imperialism is important because it robbed the Filipino nationalist movement of much of the intense anti-Western feeling and fanatical drive found in other colonial countries.

The criterion of political maturity is a particularly difficult one to test. To Governor Taft, for example, the test of self-government was defined by the degree to which the Filipinos had acquired a knowledge of the nature of individual liberty and the processes of constitutional government. In his view the future form of government, whether dominion status, incorporation in the Union, or statehood, could be left for the future to decide. In 1908 he reported to President Roosevelt that it would take at least another generation for the Filipinos to be ready for full self-government.

From the very beginning the United States had assumed that one precondition for independence would be the presence of a mature public opinion, nurtured by public education and by increasing opportunities for Filipinos to participate in the process of government. When this had been achieved, the government would be responsible to the wishes of the people. Such a condition had not been reached by 1930, according to Secretary of State Henry S. Stimson. Independence at that time, he said, would result in either chaos or rule by an oligarchy, and both were inadmissible. But how was one to judge maturity? One view was that a working electoral system was sufficient evidence; another, that maintaining law and order was sufficient. In retrospect it is easier to see now the inevitability of oligarchical rule so long as the suffrage was limited to literate males and the social and economic condition of the mass of the population remained unchanged since Spanish times, except for the spread of formal education. While suffrage was limited in effect to those who had the main stake in society, it worked against the very changes—extension of the suffrage, social mobility, responsiveness to the popular will—that were set as conditions for a healthy and informed public opinion.[7]

How shall an imperial power measure the intensity of the wish for independence on the part of a colonial people? As early American experience has shown, it is the few who are willing to fight and die for freedom, not the many. Intensity of nationalist feeling cannot be measured by counting heads, and President Coolidge vetoed the proposal for a Philippine plebiscite.[8] It could be argued that the bitter struggle of the Philippines against American conquest was in itself sufficient evidence of the desire for independence, and that this was a more significant indication of the popular will than participation in elections or the percentage of literacy or the attitudes of certain members of the elite whose economic interests were bound up with the maintenance of the *status quo*. The ambivalence of some Filipino leaders toward independence—due to the conflict between their economic interest, either private or national, and the need to associate themselves with the nationalist movement for their own political survival—was used to advantage by the United States when it wished to delay the granting of independence. But when Congress chose to act, these considerations dropped into the background.

If the popular will was a flexible criterion, so was the concept of a stable government. For those who wanted to delay the granting of independence it was natural to set up a model of excellence that would reflect the best in American political institutions, while for those who favored an early separation the standards were much lower. Although President McKinley is on record as favoring due respect for the customs, institutions, and laws of the Filipinos prevailing at the time of conquest, there is no doubt that the weight of his influence, as of his successors and of most governors-general, was on the side of imposing

[7] Georges Fischer, *Un Cas de Decolonization* (Paris: Librairie Générale de Droit et De Jurisprudence, 1960), p. 62 ff.

[8] *Annual Report of the Governor-General of the Philippine Islands, 1927* (Manila: Bureau of Printing, 1927), p. 64.

American concepts of political behavior, public administration, rights of the individual, fiscal policy, and public order. It is practically impossible, however, to separate the criteria of stable government from those of a stable economy.

Those who set up the most exacting requirements for stable government stressed the protection of private property, particularly foreign investments, and the regulation of the tariff. They wanted the assurance that there would be no unilateral repudiation of the debts of the previous regime and no sudden change in the conditions of trade to the detriment of American interests. At the same time they argued that a stable economy was a necessary basis for a stable political system.

What is a stable economy? In the case of the Philippines, there was general agreement that it required diversifying the economy and lessening its excessive dependence on that of the United States. Many American officials pointed out that the economic dependence of the Philippines on the United States was a poor basis for political independence, the stated objective of U.S. policy. Colonial policy had tended to consolidate the power of an oligarchy that profited, after 1909, from the free-trade relationship and would be likely to respect, after independence, the rights and privileges of Americans. The same policy had done more, perhaps, to increase than to decrease the gap between rich and poor in the Philippines, and the oligarchy showed little interest in raising the general living standards of the people. If the economic bonds between metropolitan power and colony were broken, if free trade were abandoned, however gradually, then the economic foundations of the existing order would also be shattered. Given the evidence of social pressures, this might lead to a change in political leadership and to different attitudes toward foreign rights and interests in the Philippines and international debts and other obligations. A stable economy—diversified and independent—might not go together with a government friendly to U.S. interests.

It was assumed in the 1930s that all responsibility for the military defense of the Philippines would cease with independence, and the inability of the Philippines to defend itself was used, on occasion, as a reason for delaying the granting of independence.

President Hoover vetoed the Hawes-Cutting Bill on these grounds, although it provided (as did the Tydings-McDuffie Act) for the retention by the United States of certain military installations in the Philippines. As a criterion for independence the defense argument is almost meaningless. How can the capacity of a weak country to survive be estimated unless it follows its own policies, makes its own alliances, takes its own chances? As events were to prove, an independent Philippines could hardly have suffered more from foreign aggression than did the Philippines in World War II at a time when it was still under American military protection. The defense argument was actually an argument for the continuation of U.S. military power in the western Pacific, for which there were other good and sufficient reasons. It had little relevance to any estimate of the ability of the Filipinos to take care of themselves. When independence came in 1946, the Filipinos were barely able to take care of internal subversion, let alone external aggression. But just as the acceptance of responsibility for economic aid compensates in some measure for the economic dependence of the Philippines, so do regional defense arrangements compensate somewhat for its military dependence, except that military dependence is even more constricting to the nationalist than is economic. Imperialism is not easy to liquidate.

The Emerging Political Structure

The American approach to the novel problem of tutelage over an Asian people was not without a basis in theory. Certain assumptions about the nature and purpose of government were considered self-evident and universal. But the process by which the great principles and practical rules of government were to be established was of necessity empirical. It took shape through a series of actions of the American Congress and of strong-minded civil and military leaders in the Philippines. There were two main lines of approach: one was to set up the institutional structure of the modern state, the other was to provide for the functional processes that would make it work.

The Constitution of the Philippines, adopted in 1935 and still in force today, was the work of an elected convention under the chairmanship of Claro M. Recto, a distinguished lawyer and politician whose turbulent career ended only with his death in Rome in 1960. The convention delegates, as Hayden points out, drew heavily on American precedents but ". . . adapted their borrowed ideas to the needs of their own country in the light of their native political experience and predilections." [9] Wherever the Filipinos departed from other models they did so in the direction of a greater centralization of power, particularly the power of the presidency. The president has great control over the budget and over local government. He is empowered to suspend the writ of *habeas corpus* and place the country under martial law. Claro M. Recto's comments on the centralization of power at the close of the Constitutional Convention are still of interest:

During the debate on the Executive Power it was the almost unanimous opinion that we had invested the Executive with rather extraordinary prerogatives. There is much of truth in this assertion. But it is because we cannot be insensible to the events that are transpiring around us . . . we have seen how dictatorships, whether black or red, capitalistic or proletarian, fascistic or communistic, ancient or modern, have served as the last refuge of peoples when their parliaments fail and they are already powerless to save themselves from misgovernment and chaos. Learning our lesson from this truth of history, and determined to spare our people the evils of dictatorship and anarchy, we have thought it prudent to establish an executive power which, subject to the fiscalization of the Assembly, and of public opinion, will not only know how to govern, but will actually govern, with a firm and steady hand, unembarrassed by vexatious interferences by other departments, or by unholy alliances with this and that social group. Thus possessed with the necessary gifts of honesty and competence, this Executive will be able to give his people an orderly and progressive government, without need of usurping or abdicating powers, and cunning subterfuge will not avail to extenuate his failures before the bar of public opinion.[10]

The first president of the Commonwealth, Manuel Quezon, was quite frank about another important deviation in a docu-

[9] Joseph R. Hayden, *The Philippines: A Study in National Development* (New York: Macmillan, 1942), p. 60.
[10] Same, p. 67.

ment that otherwise bears so many resemblances to the American Constitution. He argued that the political philosophy underlying the Constitution of the United States was quite different from that of the Philippine Constitution in that it placed the individual above every other consideration. "Under our Constitution what is paramount is not individuals; it is the good of the state, not the good of the individual that must prevail." [11]

The state, as Quezon so often pointed out, has a social responsibility. The president takes an oath to do justice to every man, a phrase that is not to be interpreted in a literal legal sense but rather as an obligation to do whatever he considers essential for the good of the country, provided the law does not actually forbid it. The presidency in the Philippines allows for a commonly held charismatic view of leadership. The leader who senses the popular will, as President Quezon well knew, is expected to act without too nice a consideration of the division of powers, of popular sovereignty, or even of the Bill of Rights. The status of the individual, for example, while stoutly affirmed, is limited by the absence of trial by jury, by *jus sanguinis* as the basis for citizenship, and by the regalian theory of natural resources.[12] The Constitution gives the government broad powers to expropriate and transfer land and to limit holdings. The right to own or exploit natural resources and public utilities is limited to Filipinos and corporations 60 per cent owned by Filipino citizens (a provision modified by constitutional amendment in 1946 to give Americans the same rights as Filipinos). The state is also empowered to expropriate utilities and private enterprises on payment of just compensation; to regulate private and public schools, provide free public primary schooling, and guarantee academic freedom in the universities.

The twenty-four senators in the Philippines, unlike those in the United States, are elected at large. This concession to Philippine conditions was justified by the framers of the Constitution on the ground that national figures would counteract regionalism. It is possible that other deviations from the American

---

[11] Human Relations Area Files, *Area Handbook on the Philippines*, v. 1 (New Haven: Author, under Sub-contract HRAF-1, Chi-1, 1956), p. 203.
[12] Same, p. 201.

model might have been written into the Constitution had not the Philippine Convention been aware that the document had to secure the approval of the American government. To judge by the Malolos Constitution, written entirely by Filipinos before the American conquest, it is arguable that the changes would not have been very serious, in fact there was a remarkable consistency between the two constitutions.[13] The Filipinos had some traditions of their own on which to build.

It might have been expected that the United States would replace the Spanish legal system with the American, but it did not do so. Because Spanish civil law remained largely untouched, the state continued to support the authority of the parent in the family and of the teacher in the school. No jury system was introduced. A supreme court on the American model, from which appeals could be made to the Supreme Court in Washington, and the writ of *habeas corpus* were the main additions on the legal side. As a matter of policy the legal system was put into the hands of Filipinos as rapidly as possible; after a quarter of a century of American rule only two out of fifty-five judges were Americans.[14]

The measures that the American authorities set in motion during the colonial period were not derived from any sophisticated theory of historical development, as are the strategy and tactics of the Communists. They reflected rather the views of political organization and of the state, of human relationships and of social values that stemmed from the experience of the Western world, particularly that of the United States. Because of these values, there was no ruthless and mechanical imposition of foreign institutions on a helpless people, yet there is no denying that the decision to make of the Philippines a democratic republic in the American image was unilateral. There was much more to this "experiment," therefore, than the imposition of democratic institutions. It was designed to be an educational, social, political, and economic revolution. A change of these dimensions was not undertaken absent-mindedly; it required great confidence and resolution. The ends desired were not always achieved and

[13] Hayden, cited, p. 33.
[14] W. Cameron Forbes, *The Philippine Islands* (Cambridge: Harvard University Press, 1945), Chapter 6.

the means employed not always coordinated, but the total impact on Philippine society was so great that there could never be any return to the conditions at the end of the Spanish period.

Education as a Means

The introduction of a compulsory system of public education was intended to be the cutting edge of the social and political revolution, the device that would make the difference between a literate oligarchy and an educated democracy. William Howard Taft, who dominated Philippine policy from 1901 to 1913, first as Civil Governor, then as Secretary of War, and finally as President of the United States, thought that the granting of independence should not be considered until the "decidedly ignorant masses" were educated sufficiently to be informed and responsible citizens. Once the United States undertook the task of making the Philippines into a democracy, such a policy was certainly the course of wisdom. But public education by itself, as the Japanese example had shown, does not necessarily lead to democracy. Much depends on what is taught and how it is taught.

In the United States the public school has been more than an academic institution; it has served as a means of molding peoples of diverse origins into a nation; the schools are the melting pots. It was natural to assume that this unique American concept of the school and of the role of education in the building of a nation would be peculiarly appropriate in the Philippines where there were also many peoples of diverse origins, differing in language and religion. The school was a device with the two essential characteristics of an instrument for revolutionary change: organizational continuity and direct access to the sources of ideology. For American purposes in the Philippines both the instrument and the point of attack, which was the values and loyalties of the ordinary Filipino, were well chosen.

A foundation already existed. The Malolos Constitution in 1899 had provided for free and compulsory education entirely under state control and for the elimination of religious instruction from the curriculum. Elementary education under the Spaniards had been largely in the hands of the church, and in spite of directives from Spain to teach the doctrine of the church in Spanish, the friars used the native dialect because they feared that a common language would encourage nationalism. A system of secondary schools and colleges had made it possible for a few Filipinos to learn Spanish and study for the professions, but for most of the population, memorization of the prayers and the *Doctrine Cristiana* was considered sufficient. Proposed reforms under the Spaniards were never carried out as intended, and, as a result, by 1898 there were 2,167 government-supported primary schools attended by about 200,000 boys and girls out of a total population of seven million.[15]

Although only a small minority of Filipinos received an education, enough had been done to stimulate tremendous interest and to create a demand that could not be satisfied. The Spanish educational system had attained its main objective, the teaching of Christianity, but had not succeeded in preparing the Filipinos to live in the modern world. The revolutionary leaders were ready for the American view of education as the handmaiden of the state, and of the school as the breeder of patriots and the training ground for citizens—though they took for granted the Spanish view that the educated man belonged to a small, privileged group.

It was the reformation of Philippine education that made other changes possible. The separation of church and state, the constitutional commitment to popular sovereignty, acceptance of social mobility, participation in the electoral process—all of these changes depended, in the long run, on the success of popular education. During the American period the rate of literacy increased faster than the increase in population. According to the census of 1948, two years after independence, 59.8 per cent of the population above ten years of age could read and write in some language or dialect.[16] Literacy in the English language was 37 per cent. When the Philippines acquired their independence more people could speak English than any other language, and with few exceptions English was still the language of instruction, even in the primary grades.

[15] *HRAF Handbook,* cited, v. 2, p. 752.
[16] Same, p. 956.

The imposition of the English language in the schools solved some serious problems but created others. It opened up to the Filipinos the world of Western learning and gave them a common language for government, the professions, business, and diplomacy. At the same time the prevalence and prestige of English made it more difficult to develop the use of Tagalog when it was chosen as the national language and impeded the emergence of a truly national literature. American-style curriculum and textbooks introduced the Filipino to a world he did not live in and placed before him traditions, heroes, and events that could never be part of his inner life and experience. This had serious consequences for the national ethos, and it accounted, among other things, for much of the ambivalence of the present day Filipino toward his native and his American heritage. In the long run, however, the Filipinos will make the educational system their own, and cultural pluralism will put the American contribution in perspective.

The most significant and lasting consequence of American educational policy is stated in Article XIV of the Philippine Constitution: "The Government shall establish and maintain a complete and adequate system of public education, and shall provide at least free public primary instruction, and citizenship training to adult citizens." The problem of financing this great undertaking has always been difficult, and at no time has the Constitution been fully implemented, but tremendous efforts have been made in response to the pressures of public opinion. Under the Americans, education became the main route of upward social mobility. While there is no exact way of measuring the social impact of the educational system it is clear that it has helped to bring new social classes into being, that the demand for education continues to be very great, and that, whatever its shortcomings, the educational system is second only to that of Japan among the countries of eastern Asia.

The shortcomings, however, are serious. The public school educational system is not doing the job for which it was intended and for which it is so admirably devised as an institution free from distinctions of class or sectarianism. The main trouble is that the public school system was never extended sufficiently to secondary and higher education. The Filipinos have a large number of college degrees, more per capita than any nation other than the United States, but this does not reflect a well-ordered educational system. It is estimated that 72 out of 100 students do not reach the sixth grade and only 5 out of 100 complete high school. While there may be enough trained Filipinos for the level of economic development today, there are not enough to furnish the need if economic growth actually takes place as planned.

The quality of education has gone down since World War II for a variety of reasons. Schools and colleges had to be rebuilt. (For instance, the University of the Philippines campus in downtown Manila was completely destroyed during the war.) The United States has given some help in reconstruction, but there is no way of recovering the loss of time, morale, and valuable collections. The salaries of teachers at the universities are so low when compared with opportunities in politics and the professions that it is hard for the University of the Philippines, for example, to keep its top faculty. In addition, the quality of education has also been lowered by the growth of large numbers of "diploma mills" on the college level, since the war. Finally, the public education system has been bypassed by the parallel system of church-affiliated schools, many of them excellent academically, but none of them, by definition, performing the essential task that only the public school can carry out. Practically all education beyond the elementary level is either private or parochial; and as it has to be supported from tuition the quality of instruction in fields such as medicine and science, which require expensive equipment, is even worse than it is in the fields of law, government, and the humanities. The only solution for this situation is to revitalize the public school system, but since many members of Congress either own or have shares in the diploma mills or support the parochial schools, this is not likely to be an easy task. Yet the future of Philippine democracy depends, in large measure, upon the quality and quantity of the public educational system.

Closely related to the emphasis on education during the American period was the development of a system of communications along American lines. As a result, the Philippines today is better provided than other Southeast Asian countries with postal, telegraph, telephone, and radio facilities, as well as with newspapers, periodicals, and books. The Philippines has had a free press longer than has Japan. There are important newspapers in the national and other languages, but English dominates the press and most of the literature, even poetry. As with many other things, the greatest concentration of intellectual communication is in the Manila area, where the literacy rate is also highest and where the political and economic decisions are made, just as they were in the Spanish period.

The Political Process

Political tutelage has ranked second only to public education among the important policies of American colonialism. The first step, the enactment of an excellent civil service law, was a bold and direct effort to implant the merit system in public administration and to train a group of professional administrators. "The Patronage or spoils system would prove absolutely fatal to good government in this new Oriental territory," wrote the Schurman Commission; public employment was not for sale to either Americans or Filipinos. At a time when, as Hayden points out, appointments in the British colonial service were handled on a patronage basis and only three states of the Union used the merit system, the United States set about introducing the most advanced concept of public administration in a country that had long been accustomed to corruption in government. American officials thought that without the civil service law and its strict enforcement American government in the islands would be "foredoomed to humiliating failure." [17] Because the Bureau of Civil Service was an independent office directly under the governor-general, it was possible to enforce the regulations with some measure of success. It is generally agreed that the administration of government in the Philippines up to 1913 was remarkably honest and efficient, with 2,777 Americans in the Philippine civil service, a little more than half the total number. When the Democrats took over in 1913 and Governor Harrison speeded the Filipinization of the

[17] Hayden, cited, pp. 88-91.

civil service, the number went down to 29 per cent and by 1921 to 4 per cent. In 1936 there were 160 Americans and 22,555 Filipinos in the civil service, or less than one per cent of the total.[18]

Much that had been achieved in the first fourteen years of American rule was rapidly undermined; these were the only years, in fact, when the United States ruled directly and had sufficient Americans in the field to do so. It was too short a period to achieve a change in the value system of a people unaccustomed to the merit principle in appointments and firmly convinced by their experience with Spain that political connections were essential for advancement and that government service was for personal profit rather than the public welfare. The Filipino concept of corruption differed radically from the American. To the Filipino, that man was corrupt who failed to pay his political debts with the spoils of office or to promote the interests of his kin group. The concept of honest and efficient administration as an end in itself, or as a necessary condition of good government, found little support in theory or in practice. Filipinization of the civil service came before the educational system had had time to inculcate the administrative concepts of the modern state.

The political training of the Filipinos in the responsibilities of national electoral office had begun with the creation of the Philippine Assembly in 1907. To be sure, the United States reserved to itself tremendous powers—Congress could annul any Philippine law on any subject, and the signature of the President was required for all laws dealing with currency, coinage, public land, timber and mining resources, tariff, and immigration. But the Assembly was in a position to have considerable influence over the executive and the civil service, especially after 1913. It was part of the process of political tutelage to encourage the growth of political parties; but one party, the Nacionalista, dominated the Assembly because of its monopoly of the issue of independence. The Assembly was the platform for two important Filipino leaders, Manuel Quezon, who led the Nacionalista party from 1922 until his death in 1944, and Sergio Osmeña. These men encouraged Filipino lawmakers to agitate for independence

18 *HRAF Handbook,* cited, v. 2, p. 967.

both in the Philippines and in the United States. They used their powers, whenever they were permitted, to dominate the executive branch of government for the remainder of the time that it was in American hands.

The policy for local government laid down by President McKinley was in line with American practice. "The natives of the islands . . . shall be afforded the opportunity to manage their local affairs to the fullest extent of which they are capable . . . In all cases the municipal officers . . . are to be selected by the people." In the distribution of powers among the governments organized by the commission, the instructions read, "the presumption is always to be in favor of the smaller subdivision" so that the central government of the Islands, "following the example of the distribution of powers between the state and the national government of the United States, shall have no direct administration except of matters of purely general concern." [19] There was a clear contradiction between the need for great authority in the hands of the executive arm of government, if it were going to be able to establish the institutions of the modern state, and the instruction to put more authority in the hands of local elected officers.

The Spanish tradition of centralization, combined with the American practice of supervising local government, ensured that there would be no revolutionary growth of local autonomy. Municipal officials were elected by the small propertied class which had the right to vote, but there was no diminution of central government control over finances and the administration of the new public services. The lines of authority ran directly through the executive departments to the president. Local government never became independent of central authority in any real sense. If the executive today carries out administrative functions at the provincial, city, and municipal levels through the departments of finance, agriculture, health, education, public works, justice, and the Office of Local Government, it is largely because the instructions of President McKinley were not and probably could not have been carried out. It has been suggested that if

[19] Dean C. Worcester, *The Philippines; Past and Present*, rev. ed. (New York: Macmillan, 1930), pp. 793, 795.

American supervision had continued longer there might have been sufficient antagonism against it to foster a stronger spirit of independence in local government, but even this possibility ceased in 1916 when American supervision of local government ceased.

The end result of American political direction was an American-type constitution but not an American form of government; the Philippine Republic is a centralized, not a federal government. The unusual concentration of authority in the person and office of the chief executive certainly did not come about by American intention, but resulted from historical factors and the structure of Philippine society. The Filipino looks for the charismatic element in leadership and is accustomed, through personal experience of the patricentric family, to accept authority. The relation between landlord and tenant, the most common of all relationships outside the family, was much more than a contractual affair. It had many of the elements of deference and responsibility that were common within the family. In the Philippines, traditions of individual initiative and responsibility in the political process had to be created as far as the masses were concerned. While it is not true to say that the ideological bases of the Western type of democracy have found no acceptance in the Philippines, they still compete with powerful forces.

The decentralization of government is probably an essential condition for economic progress along the lines decided upon by the Filipinos today. Some steps have been taken in this direction. The Barrio Act of 1960 provides the barrios with a legal personality and official powers to raise taxes, and the office of the Presidential Adviser for Community Development (PACD) stimulates local self-help projects. But much remains to be done if there is going to be a real working democracy in the Philippines. At the very minimum there must be a great improvement in the educational system to provide local leaders, a rapid building of physical communications, the provision of electric power to the barrios for light and for industry, the delegation of greater tax-raising powers to local authorities, and the abolition of the pork barrel system. The public works budget is called the Pork Barrel Bill and it amounts to around 30 per cent of the national budget.

Each congressman receives a share of these funds and is free to allocate them as he pleases in his own district, but the president controls the disbursement of the money. Obviously such a procedure means that all roads lead to Manila from whence comes all the money for public works projects, both large and small. If there is to be any growth of democracy, responsibility for most of the public works will have to be given to local agencies. And if units of local government had adequate powers, they could improve on what the central government provides for education, and they would have the incentives to better the tax collection system. The character of politics would change, and political parties, perhaps, would cease to be nothing more than coalitions of personal factions and local political bosses.

The Americans have mainly themselves to blame for the failure to build democracy at the grass roots when they had the opportunity to do so. All that they can do now is to encourage those groups and those forces in the Philippines that are moving in the right direction. Unfortunately, it is still an open question whether the Filipinos want a modern democratic political and economic system more than they want their traditional social system. They cannot have both.

Chapter 4

The Economic Record
of the United States

Economic Dependence and the Agrarian Problem

At the same time that the United States was taking steps to train the Filipinos in the art of self-government with a view to eventual freedom, it was making the colonial economy progressively dependent on its own. This was pointed up by President Garcia in his state of the nation address of January 1960, when he went out of his way to say that the Philippines became independent in 1946 but that economically it was still semicolonial, especially in foreign trade. The conditions to which he was referring go back to the establishment in 1909 of what has been called "free trade" between the two countries, meaning the free exchange of goods without tariff. The Philippine Assembly objected to this measure at the time on the ground that it would make the transition to independence in a world of tariffs all the more difficult. Even before the ten year period of grace for Spanish ships and goods came to an end ways were found to favor American goods, and after 1909 the Philippine economy became more and more bound to the American. To all intents and purposes this meant a closed, not an open, door, and raised the question whether a country could be politically free and economically dependent.

There is no doubt but that the Filipinos would feel more independent if they were less dependent on one country for their imports and exports. They would be less open to pressure from the American Congress and from those domestic industries that depend so heavily on the American market. That is why it is to the long-range interest of the United States to put no obstacles in the way of diversification.

Too much has been made of this point, however, and not enough of an even more serious defect of U.S. policy: its neglect of the agrarian situation. While the import-export pattern may modify the exercise of political independence in relation to one country, the agrarian problem raises the more fundamental questions of domestic political stability and economic progress. Something was done about the short-range problem of the friar lands, but little about the long-range problem of improving Philippine agriculture.

The United States inherited a land problem from the Spanish regime that had features peculiar to the Philippines, but in many respects land tenure was similar to that in other parts of Asia. In the pre-Spanish system, with some exceptions, ownership of land seems to have been on a community basis under the control of the *datus,* or chieftains. On this system the Spaniards superimposed the encomiendas, or land grants given to Spanish subjects, which entitled the holder to collect taxes and impress labor. While not hereditary at first, the land grants tended to become so, and there evolved what came to be called the cacique system. The cacique, or landlord, armed with patents from the Spanish authorities, took a share of the crop from the tenant and handled practically all the affairs of the tenants under his control, lending money and helping out in times of natural disaster. As a market economy developed in the late nineteenth century, an increasing number of landowners left their estates in the hands of men known as *inquilinos* (cash tenants) who paid rent in cash to the landlord, often an absentee, and in turn exacted payments in cash or kind from the share tenants. The paternalistic relation between the resident landlord and the peasantry grew weaker as a cash tenancy system spread over many areas in the Philippines. But the cacique retained the social and political authority to which the landlord had been accustomed, he was the local "boss."

The distress of the peasants on both privately held and church-affiliated lands was so obvious that during the last decades of their rule the Spaniards tried, without much success, to issue land titles. It was not surprising that the wealthy and the educated appropriated such titles as were issued, to the disadvantage of the illiterate peasants to whom the very concept of a land title was an incomprehensible innovation. Boundaries were so vague and cultivation often so shifting that, in the absence of a cadastral survey, flagrant abuses were common; the gap between poor and rich grew wider. At the time of the American conquest the number of Filipino peasants without land titles was estimated at 400,000, and there was no complete record of the titles issued.[1]

American policy was first to settle the question of the friar lands through purchase and resale. This was only partially successful because not all the friar lands were purchased and most of the land went back to tenancy. In addition, although the friar holdings were large (the Augustinians, Dominicans, and Recollects owned about 400,000 acres of good land), they were only a small proportion of the total area under cultivation. The second step was to protect the public domain. The Organic Law of 1902 set limits of 144 hectares for private and 1024 hectares for corporate holdings of undeveloped land. Third, the American administrators, bound by the Treaty of Paris, recognized the Spanish royal grants but made an effort to extend land registration for the protection of the owners. They borrowed from Australia the system of Torrens titles whereby the occupant of the land is assumed to be the rightful owner unless another owner proves his title. Courts for land registation were set up to receive applications for title based on cadastral survey of the land in question, and after due process the court issued a clear title. Not by intent, but in effect, this procedure gave great advantages to the educated and the wealthy because court procedures cost money and were incomprehensible to the ignorant peasant. Very few peasants secured title to their land, and some lost what they had.

As agriculture is still the most important sector of the Philippine economy, providing employment for 65 per cent of the labor force, contributing about 40 per cent of the national income and 75 per cent of the value of exports, failure to make any sig-

[1] Karl J. Pelzer, *Pioneer Settlement in the Asiatic Tropics* (New York: American Geographical Society, 1945), p. 90.

nificant improvement in the agricultural sector was a serious shortcoming in the U.S. record. While the Japanese were improving their crop production by applying science to agriculture, the rice culture of the Philippines remained almost static, with no increase in yield per hectare and no improvement in the peasant's standard of living. Part of the reason for failure was the fact that, because of differences in conditions, the legal provisions and individual incentives that worked in the United States did not produce the same results in the Philippines. It must also be admitted that even such measures of agrarian reform as the United States attempted to enforce were successfully blocked by the Philippine legislature.

The last significant effort of the American administration before the establishment of the Commonwealth government came in 1933 when Governor-General Theodore Roosevelt persuaded the Philippine legislature to pass a Rice Share Tenancy Act. The purpose of the act was to protect the rice-producing share tenant against abuses by the landlord. But the caciques were strong enough to have the legislation amended in such a way as to make it ineffective. When further efforts were made in 1936 to improve the lot of the share tenants, who had revolted against the landlords in certain areas, the caciques again prevented the general application of the law. They insisted on a provision that the act should take effect only by proclamation of the President of the Philippines upon recommendation of the secretary of labor, and then only when public interests so require; in other words, when the share-tenants were disturbing law and order.[2] The Tenancy Act called for reforms such as the writing of contracts between landlord and tenant in the local dialect; establishment of a one-year minimum for contracts; equal sharing of the crop and of the cost of transplanting, harvesting, threshing, irrigation, and fertilizer; a limit of 10 per cent per agricultural year on advances for cultivation; and no breaking of the contract by either party except for good reasons. President Quezon made some efforts to enforce the Act in 1937, but it was difficult to anticipate and block the many evasive measures adopted by the landowners.

The fact that the percentage of tenancy had doubled by 1935

[2] Same, p. 98.

would have been less significant if the rice tenancy legislation had been enforced. It is not the number of tenants but the conditions of tenancy that matter. Because the American administrators made so little progress in improving the conditions of tenancy—getting rid of usury, issuing titles, enforcing contracts, and limiting the proportion of the crop paid to the landlord by the share-tenants—the increase in tenancy was a serious matter. The lack of any improvement in living standards (in fact, the mass of the people may have been even worse off than before) had much to do with the outbreak of the several agrarian revolts. The Sakdal revolt of 1935 in central Luzon had very strong ideological overtones, and during World War II the Communist-led Hukbalahaps were able to recruit large numbers of peasants to their cause.

Opposition to the measures proposed by the American authorities to improve the lot of the peasant was not alone responsible for the growth of tenancy. The social and legal institutions that favored tenancy were in some cases not the old but rather the new ones, such as the attempt to issue land titles and the establishment of the Philippine legislature, which gave preponderant influence to the caciques. The comparative lack of public education in the villages left the peasant even more at the mercy of the educated and powerful men who controlled and profited from the new institutions of the modern state while still retaining the advantages of the traditional society. The high frequency of share-tenancy in the Tagalog area, closely correlated with agrarian unrest, is probably associated with its proximity to Manila; a similar commercialization of land tenure was apparent around Shanghai in prewar China.

The strong trend toward the growth of a cash economy under the American occupation also had its effects. The granting of free trade preferences to Philippine exports after 1909 stimulated the production of cash crops such as sugar, copra, abacá, and tobacco for export to the United States. At the same time it gave to American manufactured imports a competitive advantage, which led to the decline of Philippine handicrafts, an important element in the agricultural economy. This, as an American economist has suggested, led to the last important change in the economy of the Philippines: the emergence of a "colonial"-type "national" economy, heavily dependent on agricultural raw material exports and on manufactured and processed goods as well as food imports. By 1940, the "colonial"-type, export-import economy had developed to such a degree that the proceeds from the agricultural export crops amounted to approximately one-third of the total national income. It was estimated at that time that no less than six million of the total population of sixteen million were dependent on the cash crop export commodities for their livelihood. Not only was there a large direct dependency on the production of these export crops, but also there appeared to be little inclination to change the existing structure by reorienting internal production and consumption patterns. The emphasis on production for the export market, as a matter of fact, was so great that the Philippines, potentially one of the great food-surplus producing areas in the Far East, became one of the major food-deficit areas.[3]

There is little in this analysis that Filipinos would disagree with so far as it describes their relations with the United States, but not many of them pause to reflect that things might have been much worse if it had not been for other aspects of U.S. policy. The Americans did not leave the Filipinos with a huge alien population on the land, like the Chinese and Indians in Malaya, or cover the country with huge plantations worked with alien labor. As far as land was concerned, it was for the most part reserved for the use of the Filipinos.

According to former Governor-General Forbes, the limitation was due to the activities of the beet sugar lobby, which hoped to cripple the Philippine sugar industry by preventing corporations from holding enough land to supply a modern sugar central. The official reason given was that the limitation would protect the Filipinos from the speculative acquisition of large tracts of undeveloped land by American financial interests.[4] Philippine land laws made it virtually impossible for aliens to acquire pub-

[3] Thomas R. McHale, "Economic Development in the Philippines," *Journal of East Asiatic Studies*, v. 1, no. 3, 1952 (University of Manila), pp. 1-10.

[4] Grayson Kirk, *Philippine Independence* (New York: Farrar & Rinehart, Inc. 1936), p. 64.

lic land legally, and the controlling interest in corporations could be held only by Filipinos or Americans. Thus, while there was a growth of a modified plantation economy in export crops such as sugar, the firm attitude of the American Congress and the Philippine aversion to large landed estates combined to prevent the rapid exploitation of the land and its resources by American capital. There is little reason to doubt the statement of the last American governor-general, Frank Murphy: "The public domain has not been exploited. Large estate grants—a sore spot in other days—have not been tolerated. The natural inheritance of the Filipino as the owner of his fatherland has not been violated." [5] The Filipinos have not been ungrateful for the protection of the public domain.

It is easier now to see what could have been done to improve the lot of the Philippine peasantry, but there was no body of theory available at the time to provide the answers or even to define the problem. The United States itself had no fear of agrarian revolt; and the little-understood role of the Russian peasantry in the events of 1917 gave no warning of the revolutionary potential of the peasants of Asia.

Economic Growth

The emergence of a so-called colonial type, import-export economy should not be allowed to obscure the other possibly more significant developments that were made in the economic sphere during the American period. The reform and extension of the legal system in substance and in practice, an essential step for economic growth, was undertaken early and included, as we have seen, efforts to straighten out the land title situation. For where titles are unclear, banking credit is timid and usury flourishes. The limited success in this field contrasts sharply with the large measure of success in establishing the legal framework for banking, commerce, and industry. Economic growth also depends on communications and the American period saw impressive developments in journalism, literature, science, and edu-

[5] Pelzer, cited, p. 108.

cation, as well as in the building of roads, bridges, harbors, and railroads, and the construction of postal, telegraph, and cable communications. Also of great importance was the stabilization of the currency by tying the peso to the dollar, and the multiplication of banking and insurance facilities.

The United States also took it for granted that a government was responsible for providing an efficient public health service. The energy put into public health, told so well by Dr. Heiser in his *American Doctor's Odyssey*, accounts in large measure for the doubling of the population from roughly ten million to twenty million through eliminating epidemics of smallpox, rinder-pest, Asiatic cholera, and bubonic plague, and reducing the incidence of other diseases such as beriberi and malaria. The average life expectancy in 1900, which was 12 years for males and 14 years for females, rose to more than 40 years by the end of the American period.

The American administration may have created conditions for economic growth, but it cannot claim any significant progress in either agriculture or industry. There was some mechanization of agriculture, especially in the processing of sugar, and modest attention was given to the use of fertilizers and to plant and animal husbandry; but the extent of the effort may be judged by the fact that production of rice and corn, the staple crops, did not keep up with the increase in the population.

The greatest industrial advances were made in the mining of gold, copper, chromite, iron, and manganese ores. The development of power production and manufacturing was, on the other hand, extremely limited. Why was this so? It is too simple to say that American imperialism deliberately restricted the Philippines to the extractive industries and the production of agricultural raw materials, although this is what happened. If this was the objective, then it was badly conceived. A nation with this in mind would not have undertaken political tutelage and have turned over so much power so soon to the Filipinos. Nor would there have been deliberate efforts to promote Filipino participation in banking, trade, and industry by establishing a government bank of issue and a National Development Company. If economic control had been the intent of colonial policy, investments would have flowed into the Philippines. But they did not do so, a fact that the Communists are hard put to explain because they find the real explanation inadmissible: the political decision to prepare a colony for independence did not encourage investment in expensive long-range undertakings.

The failure of the Philippines to take even the first step toward industrialization—the development of light industries and power facilities—was due partly, it must be admitted, to the free trade policy that gave American manufacturers a competitive advantage in the local market. In spite of their very real control over domestic affairs during the last decades of the American occupation, the Filipinos could not impose tariffs in order to develop their own industries. But other considerations were perhaps more relevant, and the responsibility for them must be shared. One was the failure to raise the purchasing power of the peasantry by improving agricultural production and changing the social conditions in the villages. This also diverted funds to the purchase of imported food. The problem still exists. Another reason, also of current significance, was the cultural resistance to industrialization in the Philippines, which took the form of a reluctance to invest in industry and to develop large-scale business organizations. This cultural resistance stemmed from a value system built around the ownership and use of land. Social status, class identification, the patterns of production and consumption, all were associated in a peculiarly intimate way with the land. A whole way of life, built around the simple facts of agriculture, does not change unless it is undermined or challenged by stronger political and economic forces.

Whatever their formal objectives, U.S. economic policies speeded certain changes in the Philippine economy that were strong enough to put the traditional culture on the defensive. One of these was the rapid increase in the use of money. The amount of money in circulation in 1959 was fifty times as large as in 1900. Quite apart from the expansion of credit facilities and the velocity of circulation, there is clearly a qualitative difference in the economy today as compared with Spanish times. Money makes it possible for ambitious men to operate outside the traditional social and economic system, to secure status or financial security outside the bounds of kin and class. It sets up different standards of social measurement and provides a different channel to power and prestige. Relations based on status give place to those based on contract; new concepts of obligation emerge and new types of economic organization compete with the landbound family system.

Political decisions to force the pace of political tutelage in the Philippines also brought some unplanned economic consequences. By turning over to the Filipinos a large degree of control over internal affairs so soon after the conquest, the United States took into partnership in the task of constructing the modern state some of the elements in Philippine society that were least interested in change and were in the best position to prevent it. Before the other measures introduced by the American administration changed the balance of power in society, the traditional Philippine oligarchy again dominated the political process. This contributed in no small measure to a phenomenon peculiarly strong in the Philippines: the use of political influence or position for direct personal or group financial gain. One example is the use of the legislative power in the treatment of alien groups—the passing of discriminatory laws against the Chinese in order to increase the price that the Chinese would have to pay to have the laws disregarded.

Under American rule the threefold division of labor between Filipinos, Chinese, and Westerners followed roughly the pattern established under the Spaniards. The Chinese continued to prosper as retail merchants and in the processing of agricultural goods. Americans removed the legal limitations on Chinese commerce that had been imposed by the Spaniards, and with more efficient government they reduced extra-legal or indirect forms of taxation. Chinese investments in the Philippines before World War II were estimated at about half the total of American investments, being distributed among lumber, banking, retail and wholesale merchandizing, and real estate. Since American immigration laws were applied to the Chinese entering the Philippines, there was no mass importation of Chinese labor. But the Chinese population increased under American rule, and, as elsewhere in Southeast Asia, the tendency to intermarry with the people of the host country decreased and the Chinese community kept its racial and cultural identity.

Under American rule Westerners continued to specialize in banking, import and export transactions, and in other undertakings requiring large-scale capital investment. In consequence of the trade relations between the two countries, the American business community in the Philippines exercised a powerful influence on the economic policies of both governments. One year before World War II, the Philippines sent to the United States 82 per cent of its annual exports (valued at $256,064,439) and bought from the United States a little under 78 per cent of its annual imports (valued at $210,630,854). In 1960, U.S. trade with the Philippines was still substantial.

The third element in the division of labor, the traditional Philippine economy, underwent the least change during the American period, particularly in the agricultural sector, as we have seen. It had least to do with the market economy that Americans, Spaniards, Chinese, and Japanese were developing. The fact that foreigners took the leading role in the modernization of the economy had some unavoidable consequences for Philippine nationalism. The Filipino nationalist who favors a modern economy has to contend with the traditional Filipino who does not approve of the challenge to the socio-economic system and so is willing to encourage, for his own purposes, an appeal to nationalism in terms of antiforeign feelings with a reckless disregard for the economic consequences. Some, knowingly or not, may accept an alliance with radical forces that have different long-range objectives but are immediately interested in destroying the position of the aliens in the economy. The Filipinos who play a role in the new sectors of the economy are not large in number, and they vary in their degree of alienation from the traditional system; their ranks are perilously thin. They are the most important by-product of American economic policies. Much depends on the outlook, the wisdom, and the political role of this middle class—a matter taken up in more detail in Chapter 9.

Chapter 5

A Country Divided —
World War II

Communism and the Philippines

Moscow and the Comintern began to pay serious attention to the Philippines only a decade after the Bolshevik revolution took place. The delay was due more to the exigencies of the world situation than to a lack of a general strategy for the colonial world. Although Lenin elaborated the doctrinal basis for Communist policy in the "colonial and backward countries of the East," in his writings and speeches during the years 1919 and 1920, the only major application of theory to practice in the 1920s was in China. During this period Southeast Asia remained an area of secondary importance in which Moscow, unable to press such advantages as it might have had, confined itself to making useful contacts with groups and individuals in various countries by working through the Communist parties of the imperial powers.

It was at the suggestion of the American Communist party that Philippine labor unions sent delegates to the First Congress of the Oriental Transportation Workers held in Canton in 1924. Three years later the Philippine Labor Congress affiliated itself with the Red International Labor Union and began a worker's party, some of whose leaders were selected for training in Moscow. Crisanto Evangelista and Cirilo Bognot—who had already met Chou En-lai and Earl Browder—and Jacinta Manahan, were among those who went to Moscow. At the same time Filipino Communists set about infiltrating peasant organizations, one of which, the National Federation of Tenants and Agricultural

Workers of the Philippines, continued in existence until it was absorbed into the Huk organization during the war.

The Communist party of the Philippine Islands, established in August 1930, held its first Congress in secret in Manila, May 1931, bringing together 40 delegates from 13 provinces. The Congress adopted a resolution to the effect that it

fully and unconditionally accepts and approves the Program and Statutes of the Communist International (as adopted by the VI World Congress of the C.I.) and herewith makes application to the Communist International. The C.P.P.I. expresses its hope and desire that the C.I. will help the young C.P.P.I. with advice and guidance based on the rich experience of the world-revolutionary movement led by the Communist International—the General Staff of the World Revolution.[1]

The Manifesto of the Congress went on to state that the objective situation in the Philippine Islands favored the rapid development of the Communist party. However, because of the party's inexperience as well as ". . . the ruthlessness of the iron heel of Yankee imperialism and native reaction, it was essential that the Communist International and the Communist Party of the United States give special attention and guidance to this sector of the international revolutionary front." [2] Outlawed by the Commonwealth government in 1931, the young Philippine Communist party needed all the help and direction it could get. This was not long in coming. The Comintern laid down its directives for the Filipino Communists in four important articles published in *Inprecor* in 1931 entitled, "The Imperialist Offensive Against the Revolutionary Movement in the Philippines and the Tasks of the C.P.P.I.," and signed by Tim Ryan, the pseudonym of a Canadian Communist.

The main task that the Comintern assigned to the party during the 1930s was to polarize Philippine politics, primarily by capturing the leadership of all opposition to the United States and the Commonwealth government, which were always to be described as having identical interests. Techniques to be used in-

[1] Organ of the Executive Committee of the Communist Internationale, *International Press Correspondence, 1924-1935,* 11 vols. (Moscow: Author, 1924 ff.), v. 11, no. 33, June 25, 1931, p. 603.
[2] Same, p. 604.

cluded building up cells in "factories and fields," leading "local struggles around the burning needs of the masses," and linking together the "basic struggle for national independence and land." The immediate enemy to be destroyed was not the United States or the "native bourgeoisie," but those who stood for what the Communists called "national-reformism." The party was instructed to "ruthlessly expose" the demands of the National-Reformists for improvements in the land title situation—a cadastral survey, more rural credits, and other improvements—as these would take ammunition away from the Communists. They preferred to convince the peasant masses that the only correct and practical solution of the agrarian problem was the revolutionary seizure of land from the landlords. Hence, the instructions to carry on revolutionary work in all "reformist peasant organizations having a mass base."

In the Philippines as elsewhere, the policy after the Communist failure in China in 1927 was directed at undermining the moderate democratic and socialist parties so as to capture the "hegemony over the masses," and only then to correct the reformist and gradualist tendencies within the party and thus remake it into an organization of the Bolshevist type. Many of the Filipino Communist leaders had been convicted on charges of sedition and rebellion and sentenced to various terms of imprisonment. Those who remained at large went undergound and established strict discipline through inner party educational work, including study courses, discussion groups, and self-criticism. Activists were trained in numerous small engagements: strikes, attacks on landlords, mass resistance to evictions, seizure of food and seed supplies from landlords and merchants. Official policy at this time called for an attack on right-opportunism—the name given to "legalism, passivity, and an under-estimation of the willingness of the masses to struggle." The struggle against right-opportunism in the Philippines was part of the simultaneous world-wide campaign of the Communist International to eliminate Bukharinism. The directive also charged the party to use to the full any available legal means to press for repeal of the sedition law, release of political prisoners, and legalization of the party. In short, while fighting for its open existence, the party was directed to combine its "legal" activities with semi-legal ones, and its followers were given detailed instructions for both legal and underground activities.

That the Philippine Communists acted on these instructions is a matter of history. One of their accomplishments, for those who are inclined to underestimate the skill with which the climate of opinion can be utilized, was the release of the imprisoned Communist leaders. In 1938 a representative of the American Communist party, Allen by name, persuaded the Commonwealth government to set the prisoners free, and thus they became available to lead the Huks a few years later. This achievement would probably have been impossible without the new image of Communists as fighters against fascism that was skillfully developed after adopting the united front policy in August 1935.

The Communist party immediately negotiated an alliance with the Socialist party. Most of the Socialists were anti-Communists, though they had represented the left-wing opposition during the years when the Communist party was illegal. Their leader, Pedro Abad Santos (also known as Don Perico), is claimed by Philippine Communists as a party member, but according to another view he opposed any resort to violence and was used by the Communists for their own purposes. The Socialists flourished mainly in Central Luzon, the traditional center of agrarian unrest, and during this period they combined socialism with considerable violence and class warfare. Several Socialist leaders who later declared themselves Communists, including Luis Taruc, received their activist training with the Socialists in the 1930s. As might have been expected, the federation of the two parties resulted in its complete domination by the Communists.

It has long been clear that the Hukbalahap movement, during and after World War II, was no spontaneous uprising of embattled farmers. In escaping posthaste from Manila in January 1942, just ahead of the Japanese, Vicente Lava, a leading Communist, left on his desk the plans for a Barrio United Defense Corps. These plans were pratically identical with those that had been drawn up by Communist guerrillas in China in 1937, a few months after the Japanese invasion. The transfer of techniques and experience was natural, for the Chinese Communists were in constant touch with the Filipino Communists before and during World War II, and some of their publications were put to good use by guerrillas in the Philippines.[3] The Hukbalahap movement would not have been possible without the previous ten years of struggle, preparation, and organization by the Philippine Communist party under the guidance of the Communist International.

The Japanese Occupation

Three countries fought for control of the Philippines during World War II: the United States, Japan, and the Soviet Union. In this deadly and costly struggle, still very much alive in the minds of Filipinos today, Japan was politically and militarily eliminated, and the Filipinos themselves suffered a grinding attack on their social and political institutions as well as a severe test of their national spirit. When the war began, the leaders of the Philippine Commonwealth, still five years away from promised independence, found themselves in a situation of great complexity. The Commonwealth was neither in control of its foreign relations nor responsible for its own defense; the United States could legally involve the Philippines in the war with Japan and dictate the political and military strategy of the conflict. The Filipinos had to cope with the problems of allegiance to the United States, to the Philippine Commonwealth, and to the occupying power, Japan, which called on them for treasonable behavior. In addition, they also had to cope with civil conflict, for the agrarian movements of the 1930s were quickly taken over by the Communists (Hukbalahaps) and linked to

[3] As Alvin Scaff puts it in his study: "It was during this pre-war period that the class war actually started between the Philippine government and the old political leadership on one side, and the organized peasants and workers under Communist and Socialist leadership on the other. The issues were drawn; the organizations were formed; the leaders were identified. The same people and same leaders who emerged from these pre-war struggles on the side of the peasants and workers, organized and constituted the Hukbalahap at the time of the Japanese invasion. And they were the same ones in the main who carried on the fight against the Philippine government after its independence in 1946." *The Philippine Answer to Communism* (Stanford University Press, 1955), p. 18.

the international struggle between the United States, Japan, and the Soviet Union. The Communist-led revolution against the existing order was all the more difficult to handle because it operated under the cloak of anti-Japanese patriotism and claimed to be in good standing with both the Commonwealth and the United States. The Filipinos, moreover, had to deal with the problem faced by all puppet governments of establishing a policy toward those among its own people who were carrying on underground or overt resistance to the enemy, a resistance that also sheltered ordinary criminals. It is easy now to forget the extraordinary complexity of the situation that faced the Filipino leaders who remained behind and served under the Japanese, and even easier to underestimate the degree of success with which the Commonwealth government dealt with the situation.

The main facts of the Japanese conquest and occupation of the Philippines are well known. Immediately after Pearl Harbor the Commonwealth army, placed under American command, had resisted the Japanese push from Lingayen Gulf and then retreated to Bataan, where it put up a hopeless fight until forced to surrender at Corregidor on May 6, 1942. President Quezon, Vice-President Osmeña, and several members of the Cabinet made their way by submarine to various parts of the Philippines and eventually to Washington, leaving behind other members of the government to deal with the invader. The Japanese had moved into Manila, declared it an open city on January 2, 1942, in order to prevent its destruction, and had immediately announced that United States sovereignty over the Philippines had come to an end. They chose to ignore the fact that the Philippines was at war with Japan, insisting that Japan had come to free fellow orientals from Western domination and could therefore rightfully claim their cooperation. The Filipinos had no standing under international law, not even the status of an occupied people. Any Filipinos refusing to serve in a Japanese-created puppet regime were therefore treated by the Japanese as traitors and could be shot. After the Japanese executed Chief Justice José Santos on May 7, 1942, for refusing to serve under them, very few Filipino leaders declined to take office. In dealing with anything that could be labeled as anti-Japanese, the Japanese authorities were utterly ruthless and took thousands of lives without benefit of trial.

The Japanese Commander-in-Chief ordered Jorge B. Vargas, whom President Quezon had named as his personal representative, to be chairman of an Executive Commission, to which a Council of State was added in an advisory capacity. This was the shape of the first puppet government in which many of the most prominent Filipino leaders of the Commonwealth served. As in occupied China, the Japanese were incapable of leaving their puppets enough self-respect even to be good puppets, for every department of government was staffed with so-called Japanese advisers and all actions and official statements had to be drawn up or approved by them. The Japanese military administration took over all Philippine institutions and resources, forcing the puppet officials to preside over the exploitation of their own country. To control the general population the Japanese extended to the Philippines a system of collective responsibility which, under various names, has had a long history in Asia. The members of ten families were considered a unit for purposes of policing, reporting on guerrilla activities, and the enforcement of government orders. The people, in other words, were used to control themselves in a manner that was particularly degrading to Filipinos, accustomed as they were to a substantial measure of personal freedom.

The Japanese moved quickly to disestablish all political parties; they could hardly be expected to tolerate abroad what they did not have at home. As replacement they set up an organization known as the Kalibapi, said at first to be nonpolitical in character, into which they forced all government officials and practically every other existing organization, even including the Philippine Veterans Association headed by General Aguinaldo. Holding a meeting of the Kalibapi at Malolos, the birth place of the first republic, was an act of either sheer stupidity or deliberate mockery. The next step was to grant to the Filipinos their "independence," and a republic was inaugurated on October 14, 1943, with José Laurel as president. The Japanese dictated the constitution and handpicked the Kalibapi delegates who approved it; they made Vargas the ambassador to Japan. The Filipinos accepted, as they had to, the pretentious mockery, but in various ways they showed their resentment as openly as the Japanese revealed their contempt.

Step by step the puppet regime in the Philippines became more and more useless to the Japanese. According to an observer on the spot:

Crime, indeed, inside and outside the Government, inside and outside of the new Constabulary, rose to heights previously unimaginable . . . Official extortion and brutality; private thievery, robbery, and murder; quasi-judicial 'executions' of collaborators and supposed collaborators by the guerrillas—the lawlessness knew no bounds. Practice blackouts which had finally begun in May, were soon held only on moonlit nights because Japanese soldiers and civilians and Japanese 'sympathizers' were resorted to by the agencies of the 'law' . . . There was a constant invasion and searching of private homes as well as searching of pedestrians on the streets. More and more young men of prominent families were taken into various Japanese 'training' institutes or were sent to Japan as 'pensionados of the Republic,' but actually as hostages to keep their fathers in line.[4]

As the problem of food became more and more urgent, Roxas was given the job of organizing food distribution—that is, of feeding the Japanese army. Laurel, at Japanese instigation, tried to mitigate the guerrilla problem by declaring an amnesty, and by offering food and employment to guerrillas who surrendered. Although these policies met with some success, they did not affect the struggle to any serious extent.

When the Japanese conferred "independence" on the Philippines they made it a member of the Greater East Asia Co-Prosperity Sphere, which was theoretically an association of independent states with Japan as the leader. In fact, the Japanese established complete economic, political, and ideological control over their newly won territories, using very much the same pattern as in their earlier conquests. The Philippines, like the rest, came under the control of the Greater East Asia Ministry; it was to this Ministry that the Japanese ambassador to Manila actually reported, not to the Ministry of Foreign Affairs. "Independence," it was clear,

[4] A. V. H. Hartendorp, *History of Industry and Trade of the Philippines* (Manila: McCullough Printing Company, 1958), p. 129.

was to be in name only and was obviously recognized as such by the Filipinos. They had to accept "independence" whether they liked it or not, and with it a Japan-Philippine Pact of Alliance. Both parties agreed to cooperate closely in prosecuting the War of Greater East Asia, and the Philippines agreed to furnish all kinds of facilities for the military actions to be undertaken by Japan and to "closely cooperate" with Japan "to safeguard the territorial integrity and independence of the Philippines." This meant that the Japanese would continue to use the Philippines as they had before the alliance. Although the Filipinos were not requested to fight abroad for the Japanese, a matter on which they congratulated themselves, the commitment to join with Japan in safeguarding the territorial integrity and independence of the Philippines meant that, when the Americans returned, any Filipino who gave them aid and assistance would be a traitor. But there was to be no conscription, for even the Japanese realized that this would be far too dangerous a step. The republic, as was to be expected, was recognized by the Axis powers and Japanese satellites; it even asked for American recognition. In September 1944 the Japanese forced the Philippines to agree to the final indignity of declaring a state of war against the United States and Great Britain.

By this time it was quite clear that the mass of Filipinos was completely alienated from the government and would welcome the Americans back, and that the puppet regime was of no value whatsoever. The Philippine constabulary was so unreliable, with desertions amounting to 75 per cent of the force, that it was disarmed. The Japanese made desperate efforts to organize Filipinos to cooperate with them, but in 1945 they found themselves fighting alone to a suicidal end that cost the destruction of most of the city of Manila and the ruthless killing of thousands of Filipinos. Laurel and his cabinet were transported to Baguio. When the American forces approached Baguio, the Japanese took Laurel to Tokyo, but permitted the other cabinet officers to escape. On reaching the American lines, they were arrested and imprisoned, except for Roxas, who alone was exonerated of the charge of collaboration and attached to the staff of General Douglas MacArthur. The former members of the Laurel cabinet were all released when American sovereignty came to an end in 1946, and the Philippine authorities eventually declared an amnesty for the so-called collaborators. All Japanese nationals, military and civilian, were repatriated, and Japanese assets were taken over by the republic. Not until after the signing of a treaty of peace in 1952 were diplomatic relations restored between the Philippines and Japan.

The Wartime Role of Filipino Leaders

When the Japanese arrived, the first problem for the leaders of the Commonwealth government was to clarify their relationship to the United States, to which all Filipinos still owed allegiance. What was the correct policy in 1941 for the government of a country that had been promised full independence by a colonial power that had proved powerless to defend it and might never return? Some Filipinos had long anticipated the problems that would confront an independent Philippines. As early as 1927 Claro M. Recto had pointed out that the only chance of survival was the establishment of some sort of equilibrium between the power of the Western empires and the ambitions of Japan and the Soviet Union. On the day that the Western empires are ousted from the Pacific, "the Philippines, which lies in the way of Japanese expansion, will fulfill the destiny assigned to it by Count Okuma: to do homage to the mighty and to allow the strongest to rule." [5]

To Recto the coming struggle with communism was also clear long before World War II:

China and Russia, separately or jointly, are now plainly visible behind Japan, which indisputably holds the center of the stage at this time, as possible champions in the future of an Asiatic Monroe Doctrine if that idea ever materializes. The Philippines will be beset, on the one hand, by the major problem of Chinese immigration, the solution of which is not to be conjectured at this time, and, on the other hand, by the avalanche of communistic ideas which is the corner-stone of the present civilization. All this would happen if western influence were

[5] Claro M. Recto, *Three Years of Enemy Occupation* (Manila: Peoples Publishers, 1946), p. 136.

completely swept away from Asia by the great Pan-Asiatic movement directed and fostered by Soviet Russia.[6]

Therefore the Philippines, he argued, should be cautious about aligning itself with those who would drive Western power out of the Pacific completely, for as much as Filipinos might want to see an end to "the secular domination, the insulting arrogance, and the false caste privileges of the 'white man' in the East," for the small peoples of Asia, "the domination of Asiatics by Occidentals is no more odious than that of Asiatics by Asiatics." An end to the rule of the white race in the East is one thing, said Recto, and "the maintenance here of its culture and its commerce, on the basis of an equality of right and opportunities, in order to preserve the necessary equilibrium between those two great agencies of civilization, the East and the West, is another." [7] If the Philippines were to be independent, therefore, it must be militarily strong, a goal that the United States, he felt, was doing nothing to help them achieve, and politically independent, which would mean having no American military bases on Philippine soil. To be militarily weak and at the same time militarily committed to the defense arrangements of a foreign power (the United States) would invite the danger of involvement in a war of someone else's choosing and the prospect of being considered expendable.

This is exactly what happened. As General George C. Marshall later declared, the Philippines, a small military outpost of the United States, would always have to be sacrificed in a fight with a first-class power; nor could it be assumed that the United States would enter the war if Japan were to attack the Philippines but not the territory of the continental United States.[8] There was certainly no obligation to do so.

President Quezon undoubtedly had considerations such as these in mind soon after Pearl Harbor when he proposed, with the approval of his cabinet, that the United States grant independence immediately, that both the United States and Japan

[6] Same, p. 138.
[7] Same, p. 139.
[8] George C. Marshall, "Pearl Harbor Hearing," *The Manila Times,* December 8, 1945.

agree to neutralization, and that both American and Japanese troops be withdrawn from the Philippines. Neither country, he suggested, should retain any bases.[9] Quezon could have had little hope that the Japanese would accept the proposal; but if the United States refused, which it did, then it would be even more firmly committed to the liberation of the Philippines. In a radio address to the Filipino people on December 28, 1941, President Roosevelt had pledged that their freedom would be redeemed and their independence established and protected. He invited Quezon and members of his cabinet to take up residence in Washington for the duration of the war. In replying to Quezon's neutralization scheme, President Roosevelt pledged the United States to drive the Japanese off Philippine soil. General MacArthur, on departing from Corregidor, promised that he would return.

The Commonwealth government, therefore, remained committed to American allegiance and to an American victory. President Quezon's instructions to the Filipino leaders who had to remain behind were quite explicit. They were to do the best they could, make what bargains they had to with the Japanese, try to keep the Philippines in one piece, and protect the people from Japanese brutality and avarice; all this had to be done for the future of the Philippines.[10]

Of the leaders who remained, some fled to the hills where they joined or organized guerrilla units, and some served under the Japanese.

The role of those Filipinos who engaged in guerrilla warfare against the Japanese was difficult but clear. There were two main types of guerrilla operations. Many units, large and small, were under American leadership on the spot or in contact with American forces from which they received supplies and instructions. After the war, the United States made these units eligible for compensation. There were also the highly organized forces of the Hukbalahaps, which did not accept American leadership and

[9] Garel A. Grunder and William E. Livezey, *The Philippines and the United States* (Norman: University of Oklahoma Press, 1951), p. 239.
[10] Royal Arch Gunnison, "The Filipinos Fight On," *Colliers Magazine*, July 1, 1944, pp. 46, 54-55.

were not recognized as legitimate guerrilla units by the U.S. army. The guerrillas cooperating with U.S. forces were of considerable importance in providing intelligence about Japanese troop movements and in denying Japan control of large areas of the country. The Huks may have hindered the Japanese from garnering the rice harvest of central Luzon, but their main efforts were directed toward social revolution and military preparation for the eventual seizure of power.

The Filipino leaders who had to work with the Japanese included most of the legislature and such leading men as José P. Laurel, Jorge B. Vargas, Claro M. Recto, Quintin Paredes, and José Yulo, all of whom were among the 32 Filipino officials who agreed to serve in a Japanese-sponsored Philippine Executive Commission and later in a Japanese-sponsored puppet government. These leaders had a far more difficult role than did the guerrillas. As Senator Recto eloquently described it afterwards:

> They had to tax their ingenuity and make the most of their practical wisdom to meet the grave implications of the enemy invasion and occupation, in the face of the defenselessness and bewilderment of the people. They had to feign cooperation and pretend to play into the hands of the wily enemy because the latter was not only suspicious but already convinced that the Filipinos were just waiting for the opportune moment to strike back . . . In the midst of these terrible realities this handful of Filipino leaders was entrusted with the task of looking after the well-being of their own people and trying to save the country from abject misery, even possible extinction.[11]

According to Recto the only people capable of judging the behavior of those who held office under the Japanese were those who stayed in the Philippines; those who did not live under the Japanese could not possibly understand the temporizing show of cooperation and the bargains that were necessary to placate a ruthless enemy.

In spite of minimal communications, the relations between the members of the Commonwealth government in Washington and those serving under the Japanese in Manila remained intact throughout the war. When President Osmeña, who succeeded

11 Recto, cited, pp. 69-70.

Quezon, landed on Leyte with General MacArthur on November 23, 1944, he made a statement showing a high degree of understanding between the two groups:

But in our praise of the guerrillas we should not be forgetful of the loyal civilian population that was left behind to face the ire of the invader and support the guerrillas. It was not possible for all to evade the enemy; the fate of the immense majority was to bear the manacles of enslavement. Unfortunately, this has given rise to different attitudes and actions in relation to the Japanese rule causing some misunderstandings among our people. This state of affairs has created one of the most serious problems with which our government is confronted.

We cannot close our eyes to the realities of the Japanese occupation. It was cruel and harsh. An arbitrary government was imposed on the Filipino people by the sword, and the collapse of American and Filipino armies left the majority of eighteen million Filipinos no other recourse but to submit to a despotic regime if they were to survive. Not all public officials could take to the hills to carry on the heroic struggle. Some had to remain at their posts to maintain a semblance of government, to protect the population from the oppressor to the extent possible by human ingenuity and to comfort the people in their misery. Had their services not been available the Japanese themselves would either have governed directly or utilized unscrupulous Filipino followers capable of any treason against their own people. The result would have been calamitous and the injuries to our body political beyond cure.

The problem under consideration must be solved with justice and dignity. Every case should be examined impartially and decided on its own merits. Persons holding public office during enemy occupation, for the most part, fall within three categories: those prompted by a desire to protect the people, those actuated by fear of enemy reprisals, and those motivated by disloyalty to our government and cause. The motives which caused the retention of the office and conduct while in office rather than the sole fact of its occupation, will be the criteria upon which such persons will be judged.[12]

During the war neither the Commonwealth government in Washington nor the U.S. psychological warfare agency, the Office of War Information, made any accusations against "collaborators" in the Philippines. Collaboration was a matter to be decided by

[12] Same, p. 94.

the people after the war was over. To identify as enemies those Filipinos who served under the Japanese would merely compel them to stay with the Japanese to the bitter end. But after the war, as we shall see, the United States government took a hand in the problem of "collaboration" that was not entirely consistent with its position during the conflict.

What sort of posture did the Filipino leaders in the Philippines maintain during the war? To what extent were they successful in carrying out President Quezon's directives to protect the Filipino people and keep the country together? Whatever their individual motives, the record is impressive. The fact that these men were available made it possible for the Japanese to avoid direct rule or the exclusive use of such well-known pro-Japanese Filipinos as Benigno Ramos, General Artemio Ricarte, or Professor Maximo Kalaw, President of the Philippine-Japan Association and a long-standing advocate of Asia for the Asians. It was advantageous to rule through Filipinos who commanded respect, but as the Japanese military administration denied them sufficient power to keep the respect of the public, they eventually ceased to be of any political value.

Toward the end of the war the Japanese organized the Makapili, the League of Patriotic Filipinos, with Ramos and Ricarte at its head. Benigno Ramos, the founder of the Sakdalista movement of the 1930s, had spent six years in Japan after the failure of the Sakdal uprisings and had returned to Manila just before Pearl Harbor. The Japanese found him on Corregidor, where his compadre, President Quezon, had taken him to keep him under close surveillance. What little support the Filipinos might have given Ramos had already been destroyed by the behavior of the Japanese army. The Filipino militia which fought alongside Japanese troops was neither trustworthy nor well trained, and without the Japanese it could hardly have existed at all. Senator Recto has said, and there seems every reason to agree, that the Japanese set up the Makapili because they were getting so little real cooperation from the leaders of the "independent" government of the Philippines. On December 8, 1944, at the official inauguration of the Makapili, which claimed to be independent of the republic and responsible only to the Japanese military commander, President Laurel made a courageous statement in front of General Yamashita. Only a brave man could have said:

There is only one Republic of the Philippines, to which we owe allegiance, and which we must defend with our sinews and blood. This Republic is the one of which I happen to be the President. As long as I hold and exercise the authority, I cannot consent or permit any organization, political in character, by individual Filipinos or groups of Filipinos, to exist unless that organization is subject to the authority and control of that Republic.[13]

Most of the leaders who stayed behind were acting for the interests of a future Philippine Republic in a spirit of fierce national pride and independence. The record shows that some, like Recto, had been critical of America, but very few indeed had been openly favorable to Japan. President Osmeña's analysis, that some were acting for the future good of the Philippines and others from fear of reprisals, suggests two categories that were not mutually exclusive. If everyone in authority had followed the example of Chief Justice José Abad Santos, there would have been no buffer between the Japanese and the Filipino people. In a very real sense the Commonwealth leaders could claim that to be faithful to the United States was to be true to the Philippines.

U.S. Policy and the Liberation

When the United States decided to restore its sovereignty in the Philippines, it had to clarify its policies on three important problems: the timing of independence, the suspension of the Philippine constitution, and the definition of collaboration.

When the Japanese bestowed "independence" on the Filipinos, there were those in the U.S. Congress who suggested that the United States should do the same. This was not done, for it would have dignified the Japanese action by seeming to make the two actions comparable; it would have conceded the initiative to the Japanese. On another matter, the question of the Presidency, there was long and sharp debate. President Quezon, who

13 Same, p. 59.

had already served six years in office before the 1941 election, was due to retire in 1943 because the Philippine constitution put a limit of eight years on the office of president. In the normal course of events he would have been succeeded by the Vice-President, Osmeña, who was in Washington ready to take over. A few days before the deadline, by a joint resolution of both houses of Congress, the relevant clause of the Philippine constitution was put aside and Quezon was continued in office until such time as the president of the United States should determine that law and order had been restored in the Philippines and normal processes of government could be resumed.

There is no doubt that the U.S. Congress had the power to do this. Those who promoted it included the Filipino officials resident in Washington, Senators Tydings and Vandenberg, and the departments of State, War, and Interior. This powerful combination of forces argued that Quezon and Osmeña were both in favor of extending the term, and that the outstanding record and leadership of Quezon was a political asset in the struggle with the Japanese that should not be thrown away. The Japanese would interpret his resignation as repudiation. The opposition in the American Congress attacked this interference with Philippine constitutional processes as Fascist legislation in a war to end fascism, a violation of Philippine constitutional integrity. Congressman Judd argued that a Japanese wrong does not make an American right. As events turned out Osmeña took over after Quezon's death in August 1944, and at the end of 1944 he returned with MacArthur in the invasion of the Philippines. The death of Quezon saved the United States and the Philippines from one serious consequence of this joint resolution that was not mentioned in the debate. If Quezon had lived to return to the Philippines, there is no doubt but that abrogation of the constitution would have been used by his enemies as a political issue to the embarrassment of all concerned.

The United States was committed to advance the date of independence as early as possible prior to July 4, 1946.[14] After the war in the Philippines was over, President Osmeña suggested

[14] S. J. Res. 93, Public Law 380, 78th Cong., 1st sess. (December 9, 1943), *Congressional Record*, v. 89, pt. 8, p. 10489.

that this be done. President Truman refused on the ground that the Philippines needed time to set its house in order and to work out future relationships with the United States. At the same time the President took occasion to warn Osmeña that he should investigate and try "a number of persons who gave aid and comfort to the enemy and are now holding important offices in the Commonwealth Government." [15] In departing from the wartime position on collaboration Mr. Truman used the authority of his government, at this late stage, to inject a very dangerous note into Philippine politics. If independence had been granted immediately after the war, the Filipinos could have settled the collaboration issue through a general amnesty. In that case the thousands of Filipinos arrested and imprisoned by the United States forces would have been turned over to Osmeña. Whatever the outcome, the Filipinos would have been in charge of the collaboration issue, a not unreasonable responsibility for a people capable of magnificent noncooperation with the Japanese and only one year away from formal independence.

If the time before the granting of independence had been used to rehabilitate the Philippines, there would have been more justification for the delay, but it was not. The time was spent in haggling with the Filipinos about the terms of independence, which the U.S. Congress linked to the amount of rehabilitation, while the American army used the Philippines as a base for the projected attack on Japan. According to a well-informed American observer, the attitude of the High Command was expressed by General Courtney Whitney, head of the Civil Affairs Section and one of MacArthur's right-hand men: "These people are so happy to be liberated from the Japs, that if we do nothing more for them for the next six months, it will be all right." [16] Yet the army, the only agency that could have given help to the Philippines at that time, took prior claim over all existing facilities and public services and kept control over large parts of the country. Though its legal authority had been restored, the Commonwealth government lacked funds, and it took second place for office space, equipment, and supplies. Osmeña had responsi-

[15] Hartendorp, cited, p. 219.
[16] Same, p. 221.

bility without power, a dangerous role in a country emerging from war and occupation and whose people expected a miraculous return to the conditions that preceded the conflict.

Much more serious for the Commonwealth government, however, was the fact that Manuel Roxas, in effect, was singled out to receive the powerful backing of General MacArthur, while Osmeña was told that he could have neither independence nor funds for rehabilitation until he satisfied the United States that collaborators were being dealt with.

Roxas won the first election to be held after the war, in April 1946, and thus became the last President of the Commonwealth and the first President of the independent Republic of the Philippines. Osmeña accepted the peaceful transfer of power with dignity, making a contribution to the future of Philippine democracy that was generally unrecognized at the time. In January 1948 Roxas declared a political amnesty for the collaborators; it was the only wise and statesmanlike thing to do.

It is easier now than it was at the time to see that the collaborators helped save democratic institutions in the Philippines by preventing the polarization of politics. Without their willingness to suffer the humiliations and indignities of working for the Japanese army, politics might well have been a contest between the Japanese army and pro-Japanese Filipinos on the one hand, and the Communist-led Hukbalahaps on the other. The extremists on both sides would have preferred things that way; hence, the fierce attack that the Filipino Communists, in common with their fellows in other occupied countries, made on those who tried to cushion the impact of the enemy on the nation.

During the war those guerrilla units that were under American direction soon discovered that it was impossible to cooperate with the Huks on acceptable terms, and there were frequent clashes between them. American attitudes towards the Huks, however, were somewhat ambivalent. There was reluctance to disapprove openly of any forces that were fighting, or claimed to be fighting, the Japanese. In the Philippines, as in China, the Communists, as a matter of policy, made much of their actions in rescuing American airmen who came down in their territory. The apparent concern for the Filipino people, especially on the land question, was favorably regarded by many Americans. As the Huks were able to conceal or at least confuse the issue of class war against landlords by claiming that they were expropriating or killing only the collaborators—in effect, landlords who had gone to the city—it was possible for them to carry on a social revolution and even set up governmental administration in certain areas without arousing the public denunciations that such behavior would normally provoke. Everything they did was done in the name of the nation and the united front of all anti-fascist peoples. By the end of the war the Communists had a strong military force under their control and probably ruled more than half a million people. They were growing in strength as the puppet regime under Laurel was disintegrating, and if American forces had not come to the Philippines before the surrender of Japan, it is difficult to see what could have prevented them from seizing power throughout the islands.

Japanese propaganda appeals, such as Asia for the Asians, a Co-Prosperity Sphere under Japanese leadership, and "Oriental virtues," might have won more friends if they had been pressed in a friendly manner. But these appeals did not win over the intellectuals, as the writings of Recto show, and they were meaningless to the ordinary people because of the sufferings the people endured under Japanese military rule. The Filipinos were accustomed to ruling themselves through democratic institutions, a two-party system, and an almost completely Filipinized civil service. They knew what a free press and freedom of speech meant. They took for granted the right to travel, to form associations, to have access to a system of public education, and to practice their religion. The Japanese destroyed all these liberties and imposed a reign of terror without equal in all their vast empire. In the competition for the loyalties of the Filipinos, the Japanese failed miserably to make inroads against the Nationalists or the Communists. However, as in China, they indirectly promoted the growth of communism by destroying the military power of the Commonwealth, by undermining its economic life and institutions, and by pulverizing its political authority. Elsewhere in colonial countries of Asia (as in Indonesia and Indo-China) the Japanese, in their retreat, left behind large stocks of arms and other equipment which the nationalist movements could use to resist the return of the former imperial powers. This policy had no relevance for the Filipinos because the Commonwealth government had no desire and no intention of fighting the Americans. In its decision to force the general destruction of Manila by planned sabotage and a suicidal stand the Japanese army may have had certain strategic considerations in mind, but its systematic slaughtering of Filipino civilians in the last weeks of rule would seem to indicate that this act was one of sheer frustration and revenge.

The immediate consequence of the three-way struggle for the Philippines was the elimination of the old Japan as a contender. The influence of the new Japan should not, however, be written off; in fact, it may well be of considerable importance in the future. In the immediate postwar years the struggle clearly came to be one between the United States and the Soviet Union, with Japan an ally of the United States and, indirectly, of the Philippines, instead of an enemy. The long-range consequences of the wartime struggle in the Philippines are difficult to measure. The Philippines survived as a nation but with a dangerously divided ruling class. In addition to the three groups of Nationalist leaders—those who spent the war outside the Philippines, those who spent it under Japanese domination in Manila and other cities, and those who led the guerrilla resistance movement in the provinces—there were the leaders of the Hukbalahap, who spent the war constructing a political and military base from which to seize power and who claimed to be more nationalist than the Nationalists themselves.

The problem for the Nationalist leaders was how to close ranks and re-establish the authority of government, how to negotiate the terms of independence with the United States, and how to handle the internal threat from the Communists. Unfortunately, the question of collaboration, pressed by the Huks with intent to divide, was also raised by anti-Communist Nationalists, such as the guerrilla leaders, Tomas Cabili and Tomas Confesor, who later refused to join the Osmeña cabinet on the ground that it tolerated too many former collaborators, especially Roxas, then the president of the Senate. Cabili and Confesor accepted appointments as members of the Philippine Rehabilitation Commission in Washington, where they may well have done much to inspire the tough attitude that Secretary of the Interior Harold L. Ickes and President Truman took on the collaboration issue.

In negotiating the terms of independence the Philippine Nationalists had never been in a worse bargaining position, except for the fact that it was now politically impossible for the United States to delay the granting of independence beyond the long promised date of July 4, 1946. On the other hand, they were completely dependent on the United States for assistance in restoring their economy and making good the damage that had been done to their buildings, communications, cities, plants, industries, and mines. Utterly defenseless, this was no time for them to insist on neutrality as a national policy or to resist the re-establishment of American bases on Philippine soil. Philippine leaders were only too anxious to commit the United States to providing an effective defense of the Philippines and to supporting the rehabilitation of its economy. The problems that would arise from these arrangements could be and were left to the future.

Chapter 6

The Launching of the Republic

The Liberated Philippines

After liberating the Philippines the United States made a settlement that was marked by lavish expressions of mutual good will, by partly fulfilled promises, and by a restoration of the old relationship in almost everything except in name. Many of the issues that both countries face today arose from the policies of the United States at this time, such as the treatment meted out to collaborators, the insistence on special privileges for American businessmen, the handling of the back pay for guerrillas, determination of war damage claims, the pegging of the peso to the dollar, the status of American bases, the tariff, and regional security. Today many of these decisions take on a different cast in the light of new attitudes and new purposes. But nothing can conceal the fact that instead of a bold and imaginative program based on careful planning during the war years, such as was devised for a defeated Japan, the U.S. Congress served up a sterile compromise based on the restoration of prewar economic dependence. The Filipino representatives on the Rehabilitation Commission, able members of the political elite, were in no position to insist on changes radical enough to ensure an independent and democratic Philippine republic. Until July 4, 1946, the main responsibility for the future of the republic fell on American soldiers, yet not one recommendation seems to have been made resembling those that came so freely a few years later. This was a restoration, not a revolution.

The agrarian situation obviously demanded attention. These were days when land reform was in the air, and the threat of the

Hukbalahaps was there for all to see. So was the answer. The U.S. government at this time was recommending land reform for Japan, which was carried out later to the economic and political advantage of that country. Many demands were made of the Filipinos for the commercial advantage of the United States, but none for the social and political advantage of the Philippines. Yet drastic changes in the land system were desirable at this time to deny the peasantry to the Communists and to make possible a program for economic growth.

The public educational system was one of the chief casualties of the Japanese occupation of the Philippines. Right after the war would have been the time to insist on the rapid rebuilding of schools and the rehabilitation of the teaching profession through financial aid and a massive exchange of teachers to overcome the long years of isolation.

Instead of doing anything serious about education or the land system, the U.S. Congress spent much of its time haggling over the question of short or long tons for the sugar quota. The Congress came up with a series of legislative acts which, in effect, protected American agricultural interests through quotas, protected American manufactured goods through tariff agreements, and protected American investments through currency controls and parity with Filipinos for U.S. citizens doing business in the Philippines. Part of the purpose of the payment of war damage claims was to restore former American businesses in the Philippines to their prewar status. The key problem, however, was that of the long-term economic development of the Philippines, and to this no branch of the government gave effective consideration. The United States lost the opportunity for leadership while it still held the reins, using its great power instead to bully and blackmail the Filipinos into concessions to special interests. It was not until five years later that the United States recovered its sense of direction and proportion in its relations with the Philippines.

The most important decision in the immediate postliberation period was to fulfill the promise of independence. Whatever may be said about the terms on which independence was granted or about promises that the United States did not fulfill, this one political fact dominates most other considerations in its influence on the character of U.S.-Philippine relations. To the United States it was worth the equivalent of several divisions of troops in the war with Japan. It continues to be a source of mutual congratulation.[1] Philippine oratory and American self-righteousness never tire of the theme that Filipinos and Americans fought side by side for Philippine independence during the war with Japan. Bataan, Corregidor, and July 4, 1946, were potent political symbols because they belonged to a relationship that was based on ideas rather than on race. In 1946 they were particularly powerful.

It would have been better for Philippine-American relations if there had been an equally consistent policy on the highly volatile subject of "collaboration." During the war American official propaganda left the question of collaboration for the peoples of each occupied country to decide. Afterwards, however, President Truman criticized President Osmeña for not proceeding more hastily with the punishment of collaborators. But who were they? Truman defined a collaborator as a person who was disloyal to both the United States and the Philippines by assisting the enemy in the formulation and enforcement of political policy and the spread of propaganda. While the United States flag still flew in the Philippines, Truman was within his rights in charging with collaboration anyone who aided the enemy. But who, if not the elected representatives of the Filipinos, was to say what disloyalty to the Philippines might be? Who was to

[1] Senator Tydings told the Congress on the occasion of the American entry into Manila in February 1945: "Would that Almighty Providence might endow other parliaments and legislatures with equal vision and equal impulses directed to such worthy ends, for, if such were the case, in my humble judgment there would be laid a more lasting foundation for peace —because it would be built on absolute justice—than all the armies . . . in Christendom could ever erect or maintain." President Quirino, in accepting the return of Corregidor from the Americans said that this was a chapter in a new history, ". . . the history of a beautiful and touching relationship of two brave and noble peoples—Americans and Filipinos because they have as nobly written their loyalty and devotion in blood." Corregidor, said Quirino, was a "common shrine" to American and Filipino dead, "distinct in race yet the same in ideals." (*Senate Report 775*, 79th Cong., 1st sess., on S. 1610, the Rehabilitation bill. See also *Congressional Record*, 79th Cong., 1st sess., pp. 11464-69.)

distinguish between those who served under the Japanese to protect their people and those who were merely protecting their
own skins? Osmeña was compelled by the United States to set
up People's Courts, but the issues were highly confused and proof
was hard to provide, except for straightforward cases of participation in Japanese military measures against the Filipino people.

General MacArthur exonerated Manuel Roxas on the ground
that he acted under duress and with the interests of the people
in mind. As already noted, this unilateral decision did much to
assure the election of Roxas as first President of an independent
Philippines. Aguinaldo, the grand old man of the first Philippine republic, is among those who argue that the collaboration
issue lost Osmeña the election of 1946. The issue split the Nacionalista party and turned many of Osmeña's possible supporters to
Roxas, who defended those faced with prosecution for treason
by declaring that collaboration was a myth, that there were mistakes of the mind but not of the heart. Osmeña took a position
much closer to the official American line and lost the election
to the man MacArthur had singled out as not being a collaborator.

Aguinaldo recalled the U.S. army announcement of the surrender of the cabinet members of the Japanese puppet regime: it
stated that Manuel Roxas had been rescued and his companions
had been captured. Those who were put into prison included
a large part of the Filipino elite—Vicente Madrigal, the richest
Filipino, Claro Recto, and many of the other ministers, former
senators and congressmen, three former speakers of the House
of Representatives, newspaper and magazine editors, and Aguinaldo himself. "The economic, political and legal elite of the
country confined in the very prisons to which, as lawmakers,
prosecutors or judges, they had themselves sent ordinary criminals. It was the ultimate of humiliation." (José P. Laurel, Jorge
B. Vargas, Camilio Osias, and other puppet officials caught in
Japan were imprisoned there.) Although the prosecutions turned
out to be a farce, Aguinaldo wrote, the damage inflicted on dignity had never been completely healed. This act "was the start
of what I believe was General MacArthur's greatest error from
the standpoint of Philippine-American friendship . . . My own

wish is that he should have finished it. Because he failed to do so, we Filipinos continue to have no clearcut concept of treason and loyalty." [2] According to Aguinaldo, some of the anti-American outbursts that sour Philippine-American friendship today can be traced at least in part to the deep-seated resentment aroused by General MacArthur's arbitrary and discriminatory policy.

What was treason? The only test that the United States could apply was that of loyalty to the United States. It is no accident that the Hukbalahaps were not counted as loyal because, although they fought against the Japanese (the real test in the minds of many), they also refused to cooperate with the United States. The Filipino elite applied the test of loyalty to the Philippines, and the Huks did not pass that test either because they wanted a different kind of Philippines from that of the ruling elite. In practice the United States put the burden of enforcement on the returning Commonwealth government but did not actually give it effective civil control.

It was MacArthur who insisted on reconvening the Philippine Congress elected in 1941, even though its term of office had run out. He must have known that a majority of its members had held office under the Japanese or had served them in other ways. Osmeña had not intended to call Congress into session, for it was controlled by Roxas and could be expected to be recalcitrant. With Truman ordering him to speed up the People's Courts and MacArthur forcing him to call into session a hostile Congress full of candidates for prosecution, Osmeña was in difficult position.

It is quite possible that MacArthur disagreed with his instructions to arrest leading Filipinos on charges of war guilt and that he imprisoned the puppet leaders in order to protect them. Some years later he claimed that he was under instructions to try Laurel and others as war criminals, but he insisted, "There was never any doubt in my mind but that you [Laurel] and the others who worked with you during the Japanese occupation acted in what you believed to be the best interest of your country. Presi-

[2] Emilio Aguinaldo and Vicente Albano Pacis, *A Second Look at America* (New York: Robert Speller & Sons, 1957), pp. 231, 233.

dent Quezon completely approved of your actions." [3] Whatever
the merits of the case, important voices were raised against the
Filipino elite on the grounds that their social and economic attitudes were reactionary, "fascist," and likely to lead to the denial
of freedom and opportunity to the Philippine people. Harold
L. Ickes, for example, gave his blessing to Hernando J. Abaya's
Betrayal in the Philippines, a book that fiercely denounced Roxas
and all collaborators and presented favorably the political aspirations of the "progressive movement" in the Philippines, the
so-called Democratic Alliance, which included the Hukbalahap.

The Alliance had been launched as a political party in July
1945 under the leadership of Luis Taruc, Commander in Chief
of the Hukbalahap, Dr. Vicente Lava, political adviser of the
Huks, some labor leaders, and a few fellow-travelers. Ickes agreed
with this group on at least one thing—the determination to pun-
ish collaborators—and as Secretary of the Interior he tried to
make it a matter of policy that no U.S. rehabilitation funds
would be given to collaborators. Fortunately the U.S. government officially proclaimed in February 1946 that the promised
aid would be given to the Philippine people regardless of whom
they chose for president. If the United States had pressed the
collaboration issue with the threat of withholding financial help
unless all collaborators were tried and punished, the Communists
would have ridden to power. In avoiding this course, the United
States may have antagonized many staunch anti-Communist Filipinos who felt strongly on collaboration, but there was no practical alternative except to use the same financial pressure on the
traditional elite to exact some measure of reform. This was not
done until five years later when the Bell Mission, in different
language, agreed in essence with many of the charges that had
been levelled against the Filipino elite at this time and suggested the use of financial pressure to bring about reforms. To
some Filipinos it appeared that the United States had no clear-
cut policy on collaboration, and there are many today who
still feel that loyalty went unrewarded while opportunism received respect and honor.

The scars left by the collaboration issue are still unhealed be-

[3] Same, p. 234.

cause the political question of loyalty is confused with the financial question of eligibility for back pay for guerrillas. According to many Filipinos, the U.S. army authorities did not give recognition to the vast bulk of true Filipino guerrilla fighters but instead honored and paid many collaborators. Ramón Magsaysay himself did not receive recognition for his guerrilla activities, although some awkward attempts were made to take care of this unfortunate omission later on. Admittedly the army had no easy problem on its hands. The legislative definition of a veteran included membership in organized guerrilla forces under commanders appointed or subsequently recognized by the United States. This opened up the opportunity for claims by thousands of Filipinos who may or may not have been attached to *bona fide* guerrilla units as defined by the U.S. army. There were also many guerrilla units that had not been affiliated with the U.S. army during the occupation and could not be recognized *ex post facto* without opening up unlimited claims. The army undoubtedly made mistakes of its own, but the situation provided opportunities for misrepresentation and graft on a vast scale. The genuine but illiterate guerrilla was open to two kinds of disappointment: failure to prove his service and therefore to receive back pay, and loss of money to bogus agents whose offers of assistance so many accepted.

The combination of hasty administration of back pay for guerrillas, of uncontrollable expectations on the part of those who could not qualify, and of heartless exploitation of the ignorant by both Americans and Filipinos left a contentious legacy for the future. The reconvened Congress voted itself back pay without hesitation, and the civil servants sold their votes to Roxas in the spring election of 1946 for the promise of back pay, while Osmeña pointed to the empty treasury. As the direct and indirect source of hope for financial reimbursement, the United States could not fail to become the scapegoat. Beneath the surface resentment still runs high.

In view of the shortcomings of U.S. policy and the difficulties of the postwar period it is amazing that the Filipinos achieved as much as they did. Yet the Filipino elite closed ranks to reestablish the Commonwealth government, accept a peaceful transfer of power after the national elections, and prepare for the coming of full independence. These accomplishments were all the more impressive because the Philippines had to deal with the many problems that had been created by an enemy occupation, as well as with those of a people achieving independence after hundreds of years of colonial rule.

The liberated Philippines had to deal with two pressing and related issues. One was the threat from within presented by a well-armed and well-directed subversive movement, the Hukbalahaps. In order to counter the Hukbalahaps it was necessary for the government to restore law and order, disarm the people, open up the channels of internal communication, revive trade with the United States, and take over the responsibilities of independence. To accomplish the latter tasks required the cooperation of the United States. The other issue was the terms on which independence would be granted in view of the economic consequences of the war. The more successful the Filipinos were in reconstructing their government, the better the chances of a satisfactory settlement with the United States.

The threat from within was very serious. The Philippine Communist party, mainly under the leadership of Luis Taruc, tried to achieve in the Philippines what Mao Tse-tung achieved in China. It aimed to carve out, in central Luzon, a guerrilla base under complete Communist control for purposes of administration, taxation, and military deployment. It was clear that the Communists wanted to have at the end of the war a position from which they could challenge the legitimate government and, under favorable circumstances, take over control. In attempting this they received propaganda material and advice on strategy and tactics from the Chinese Communists and financial support from the Philippine Chinese. As in China, the Communists in the Philippines appealed to nationalism and played up Japanese atrocities—in fact, provoked them. They claimed that they were supporters of the Commonwealth government and of the United States because they were part of the world-wide United Front movement against fascism. Like the Chinese Communists, the Huks tried to deny to the Japanese the food supplies of the area they dominated, but their objective in harassing Japanese troops was not so much to drive the enemy away as to train and "blood" their own troops. They took over the land of landlords who had fled to the cities, and they liquidated Filipinos they asserted were traitors. Of some 25,000 persons they claim to have killed during the war, only 5,000 were Japanese; the rest were Filipino victims of the class war. Anyone who stood in the way was labeled a puppet. Until the liberation the Huks had the largest, the best-trained, and the best-equipped Philippine army in the country—an army estimated at 10,000 men, with some 100,000 militia to back it up. Unlike the Chinese Communists, however, they were on the route of American forces that were moving step by step to invade Japan.

During the immediate postwar period the policy of the United States in the Huk affair was similar to its policy toward Communists in other parts of Asia. But as Scaff points out in his book, *The Philippine Answer to Communism,*

> Little suspecting a full-scale Communist revolution, the American forces were careless in the distribution of arms and ammunition. Much that was air-dropped or passed out to guerrillas found its way into the hands of the Huks. Sympathetic G.I.s traded their new weapons for old ones and souvenir pieces. Other weapons were exchanged by hungry soldiers for fresh fruits and poultry. Thefts from ammunition dumps carelessly guarded were common. While the Huks were busy equipping themselves with modern guns and plenty of new ammunition, the newly reorganized Philippine army at the time of independence in 1946 was supplied with war-worn hand-me-downs.[4]

The U.S. army supported Osmeña in his refusal to accept Huk-appointed civil officials in central Luzon, and it rounded up many Huk leaders, including Taruc and Castro Alejandrino, on charges of killing Filipinos in defiance of orders to cease civil conflict. The Huk leaders were sent to the penal colony of Iwahig on Palawan where they rubbed shoulders with Recto and other members of the elite, but they were released before the formal transfer of power from the United States to the Philippines. It was during this period that General MacArthur was releasing Japanese Communists from jail and General Marshall

[4] Alvin Scaff, *The Philippine Answer to Communism* (Stanford University Press, 1955), pp. 26-67.

was trying to dissaude the Chinese Communists from pressing their bid for power. The U.S. army undoubtedly disapproved of Communists but had no conception of how thoroughly they prepare for the seizure of power. Thus, at the outset the new republic found its most determined and resourceful enemies released from jail and again free to attack both its own government and that of the United States.

Those were days when it was difficult to think ill of anyone who was anti-Japanese, as the Huks claimed to have been although, in fact, they had fought Filipinos much more vigorously. Since many influential Americans and Filipinos thought of the Huks as warm-hearted agrarian reformers who should be talked out of their unfortunate addiction to violent methods, it was difficult for Osmeña to start a vigorous campaign against them, even though the landlords who had tried to take up their positions in Huk territory were well aware of the nature of the threat. The American attitude toward the Huk problem in the early stages was not always based on a realistic estimate of the danger.

The economic problems of the Filipinos, in contrast, were there for all to see. The Japanese Co-Prosperity Sphere had not worked any better in the Philippines than elsewhere, partly because the Japanese military controlled economic planning and partly because the fortunes of war did not permit time for the fruition of long-range planning, either good or bad. At the same time the Japanese army looted and expropriated, circulated its military script in inflationary quantities, and killed an estimated million Filipinos. In his State of the Nation address President Roxas said: "Our people are to inherit a prostrate and war-devastated land. The extent of that devastation was total." The government, he continued, was without the financial means to support even its basic functions; for a budget of 250 million pesos, anticipated revenue was only 40 million pesos. Exports before the war were 240 million pesos, whereas for the coming year they might be 30 million pesos as against imports of 300 million pesos.

Practically all of our tractors and 60 per cent of our work animals disappeared through the war . . . Our transportation facilities . . . have been completely disrupted . . . Public health and sanitation have retreated far from the level which existed before the war. Epidemic is a constant threat. The three great pests of our land—the rat, the mosquito, and the locust—have thrived on our misfortunes and threaten us with both disease and hunger . . . Famine is a strong possibility . . . Today 60 per cent of our sugar mills are destroyed . . . Our gold mines are still flooded . . . The cruel scythe of war has left in its wake a chaff of violence and terror. In the central Luzon provinces . . . force prevails rather than law . . . It is estimated that over 300,000 arms are illegally held in the Philippines today.[5]

Facing these mountainous problems, the Filipinos felt that the United States should bear most of the cost of rehabilitation, and there were enough statements from the highest American officials to assure them that the United States was committed to making good the damages of war.

Formidable as the task of rehabilitation was, of even more consequence would be the future conditions of trade between the two countries. The war had rendered irrelevant the assumptions on which the Tydings-McDuffie Act had been based, and the country obviously needed a new period of economic adjustment as it became accustomed to the exercise of political sovereignty. The Filipinos were not in the best of bargaining positions. But on their side was the knowledge that the United States would wish to restore the market, as one American congressman put it, of its sixth best customer. There was also a political factor, for the United States had a strong interest in a successful Philippines. There were strategic considerations. The United States wanted bases in the Philippines, and the Filipinos also needed protection. Time was short; the Philippine problem was only one among many pressing on the American administration, and the need for action was urgent.

The Terms of Independence

It was one thing to grant formal independence, but it was another to disengage the American and Philippine economies, for as Commissioner Paul V. McNutt pointed out at the time, the Philippine economy was dependent on the United States to a

[5] Message of the President of the Philippines to the Second Congress, June 3, 1946 (Manila: Bureau of Printing, 1946), pp. 3, 5-9.

greater degree than any single state of the union is economically dependent on the rest of the country.

Many of the problems that dominate U.S.-Philippine relations today owe their origin or their current interpretation to the arrangements made in 1946. The terms of independence were hotly disputed at the time; and although they have been modified by subsequent legislation, they are still a source of political dispute.

One of the two most important pieces of legislation, the Philippine Trade Act of 1946, went through five versions and seven months of acrimonious debate. The other, the Philippine Rehabilitation Act of 1946, was made contingent upon acceptance by the Philippines of the "parity" clause of the Trade Act. The Trade Act continued free trade for another eight years, and for twenty-five years thereafter there was to be a gradually-increasing tariff on American goods entering the Philippines and Philippine goods entering the United States. This gave thirty-three years for adjustment of the free-trade relationship. With good reason the Philippine Assembly had objected to free trade when it was first introduced in 1909, fearing that it would prolong the dependence of the Philippine economy on that of the United States and perhaps make the acquisition of independence the more difficult. When the Trade Act was being drafted, McNutt asked for twenty years of free trade, possibly expecting that the Philippines would eventually ask to re-establish political ties in some form. The eight-year period was a compromise between opposing economic interests, both American and Philippine, tempered by new political and strategic considerations.

The Trade Act set absolute quotas for twenty-eight years on exports to America of sugar, cordage, rice, cigars, scrap and filler tobacco, coconut oil, and pearl buttons. Exports in 1940 were the basis of the quotas. The peso was pegged to the dollar, and its exchange rate could not be altered without the consent of the President of the United States. This unusual arrangement with another sovereign state was supported as being in the interest of Philippine economic recovery, as was the other, more famous clause in the agreement which gave to American citizens and corporations the same rights as Philippine nationals in the exploitation of natural resources and the ownership and operation of public utilities—the so-called "parity" arrangement. The President of the United States could revoke any part of the Trade Act if the Philippines discriminated against American citizens and corporations. The parity provision required an amendment to the Philippine Constitution, which passed by an overwhelming majority, possibly because the Filipinos were in no position to deny themselves the contingent financial support.

The Philippine Rehabilitation Act of 1946 provided for the payment of war damages, a concession that the United States had usually been reluctant to grant. But too many promises, including one to replace the last carabao, had been made during the war to escape the obligation. War damages were set at $400 million. In addition, the act transferred $100 million in surplus military property to the Philippine government and $120 million for use until 1950 in the construction of public facilities. The act included a provision (opposed by Senators Taft, La Follette, and Tydings) which prohibited payment of private war damages to any claimant in excess of $500 until the Trade Agreement became effective—in other words, until the Philippine constitution had been amended. The payment of war damages opened up a source of dispute between the two countries because the Filipinos were not satisfied with the amount of the payments. These came to a little over half of the adjudicated awards of damage to private property at 1941 prices, which were much lower than replacement costs in 1946. According to Waring, one of the War Damage Claims Commissioners, 80 per cent of the claims were for $500 or less, and 99.4 per cent of the claims were from Filipino citizens or corporations. These received 90 per cent of the total, an amount, he said, that was far short of that needed for total rehabilitation.[6]

The passage of the Act was marked by a grim battle of special interests that would have gone on much longer if there had not been a fixed date for independence. The State Department unsuccessfully argued that absolute quotas were contrary to U.S. foreign economic policy and that preferential treatment of the

[6] *House Report, 1921,* 79th Cong., 2d sess., on S. 1610, the Rehabilitation bill; or *Congressional Record,* 79th Cong., 2d sess., pp. 34449-34450.

Philippines would make it more difficult to persuade the British to give up their empire preferences. Policy on quotas should be the same for all countries. In addition, the State Department opposed the parity clause as this would require from the Philippines more concessions than the United States would be willing to grant to a foreign power, including the Philippines; the United States should assist the Filipinos rather than demand special privileges from them. The Assistant Secretary of State for Economic Affairs, Mr. Will Clayton, argued that the allocation procedure for quotas would deprive the Philippine government of a sovereign prerogative and give prewar producers a virtual monopoly on most of the important Philippine exports for twenty-eight years. It would enable them to prevent the investment of capital by new American enterprises in the export industries and prevent Philippine producers from competing freely in their own country. Nor would absolute quotas force diversification of production, for the act empowered the United States to impose absolute quotas on any goods in competition with similar American goods. Such measures, according to Clayton, were designed to protect U.S. interests since they were not applied to imports from any other country in the world. The pegging of the peso to the dollar and other fiscal arrangements also protected American investing interests in the Philippines for a period of thirty-three years,". . . so that when the capital decides to revert to the United States it may come to the United States without depreciation," as Congressman Mills put it.[7] The State Department protested in vain.

The Filipinos accepted the Trade and Rehabilitation Acts because they preferred action to inaction. They accepted the quota provisions under protest. Like the U.S. State Department they would have preferred the rights of American citizens to have been detailed in a Treaty of Friendship; they wanted no quotas and disapproved the currency regulations. Unlike the State Department, they wanted free trade in perpetuity. They would have agreed with Congressman Jere Cooper of Tennessee when he said, "The people of the United States, in all fairness, stand a far

[7] *House Report, 1821,* 79th Cong., 2d sess., on H.R. 5856, the Trade Relations bill. See also *The New York Times,* September 18, 19, 1946, pp. 4, 8.

greater chance and opportunity to benefit under this legislation than do the people of the Philippines." [8] Be that as it may, the provisions of the two acts were soon to be the subject of renegotiation between the two countries under very different conditions from those that prevailed in 1945-46.

The Philippines assumed its sovereignty as dependent on the United States for military as it was for economic assistance. No country can be independent if its army is unable to combat internal subversion, and the Philippine government was in no position to disarm the sizable forces of the Hukbalahaps. So long as American troops were stationed in the Philippines the Huks could be contained, but the move to bring American servicemen home, encouraged for obvious reasons by Communist elements in the U.S. army in Manila, was irresistible. Besides, the new government was committed to provide 50,000 troops for occupation duty in Japan. Romulo appealed for immediate military assistance to enable the Philippines to have something of a force when independence came.

When Congress passed the Military Assistance Act in 1946, it meant that the close association of the American and Philippine military could continue after independence. The significance of this aspect of the relations between the two countries is often underestimated, yet in the long run the military relationship may be more important than the political and economic because it is more closely associated with national pride and prestige.

Under the Military Bases Agreement, which went into effect March 1947, for a five-year period, the United States secured a ninety-nine-year agreement providing for twenty-three army, navy, or airforce bases at various points in the Philippines and the right to use part of the Manila port area on the same basis as any private party.[9] The bases were for mutual protection and

[8] Shirley Jenkins, "Great Expectations in the Philippines," *Far Eastern Survey*, v. 16, August 13, 1947, pp. 169-174. See also Chapman, "American Policy in the Philippines," *Far Eastern Survey*, v. 15, June 5, 1946, pp. 144-160.

[9] *Agreement between the Republic of the Philippines and the United States of America concerning Military Bases*, Department of Foreign Affairs Treaty Series, v. 1, December 1948, pp. 144-160.

the maintenance of peace in the Pacific. The Philippine government retained the right to exercise jurisdiction over all offenses committed outside American bases, except in cases where the offender was carrying out military orders or in cases where only Americans were involved. These are the provisions which later came under fire as imperialist insistence on extraterritorial rights. The United States agreed to provide a Joint Military Advisory Group (JUSMAG) and military assistance in the training of troops and the loan of weapons and equipment. This equipment could be turned over to the Philippine government by sale, loan, or gift, and the sum of $19,750,000 was allocated for these purposes. The Philippines agreed to purchase the bulk of its military equipment in the United States, and to secure U.S. approval of purchases that were made elsewhere. This provision gave the United States a very considerable influence over the size and character of the Philippine military forces.

Most important of all, it was agreed that there would be negotiations concerning problems of security. In those early years the Filipinos felt that the United States, far from interfering in the affairs of the Philippines, was not doing enough to develop its bases and provide for the security of the new republic. The United States had not undertaken a formal guarantee to come to the aid of the Philippines if it were the victim of aggression; it had merely assured the Filipinos that any attack on them would be considered dangerous to American peace and safety. The Filipinos pressed for a binding guarantee from the United States to come to their defense in case of attack. Not until the Korean War broke out did they secure a firmer assurance of protection.

Failure to include such guarantees in the first military agreement stimulated discussion of neutralism as an alternative. As Claro M. Recto, always an able advocate of neutralism, later argued:

If America really believes that war is inevitable, then let her give Asia a resolute leadership we can trust; let her give the same unconditional pledges and guarantees and the same actual evidence of a spiritual equality and common fate that she has given to her kinsmen and allies in the Atlantic community, and we shall have justification for the risk

of war and incentive to make common cause. Otherwise we must re-
strain our enthusiasms, dissemble our sympathies, moderate our words
and actions, and in fulfillment of the primitive duty of self-preserva-
tion, make no enemies where we can make no friends, and hold our
peace . . .[10]

Because of the economic and military facts of dependence at the
time, no Philippine government except a Communist regime
could have broken with the United States. But although Senator
Recto was in opposition he was expressing a very general Filipino
attitude toward the problem of security, one that was not resolved even by the Defense Treaty of 1951.

Not all promises made in the heat of battle are kept after the
battle is over. In February 1946 General Romulo read into the
Congressional Record a list of commitments made by the United
States to the Philippines during the war, not so much, perhaps,
in the hope they would all be fulfilled to the letter as to put
moral pressure on Congress. In 1946 the United States was concerned with the devastation of war in many parts of the world
and had little time for the Philippines. To many Americans, and
to some Filipinos, it looked as though independence would be
a hazardous undertaking in view of the breakdown of law and
order, the social malaise, the economic devastation, and the
threat of civil war. How safe would life and property be, let
alone investments and businesses? On the face of it there was
a good argument for special privileges for Americans doing business or investing in the Philippines, as there seemed to be no
other source of managerial skill or capital investment immediately available for the job of reconstruction. There was also a
case for continuing free trade in order to restore, as quickly as
possible, the traditional sources of employment and national
income.

The whole range of actions taken at the close of the war indicated some new trends in American policy. The political reasons
for Philippine independence were now more compelling than

[10] Senator Claro M. Recto, "No U.S. Definite Committment for Philippine
Defense," *Manila Times*, June 1, 2, 1960. See also Claro M. Recto, "Foreign
Relations and National Survival," *Manila Times*, May 26, 27, 1960, April 14,
16, 1960.

were those of special economic interests; definite promises had been made during the war that we would keep our word, and too many changes had taken place in Asia to permit reconsideration. By the same token it was necessary, for reasons of prestige, to put the new republic on its feet economically and to provide it with the means of restoring law and order. Owing to the shift in the world balance of power, the strategic importance of the Philippines had changed considerably since the passage of the Tydings-McDuffie Act, and for strategic as well as political reasons it was important that the new republic should succeed. But it would be too much to say that apart from these general considerations there was very much agreement in the American government on how to proceed.

The executive branch, especially State and Treasury, was more sensitive about demanding special privileges for Americans in the Philippines than was Congress. For the first time there was a disposition to think seriously about the contrast between the economic dependence of the Philippines, for which the United States was entirely responsible, and the achievement of political independence, for the success of which the United States was now concerned to a degree that could never have been anticipated before the war. Not every senator or congressman in the debates on Philippine policy during 1945 and 1946 realized fully the changes that had taken place in the world position of the United States in the ten years since the Tydings-McDuffie Act—hence, the peculiar mixture of old and new thinking in the handling of Philippine independence. But it was clear to most that special economic interests, however legitimate, had to be considered in a new context of high international responsibilities, a context very different from the neutralism of the 1930s.

The terms on which the Filipinos secured their independence brought varied reactions. To Americans the dominant consideration was that a promise had been fulfilled, the terms being a compromise that satisfied no one completely but expressed the national interest as then conceived. The Filipinos were impressed with the fact that the promise was fulfilled on time. They were generally disappointed at the financial settlement and critical of the special privileges accorded to Americans, except insofar as they might speed up recovery and help to commit the United States to further aid. The Soviet Union was critical indeed of the terms of independence. *Pravda* told its readers that the United States depicted the solution of the Philippine question as a perfect model, an ideal example of new relationships which all other colonial powers should emulate. At the same time, American troops remained in the Philippines and the movement for "national liberation" (Hukbalahap) was being suppressed. New forms of alien bondage—political, economic, and military—were being clamped down on the Filipinos. The United States was trying to preserve the colonial character of the Philippine economy, perpetuate the economic dependence of the Philippines on American capital, and transform the Philippines into a permanent auxiliary base for the American army and navy in the Western Pacific. *Pravda* was especially angry at the use of American troops to suppress the Huks. Roxas, according to *Pravda,* was freed on condition that he would hand the Philippines back to American capital, grant bases to the American militarists, and strangle "the People's opposition movement."

The Soviet analysis of the situation in the Philippines, repeated constantly year after year, provided a pattern that had an impact on other countries besides the Philippines. Nehru of India openly criticized the terms of Philippine independence. As the first of the postwar colonial settlements, it probably had some demonstration value for the rest of Asia. The terms were very different from those made by Great Britain a few years later; the British secured for themselves no special privileges in India, or in Burma, which had been occupied by the Japanese and was then a close parallel to the Philippines. The British and others have often pointed to the contrast in policy, especially when they were irritated by the more self-righteous statements emanating from America about "our record in the Philippines."

The most serious shortcomings of the American record became apparent within a few years of independence when the Bell Mission made a systematic review of the situation in the Philippines and prepared a detailed report on what had to be done by the Philippines and the United States if the republic were to survive the crisis of 1950. Although intended mainly as an economic survey, the discussions and recommendations of the Bell Mission extended to the social and institutional changes that were necessary for economic growth. Many of the changes, especially those relating to land tenure and productivity, could have been brought about during the fifty years of American occupation. Gradually it became clear that the U.S. interest in a stable Philippine economy, strong enough to provide the basis for political independence, must take precedence over special concerns. It also became clear that the United States had to devise a new approach and use new techniques to help bring this about. The approach of the Tydings-McDuffie era, which so strongly influenced the Trade and Rehabilitation Acts, was already out-of-date before World War II was over. By 1950 it was obvious that when the U.S. Congress was fulfilling the promise of independence in 1946, it was not laying the foundations for the development of a strong and independent Philippines. The Filipinos got off to a very bad start on the road to independence.

Chapter 7

Partners in Crisis

Many of the objectionable features of the terms of independence have now been modified or have disappeared altogether. Since 1946 there has been a measurable growth in Philippine nationalism and an increased willingness on the part of the United States to accept the Filipinos more as partners and less as wards. That these changes have come about is largely the consequence of a domestic Philippine crisis coinciding with a crisis in the relations of the United States with Asia.

By 1950, as a result of the conditions under which the Philippines acquired independence, the country was practically bankrupt and the government was fighting for its life against Communist efforts to seize power. The vigorous U.S. effort to help save the situation brought the two countries together in an economic, political, and military partnership that could hardly have been more intimate, arduous and often difficult though the partnership has been.

The revolution in U.S. policies that changed the relations between the two countries came about as a result of the Communist conquest of China, the granting of independence to colonies in other parts of Asia, the signing of a peace treaty with Japan, the Korean War, and the struggle in Viet-Nam. These events led to adjustments in military aid and alliances, economic and technical assistance, and cultural propaganda. The world-wide nature of the protracted conflict with the Soviet bloc put all important policies toward the Philippines into a regional if not a global setting. As a result the Philippines has decreased in relative but gained in absolute importance. Accommodation to the new situation by Americans and Filipinos has come in stages mainly as the result of intimate partnership and often acrimonious negotiation.

The Economic Crisis: The Bell Mission

The first important revival of American interest in Philippine affairs came in 1950 when President Elpidio Quirino asked the United States to send an Economic Survey Mission to the Philippines to advise on the establishment of a sound and well-balanced economy. The group sent by the United States was known as the Bell Mission after its chairman, the former Under-Secretary of the Treasury, Daniel W. Bell.

The new republic was in trouble. Agricultural production had reached prewar levels in 1949, but the economy as a whole was not healthy. Although wages were not up to prewar levels, prices were rising and unemployment spreading. Severe import controls imposed in the previous year had slowed down the extravagant importation of consumer goods, but this did not of itself promote industrialization. Government deficits were running high, and there were inflationary pressures. For lack of funds the government stopped financing public works and fell into arrears in paying its civil servants. To make things worse, the cost of supporting the army in its none-too-successful campaign against the Hukbalahaps was eating up more and more of the national budget.

The situation did not improve during the summer of 1950, and by October Miguel Cuaderno, Governor of the Central Bank, had to go to Washington to borrow $50 million in order to pay the civil servants, teachers, and soldiers. The crisis in government finances, combined with the rising threat from the Huks, called for immediate financial assistance. The United States decided to use its one means of influencing Philippine affairs, financial help, to bring about the reforms necessary to promote the growth of a balanced economy and sound governmental operations.

Important for its analysis of Philippine problems, for its recommendations, and for the reaction of the Filipinos to its findings, the Bell Mission's report is still an issue in current discussions of Philippine-American relations. The report was neither the first nor the last American study of the Philippine economy nor necessarily the best, but it was the first large-scale, systematic postwar survey made by highly competent personnel over a reasonably long period of time. It was the first effort by the United States to bring about changes in the political and economic policies of an independent Philippines in full view of public opinion in both countries, and the occasion for extending to the Philippines what was then called the Economic Cooperation Administration for technical and economic assistance. Thus it marked the beginning of a new era in U.S.-Philippine relations.

The Bell report is generally considered to rank high as an objective analysis of Philippine economic conditions.[1] The basic economic problem of the Philippines, it suggested, was inefficient production and very low personal incomes. The standard of living for most people, it found, was below the prewar level. Why? In the first place little or nothing had been done to increase productive efficiency and to diversify the economy. The area formerly under cultivation had been restored, but the population had increased by twenty-five per cent during the previous ten years. Almost nothing had been done "to open new lands for the increased population, to improve the methods of cultivation, or to better the position of farm workers and tenants." In trade and industry, production had been restored along prewar lines as a result of the pressures from established interests in both countries. While a few new enterprises had been started, there had been little real progress in opening new work opportunities and in strengthening the economy. "The country still relies too heavily on the export of a few basic agricultural crops—coconut, sugar and hemp—which provide a meager livelihood to most of the people engaged in their production." All this in spite of the fact that some of the conditions for economic growth—namely, a high rate of investment and high foreign exchange receipts—

[1] *Report to the President of the United States by the Economic Mission to the Philippines* (Washington: GPO, 1950). This is the *Bell Report*, or *The Economic Survey Mission to the Philippines*, released to Philippines October 29, 1950. The quotations are from pages 1-3.

were present during the immediate postwar period. But investment went more into real estate and commerce than into agriculture and industry, and much of the available foreign exchange was frittered away in imports of luxury and nonessential goods, "in the remittance of high profits and in the transfer of Philippine capital abroad." At the same time inequalities of income in the Philippines had become even more marked. While the average standard of living had not reached prewar levels, "the profits of business men and the income of large landowners have risen very considerably." This was partly due to unequal bargaining power between workers and tenants on the one hand and employers and landowners on the other. Under these conditions rising prices had the effect of transferring real income from the poor to the rich.

Although the dangers inherent in this "pervading economic unbalance between production and need, between prices and wages, between Government expenditures and taxes, between foreign exchange payments and receipts" were understood by some Filipino officials, nothing was being done to stop the deterioration of the economy. In consequence, there was widespread disillusionment about independence and democracy; lack of confidence in the economic system on the part of businessmen, workers, and peasants; a growing unemployment; open support for the Hukbalahaps in the countryside; and a widening rift between government and people. Import and exchange controls and price controls were no cure. A permanent solution would be found only through a determined effort on the part of the people and the government of the Philippines, with the aid and encouragement of the United States, "to increase production and improve productive efficiency, to raise the level of wages and farm income, and to open new opportunities for work and for acquiring land." In essence, the report indicated that the Filipino elite must develop a sense of responsibility for improving the economic condition of the mass of the people.

Specific and detailed recommendations flowed from this analysis. The basic recommendation was to increase the productivity of agriculture in order to support the development of industry. This approach to economic growth, typical of the industrially advanced states of the free world, is denounced by the Communists who say that it shows how the "imperialists" keep their former colonies from industrializing. The unstated assumptions of this approach are that the conditions of agricultural production will favor individual initiative and that the primary producer will receive an adequate share of the rewards. These assumptions are important because, if they do not hold, the further recommendations are not likely to be effective.

Put very briefly, the mission suggested financial reforms, such as revision of the tax structure, more efficient tax collection, and improved credit and investment policies. It estimated that only twenty-five per cent of taxes due were actually collected and that the elite was guilty of excessive evasion.[2] For agriculture the mission recommended measures for crop improvement and extension of rural credit, and the purchase of large estates and their resale to the tenants. It pointed out that the necessary laws were on the books and that any failure to apply them was due to social and cultural factors rather than to lack of technical knowledge and skills. This situation lay behind the statement of the report that the government itself, "composed in good measure of large landowners, has not only failed to enforce the new regulations [for a 70-30 division in favor of the tenant] but has tolerated the organization of private police and civil guards to fight the tenants' demands."[3]

The mission again indicted the Filipino elite in the section on trade. It recommended a re-examination of the Trade Act of 1946 and strongly supported the extension of the period of free trade but pointed out that "the evidence of the past indicates that such will benefit American interests and the Filipino upper class rather than the average Filipino."[4] Hence the need to diversify industry, develop power, and improve transportation facilities. Particular attention should be paid to rural industries geared to seasonal labor and requiring low capital outlay. Such an approach, the report argued, might avoid in part the profound reorientation of social life and values normally in-

2 Same, p. 18.
3 Same, p. 19.
4 Same, p. 20.

volved in industrialization. Indeed, here the report pointed out with insight the relation between economic growth and cultural factors:

The apparent social disorganization of American life, the reduction of family loyalties, the secularization and material competition, are all characteristics of American life which Filipinos profess to despise, yet they are beginning to develop in industrial centers in the Philippines and will spread with further industrialization. For this reason it is particularly important that the problems of industrialization be thoroughly analyzed and presented before final programs are adopted.[5]

In other words, the Filipinos had to decide which they wanted more, their traditional value system or adequate economic growth. It was not possible to have both.

The report called for social reforms to bring about a rapid change in the condition of the peasants and workers. In particular, it stressed the need for legislation to improve health, education, and housing, to establish minimum wages in agriculture as well as in industry, and to give workers the right to organize free trade unions.

The most controversial recommendations dealt with public administration. Steps had to be taken to ensure honesty and efficiency in the operation of the government. The report actually said very little about corruption in high places, and what it said was mild compared with some of the strictures of the government in the Manila press. Coming from a foreign source, however, it attracted attention far out of proportion to its importance. Tension ran high because the recommendations of the mission were known to be an expression of U.S. policy.

Though the United States proclaimed its reluctance to interfere in the internal affairs of sovereign states, this was intervention on a grand scale. The Bell Mission recommended that the United States make loans and grants of $250 million, provided the Philippine government took steps to carry out the recommendations of its report. This meant the enactment of tax legislation and other reforms, such as a minimum wage law; acceptance of supervision over the expenditure of dollar grants and peso

[5] Same, p. 20.

counterpart funds; coordination by the Philippine government of its own funds for economic and social development with American funds that were available for the same purpose; and a final settlement of all outstanding financial claims between the two countries.

The Quirino administration hit out hard against the charges of corruption and objected to American supervision. Some of the psychological problems that arise in the relations between a large power and a small one were revealed in a famous statement written by Federico Mangahas, private secretary to Quirino, and issued from Malacañang, the presidential palace. The commentator wrote, in part:

What is not widely understood is that Philippine "bankruptcy" and "corruption" have an intimate relation to American example in racketeering and to the insidious inspiration provided by conspicuous consumption otherwise known as the so-called American standard of living. It still remains to be generally appreciated that, in the matter of graft and corruption, Filipinos are mere pikers compared to their more accomplished and eminently successful mentors who had had, and still have, a vast continent in which to base their operations. The Filipinos, there is no question, are inefficient all right—even in their grafting—due, no doubt, to simple lack of sufficient experience. With more time and greater chances, they will yet show they can equal, or even surpass, the stink familiar and now taken for granted in Washington and such very proper, exemplary centers of power, prosperity and culture. Those who talk so glibly of 2 billion U.S. dollars poured into the "rathole" that is the Philippines . . . seem extra careful not to remember the billions of dollars worth of property and life the Filipinos paid for the luxury of welcoming General MacArthur's triumphant return to their violated shores . . . Filipinos are now getting it in the neck because they are not rich enough to cover up their own stink and to be lofty and moral about it before a devasted and hungry world . . . When you are wealthy, such as America is, you can afford to step on anybody without so much as saying, by your leave. You can elaborately pretend to the loftiest principles and idealism and so conveniently forget about the whited sepulchers filled with dead men's bones. Filipinos can, and do, admit that there is something wrong with them . . . and they want to do something about it . . . but they cannot be bullied to accept that their friends, however well-meaning and altruistic, have cornered all the stock there is of efficiency, competence, vision and integrity in the world . . . The U.S. is so well-endowed and powerful that it should not be too awkward and embarrassing for her to display a little more becoming grace and modesty of spirit for the benefit of a needy and sorely distracted world . . . even if only for the purpose of Public Relations, Incorporated.[6]

President Quirino avoided responsibility for the statement, and President Truman handled it with dignity but decided to publish the Bell report in full instead of in summary form. The agreement that the two governments finally reached on their mutual undertakings arising out of the Bell Mission was one of the few examples of an open covenant openly arrived at. It took time. Quirino called a special session of Congress and the Resolution of Intent passed in February 1951. It was much harder to get passage of the specific measures called for in the report. Bills increasing individual and corporate income taxes and establishing sales, privilege, luxury and excise taxes were eventually passed, but discussions on them revealed some of the problems that arise for American policy. There was opposition to new taxes on the ground that the United States would have to assist the Philippines in any case as it could not allow the "showcase of democracy" to go bankrupt, and U.S. strategic interests were becoming more and more apparent as the international situation grew worse. There was the reluctance of the Philippine government to put pressure on the Congress to raise taxes in order to get the financial aid promised in the Bell report.

In the political struggle to secure passage of the tax measures and the minimum wage law, both prerequisites for U.S. assistance, there were factors other than their unpopularity at issue. The tax laws became involved in a fight over a bill to abolish bloc voting, the system by which one could vote for the candidates for all offices merely by writing down the name of the party. The advantage to the dominant party was obvious. The Senate refused to vote on any House-approved bills until the House passed the bill against bloc voting, so the president had to accept its abolition in order to get the tax bills passed.[7]

[6] *Manila Chronicle*, October 26, 1950.
[7] Leon O. Ty, "Inside Congress," *Philippine Free Press*, March 24, 1951, p. 5.

On the minimum wage bill the story was different. The Senate passed it but the House held it up for three months, due largely to the efforts of the sugar bloc to protect what it conceived to be its own economic interests. The planters were strong in the House while the big sugar *centrals,* the millers, were stronger in the Senate. Although it was politically impossible for an elected representative not to speak in favor of a minimum wage law, it was quite possible for him to emasculate it by suggesting such apparently reasonable devices as provincial wage boards to decide on its local application. The act that was finally passed met the specifications of the Bell report, but it would not have done so without American pressure.[8]

Although the Philippine government did not meet all of the conditions laid down in the report, it met enough of them for the United States to proceed with economic and technical assistance. The terms of cooperation were incorporated in an Economic and Technical Cooperation Agreement, known as the STEM Agreement (because the Philippines agreed to receive a Special Technical and Economic Mission).

When it came to making use of the aid funds, the two countries did not find it easy to agree on their structural and functional relationships or on the role of American advisers. The basic agreement had been reached in November 1950 by President Quirino and William C. Foster after much public discussion and private negotiation. The point at issue was the degree of control and supervision that the ECA representatives would exercise, the real meaning of "advice and consultation." One of the main concerns of American policy was to see to it that not only the Quirino government, which the press openly accused of corruption, but also any future administration would be unable to funnel American aid into private hands or use it for electioneering purposes. The Philippine government wanted to go as far as possible in saving face, but it could not avoid the final control

[8] Emiliano Morabe, *The Minimum Wage Law* (Manila: Colcol Publishing Co., 1954), pp. 3-19. See also: Leon O. Ty, "Interview with Quirino," *Free Press,* March 10, 1951, p. 4; "Editorial: Minimum Wage Legislation," *American Chamber of Commerce Journal,* v. 27, January 1951, p. 1; *Manila Chronicle,* December 31, 1950, January 7, 23, 31, 1951, and Editorial, April 30, 1951.

by the United States over the use of the funds. The alternative was for the United States to ask the Philippine government to list its projects and estimate the cost, and then hand over the money. This was out of the question. An editorial in a Manila daily pointed out at the time: "Mr. Foster coined the word 'equal partnership' as the basis of Fil-American collaboration in the implementation of the Bell report, as if 'equal partnership' with . . . Uncle Sam, the partner who holds the purse-strings, could be taken literally . . . it is always the one with the purse-strings who has the most say . . . if we finally accept it is because we have no other choice." [9] There may not have been a choice but there was plenty of room for maneuvering.

At one stage the Filipinos suggested a mixed commission, just as they had suggested a joint undertaking at the time when the Bell Mission was set up. The commission, to be appointed by the Philippine government and with a Filipino majority, would send its proposals to the ECA for transmittal to Washington for final action. The U.S. government, however, was reluctant to put Americans in a position where they would share the responsibility but be in a minority, and where the ECA mission in Manila would merely forward to Washington projects formulated by a Philippine government agency. The Quirino-Foster Agreement followed very closely the pattern suggested by Foster of two bodies, each directly responsible to its own government— a pattern that was characteristic of ECA operations in most of the rest of the world. Quirino set up a Philippine Council on U.S. Aid (PHILCUSA) in November with José Yulo as chairman. The ECA, the American counterpart, set up an office in Manila with Vincent Checci in charge. Its functions were "to advise with the Philippine Government, through the said Philippine Council, in planning the use of American social, economic and technical assistance and cooperation, and in advising and assisting the Philippine Government in carrying out the general aims and recommendations of the Economic Survey Mission to the Philippines." [10] The Philippines accepted no more

[9] *Manila Chronicle*, Editorial, November 10, 1950.
[10] *Quirino-Foster Agreement*, November 14, 1950.

supervision and control than many other countries, including India, and far less than some, such as Greece.

Several reasons account for the United States and the Philippines reaching an arrangement satisfactory to both sides. The desperate economic situation in the Philippines overcame a strong nationalist pride, and the essential soundness of American policy made the adjustment much easier. The Philippines was not being asked to accept arrangements that other independent and even neutral countries had not accepted, and there was a great deal of support for the conditions laid down by the Bell Mission. Very important was the political skill of President Quirino and several outstanding congressmen and senators. On the American side there were the political and negotiating skills of Ambassador Myron Cowen, of Foster, and of Checci, all three of whom played a decisive part.

The Bell report was an example of a thoughtful, carefully prepared statement of policy based on a well-documented survey of the situation and an integrated view of Philippine society. The goals were socio-economic in the broadest sense of the term; in fact, they were revolutionary in the Philippine context. This was a direct effort to reform a conflict-torn society in order to create a sound basis for political democracy, and it involved the use of economic leverage in order to bring about legislation that otherwise would never have been passed. The strength of the Bell Mission lay in the integration between the goals and the way they were to be attained. The Department of State was in control of policy and negotiation, and it did not then have to take into account large-scale ECA or military missions with millions at their disposal and ends and techniques of their own, factors that complicated subsequent negotiations and permitted the Philippine government to play off one group of Americans against another. The situation, it must be agreed, was much simpler than at any time since, but it can be argued that the measure of success achieved was due largely to the unusual integration of means and ends.

Looked at in the perspective of American policy, the Bell Mission was a last minute effort to correct the results of fifty years of neglect in the Philippines. The responsibility for the low incomes, inefficient production, and gross inequalities in wealth cannot be put entirely at the door of the Filipino oligarchy. The United States had made no serious or effective effort to build a sound economic base for political democracy in its half-century of rule. The United States did not turn over to the Filipinos an economy marked by a diversified use of natural resources for the benefit of the Filipino people. As late as 1941 High Commissioner Francis B. Sayre reported that "neither a sizable independent middle class nor an influential public opinion has developed. The bulk of the newly-created income has gone to the Government, to landlords, and to urban areas, and has served but little to ameliorate living conditions among the almost feudal peasantry and tenantry." [11] For the United States to change all this in 1950, when it had all the disadvantages of being the former imperial power, was obviously impossible. What could be done was to commit the Philippine government on paper to the concept of using the resources of the land to bring about the social and economic well-being of the Filipino people; to save the economy from its current crisis, establish new goals and a new sense of direction; to shift the internal balance of power a little more toward those groups that were anxious to face up to the problems of the Philippines. This the United States accomplished through the Bell Mission.

In addition, the Bell report, by indicating a willingness on the part of the U.S. government to meet some of the Filipino objections to the Trade Act of 1946 and other matters, made it clear that U.S. policy was adjusting more than ever before to the fact of Philippine independence, to the difficult task of helping the Filipinos to help themselves. The reformist element in U.S. policy, which some Filipinos pointed to with apprehension and resentment, took a new lease on life and soon expressed itself in vigorous proposals for land reform and other objectives that revealed a serious divergence between the Philippine and American view of what was best for the Philippines. In all these matters the ECA came to be the cutting edge for U.S. social and economic policies.

[11] Human Relations Area Files, *Area Handbook on the Philippines,* v. 3 (New Haven: Author, under sub-contract HRAF-1, Chi-1, 1956), p. 1274.

The Security Crisis: Domestic and Foreign

The second important development at this time, matching the new economic relationship, was in the military field. To the internal threat from Communist-led Hukbalahaps, in itself one of the main factors contributing to the economic crisis, there was now added the intensification of the cold war that followed the opening of the struggle in Korea. The Philippines, always high in strategic importance for the American navy, took on a new significance for other branches of the armed services. The Philippines was now referred to as the anchor in a chain of islands or offshore bases running from Japan in the north, through Okinawa and Formosa to the Philippines.[12] U.S. naval and air power was to rest on the use of military bases which were established by treaty agreements with governments in whose attitudes and competence the United States by virtue of such agreements had a vested interest. To the political and economic argument for interference in Philippine affairs there were now added the military and strategic considerations.

Continuation of the close relationship between the American and the Philippine military establishments was assured by the Philippine Military Assistance Act of 1946, which authorized the postwar U.S. military assistance program. On the assumption that the Philippine government had decided to "lean to one side," the terms of the agreement were to the mutual advantage of both parties. Filipinos could feel that they were paying for military assistance by granting the use of bases and that they were partners, however weak at the time, in mutual defense and in the preservation of peace in the Western Pacific. No relationship between two powers can be more intimate than one involving a common military program with standardized training and weapons. It touches the core of nationalistic feeling and sensitivities about sovereignty more than does commercial and political dependence. Although the same degree of American control was not incorporated into later military agreements between the two pow-

[12] See, for example, statement of General Bonner Fellers, *Congressional Record*, v. 96, pt. 16, July 13, 1950, p. A-5097.

ers, it is well to remember, now that the bases are a source of political contention, that the original concept in 1946 was one of mutual security based on a division of labor, the Philippine government being responsible for internal and the United States for external security. Such an arrangement presupposes agreement on foreign policy.

The relationship between the armed forces of the two countries has been marked by comparatively little recrimination. The chief complaint in the early years after independence was directed not at Philippine dependence on the United States in military matters but at the alleged reluctance of the United States to turn over first class equipment to the Filipinos. There was a certain amount of justification for some of the charges up to 1949, mainly because the Philippines could afford to buy little new material and the U.S. surplus equipment was designed not for a Philippine army but for the invasion of Japan. In the spring of 1950, before the outbreak of the Korean War, the Philippine government requested and secured the renewal of the original five-year agreement for military aid (1946-1951) to July 1953.

In August 1951, one year after the Korean War began and less than a year before the Japanese peace treaty came into effect, the United States and the Philippines signed a Mutual Defense Treaty. Article IV states: "Each Party recognizes that an armed attack in the Pacific area on either of the Parties would be dangerous to its own peace and safety and declares that it would act to meet the common dangers in accordance with its constitutional processes." [13] This was a guarantee, more binding than anything in previous treaties, of American willingness to protect the Philippines. Magsaysay later referred to it as a binding agreement under which the United States was committed to act immediately in case of an attack on the Philippines. "This pledge is contained in written commitments solemnly made and is inherent in the existence of United States military bases in our country." [14]

[13] *Mutual Defense Treaty, 1951,* between the Republic of the Philippines and the United States of America, Department of Foreign Affairs Treaty Series, vol. 2, January 1953, p. 14.

[14] President Magsaysay's Policy Statement, April 18, 1954, *Official Gazette,* Republic of the Philippines, v. 50, April 1954, p. 1540.

It is doubtful whether the treaty made it more or less likely that the United States would act immediately in defense of the Philippines, as it is difficult to imagine an attack on that country that would by-pass twenty-three American bases on the islands or would not involve action under the United Nations Charter, but there were good reasons for the Filipinos to want the extra assurance. They had been occupied by Japan at a time when the United States was responsible for Philippine security, and the experience was very fresh. Filipinos resented the changed position of Japan in relation to the United States, particularly the granting of economic aid to make her the workshop of Asia and the signing of a peace treaty without a previous reparations agreement with the Philippines. They needed an answer to the arguments of Senator Recto and his supporters on the disadvantages of the American connection. They needed all the American help they could get at a time when the Huks were still a threat and the Korean War was in progress. The treaty, said General Romulo, is one between two independent sovereign nations, a clear-cut military alliance.

The Mutual Defense Treaty with the Philippines was only one expression of the revived concern of the United States for security in the Pacific after the Korean War. The system of security pacts was extended to include Japan, Formosa, the SEATO powers, and Australia and New Zealand. But the most significant changes in American policy arose out of the new emphasis on strengthening the military forces of Asian countries that were exposed to Communist aggression and were willing to accept U.S. aid. To achieve this objective it was essential for each country to have an economy that could support the additional military burdens, and to have a stable political situation. As a result the U.S. policy of assistance to the new nations of Asia combined two purposes: to help them make a successful political and economic adjustment to independence; and to help them become militarily strong enough to take care of internal subversion and contribute to collective security against the most likely aggressor, the Communist bloc. From the American point of view nothing could seem more reasonable than for a newly independent country to desire all these things for itself and to accept assistance from the United States in order to achieve them. The Philippines came as close as any country to being the ideal image of a deserving and right-minded Asian country, and in many ways it was. But even under ideal conditions it was soon found difficult to keep in balance the promotion of economic growth, military growth, and political stability, especially when one of them was given priority over the others.

The new U.S. emphasis on military aid can be measured quantitatively. In 1950 military assistance, on a world-wide basis, represented about one-quarter of the total of American aid, but by 1952 it was over two-thirds. As the programs developed, a considerable amount of economic assistance was included in military aid under the heading of "defense support." The U.S. Congress sought to bring some order out of the many different programs when it passed the Mutual Security Act of 1951.

The Act had specific recommendations for Asia and the Pacific, especially for the nations that were close to the Sino-Soviet orbit and were important to the United States by reason of their strategic position, large population, production of essential raw materials, and vulnerability to external aggression and internal subversion. The sum of $535.25 million was authorized for military assistance to Thailand, Formosa, Indochina, and the Philippine Republic. For economic and technical assistance, Congress authorized $237 million for all of Asia, except Korea, and the Pacific. President Truman spoke of "the now inseparable goals of military strength and continuing economic stability." [15]

For the Philippines the immediate impact of the new emphasis on defense was an increase in military assistance. The military mission, JUSMAG, set up in the Philippines in March 1947 when the Military Assistance Agreement between the United States and the Philippines went into effect, was taken as the model when mutual defense assistance treaties were signed with other countries in Asia. In its first decade JUSMAG administered $169.3 million to support a wide range of purposes; these included the training of jet pilots at Clark Field; the delivery of training jets, minesweepers, and ammunition; the improvement of

[15] William Adams Brown, Jr., and Redvers Opie, *American Foreign Assistance* (Washington, D.C.: Brookings Institution, 1953), p. 502.

airfields; and the construction of warehouses and divisional training sites.

The military mission also contributed a considerable amount of advice and equipment to the struggle of the Philippine army and constabulary against the Huks. This help was probably as important as any other single factor, except Magsaysay's remarkable leadership, in breaking the military forces of the insurgents. It is generally believed that members of the mission also had something to do with the adoption of the new program of social and economic reform that was an essential part of Magsaysay's approach to solving the Huk problem. As the reputation built up by Magsaysay in the Huk campaigns was the basis of his successful bid for the presidency in 1953, the most startling political development of the period, his election may be said to have been due in some measure to the program of American military assistance.

U.S. assistance to the Philippines in the fight against communism within was more than matched by the reinforcement of American units based in the Philippines for defense against the threat from without. Immediately following the outbreak of the Korean conflict, the United States increased its air and naval forces in the Philippines, and Clark Field became one of the great air commands of the western Pacific. So much was said about the strategic importance of the Philippines as the anchor of the island chain that it became safer for Filipinos to put more pressure on the United States than they had before over such issues as the status of the military bases. The situation and the bargaining position of the Philippines had changed. It was now clear that the United States wanted the bases for its own defense and could always be counted on to come to the rescue of the government in power at a time of economic crisis. When a strong power is in partnership with a weak one, the bargaining positions are not necessarily a direct reflection of their relative military and economic strength.

Part II

Independence and Partnership

Chapter 8

The New Nation

While Filipinos have been technically at liberty to run their own affairs since 1946, it was not until the defeat of the Huks and the economic recovery of the early 1950s that they really began to take hold of themselves and their country. The turning point came, perhaps, with the Magsaysay election in 1953, which brought to power a man who was the first Philippine president to attempt to persuade the common people that the government should be responsive and responsible to them, who began to tackle the mighty problem of agrarian reform, and who firmly but tactfully impressed on the United States the fact that the Filipinos intended to be treated as an independent people. In the field of foreign affairs, the Garcia administration (1957-61) carried on the same tradition, and the successor Macapagal administration has been marked by an air of self-confidence and self-assertion that is in sharp contrast, for example, with the immediate postwar administrations of Roxas and Quirino.

The question today is not whether the Filipinos are capable of self-government, but rather what sort of government they are going to run and in which direction they are going. Everything up to the present has been a prelude to the coming drama; the vital struggles in Philippine politics are only now beginning. Key factors in Philippine political development that will affect these struggles are the place of politics in the Filipino value system, the nature and extent of nationalism, the political potential of old and new social classes, and the political role of the military.

Social Values and the Political Process

The over-riding problem of Philippine democracy is the tension between the democratic political institutions and the traditional value system. Democracy as a way of life grows more slowly than as a set of political institutions; it is the product of an intellectual tradition that must be absorbed by those who would make the institutions work. The process can be speeded up to some extent by the imposition of democratic institutions, especially when the timing and the style are acceptable, as they were in the Philippines during the colonial period. The writers of the Malolos Constitution had already committed the oligarchy to constitutional government. But as the traditional social values and institutions of the Philippines have little in common with democratic life, much now depends on the extent to which they have changed under the impact of events.

While it is difficult to offer quantitative proof of the changes that have occurred in social values and political ideology, there are ways of indicating the fact of change. Most obvious of these are: the public commitment to political democracy and the demonstrated measure of success in its practice, the continued separation of Church and State, the peaceful transfer of power and the orderly election process, the subordination of the military to civil authority, the freedom of the press, the widespread demand for education and the government's effort to provide public instruction, and the deepening sense of national unity. Changes of this magnitude indicate considerable shifts in the Filipino way of life and in certain respects put the Filipinos far ahead of some of their neighbors.

The traditional Philippine socio-economic system, however, casts a long shadow over the practice of politics in the Philippines today. The tough old family unit is still very powerful. The New Civil Code of 1953 goes out of its way to state in Article 216 that the family is a basic social institution which public policy cherishes and protects, and in Article 220 that in case of doubt all presumptions favor the solidarity of the family. "Thus every intendment of law or fact leans toward the validity of marriage, the indissolubility of the marriage bonds, the legitimacy of children, the community of property during the marriage, the authority of parents over their children, and the validity of defense for any member of the family in case of unlawful aggression." Marriages are still considered familial alliances, and divorce is not recognized by law. The position of women, always prominent in Philippine custom, was depressed by the Spaniards, who gave legal and social support to the husband and father, but today the Filipino woman enjoys the same privileges as her husband in all such matters as education, suffrage, property, and respect for age.

The Civil Code supports the hierarchy of obedience by stating specifically that "grandparents should be consulted by all members of the family on important family questions." The wealth of a family is divided equally among the children; the family takes care of the social and economic well-being of all its members. The problems that are met in the United States by old-age insurance, unemployment compensation, and rehabilitation of the wrongdoer are taken care of in the Philippines by the family. There is only one old people's home in the Philippines. Of considerable influence in political and economic life is the fact that the Filipino tends to bring personal relationships outside the family into the web of kinship through the formality of the *compadre* system, which establishes reciprocal duties and obligations.[1] This is the practice of selecting a godparent, not a member of the family, to cosponsor a child during the sacrament of baptism.

The bilateral kinship system, which is not usual in Asia, has many political, economic, and social implications. It is undoubtedly an important contributing factor (though not the only one) to the relatively open and loosely structured society of the Philippines. The Filipino is no stranger to group loyalty, but his is a loyalty to the small kinship group. Within the group his code of personal honor is of the highest, but on behalf of the group he will rob the public treasury with full assurance that this is expected of him as the natural course of action. Members

[1] Human Relations Area Files, *Area Handbook on the Philippines*, v. 1 (New Haven: Author, under sub-contract HRAF-1, Chi-1, 1956), p. 423.

of other similar groups do the same. Private virtues, however, are public vices. The formula has not yet been found that will allow the Filipinos to keep the warmth and charm of personal relationships within the kinship group while consolidating a larger community for economic and political purposes. Yet it has been suggested that the bilateral kinship system is more likely than the unilateral to favor the growth of democracy, industry, freedom of religious belief, and political dynamism. It is not easy to establish a correlation between unilateral kinship systems and authoritarian poverty and backwardness, but societies that give their women equality, education, and freedom have a definite advantage over those that do not.

The disadvantage of the bilateral system must be reckoned, too. It limits the sense of community and discourages the growth of large-scale business organizations. The strength of the family contrasts sharply with the weakness of extra-family relationships. Because the suspicion and insecurity that mark all dealings with the outgroup do not encourage attitudes that are useful to the capitalist entrepreneur, Filipinos engaged in modern political and economic life have difficulties that Americans do not have. The Filipino sense of personal dignity, for example, makes it a serious matter to lose an election, to be fired from a position, to be embarrassed in public debate, or to insist on the payment of debts. To be a borrower is to accept an inferior position. Employers are reluctant to dismiss an employee or to criticize his work as this will damage his self-esteem and that of his family. Therefore, in order to play a role in the modern economy or even in government, the Filipino must in some degree alienate himself from the traditional socio-economic system. He can operate on a small scale (as in a family business) while remaining a conformist, but not on a large scale, for this requires different attitudes and values.

The family system is usually blamed for the character of political life, including corruption. The bilateral family is a sizable group, possibly amounting to 30 persons for a prosperous middle-age couple—2 parents, 4 grandparents, 12 uncles and aunts, 7 children, 2 children-in-law, and 3 grandchildren—not to mention all the kinsmen added through the *compadre* system. The reciprocal obligations between kinsmen are extensive and exacting. The wealthier kinsmen acquire status and a large following by creating as many debts of gratitude as they can afford; the acceptance of a favor involves a willingness to repay which it is very shameful to avoid. So the politician builds up a following by giving jobs, money, or other gifts to individuals, or public works to a constituency. What more natural than to repay gifts with votes? Filipino politics has been compared to a huge Tammany-Hall type of operation. There are those who feel that up to one-fifth of the votes in an ordinary election are bought with hard cash, possibly at a price of 5 pesos to 50 pesos a family unit. There is no doubt that large amounts of money change hands in an election, much of it public money, but the candidate also expects to spend more of his own money than he can hope to receive in salary. If elected, he expects to recover his losses through graft and corruption when in office, and there are many opportunities for him to do so, although one of the main sources of graft came to a close in the spring of 1962 when President Macapagal devalued the peso and practically eliminated controls over foreign exchange.

Politics is a major industry for the Filipinos; it is a way of life. Politics is the main route to power, which, in turn, is the main route to wealth. Power is as important to the making of money as it is to the keeping. Those who have political power can evade payment of taxes and customs dues, block investigations, break competitors, and ruin political opponents. More money can be made in a shorter time with the aid of political influence than by any other means—this is one reason for the landlord's neglect of agricultural improvement and avoidance of the risks of the entrepreneur.

The Filipino thinks of political parties as large impersonal machines to which he has little or no loyalty; he tends to relate himself to a person, rather than to a principle or an institution. The viable political groups therefore tend to be small personal machines based on kinship, favors, and the relationships between leader and followers. The power of the local boss is based partly on economic influence and the immobility of labor, partly on the control of information and of access to the outside world.

This is especially true in the isolated village or barrio where the literacy rate is low and where linguistic differentiation and poor communications limit sound political growth. With some 20,000 towns and barrios in the Philippines, the national candidate is clearly not able to reach the people without going through several layers of leaders—provincial, county, barrio. In return for favors, votes are produced. A national election can be visualized as a process in which a large number of building blocks of various sizes are gradually assembled into two large piles and perhaps one or two small ones. The problem for the Filipino politician is to guess which pile is going to be the bigger and attach his building block to it; the objective is not party or policy but victory.

This simplified picture of Philippine politics needs considerable modification. The history of national elections shows that the "building blocks" shift from one pile to the other; in other words, between the Nacionalista and the Liberal parties. The question is why? Can it be entirely a matter of money and favors? If so, how can an administration in power ever be voted out, considering the enormous pork barrel it can dispense? Obviously, other factors are at work. The late Senator Recto had no machine and few favors except those he could promise if elected; yet he could always count on a hard core vote of nearly half a million people, mainly from the Manila area, who apparently thought that they were voting for a set of principles, a definite image of their country, and an incorruptible Filipino nationalist. Although Ramón Magsaysay was elected with the massive support of the Nacionalista organization, there was an element in the election of charismatic leadership and reforming zeal that undoubtedly accounted for many votes and the enlistment of many helpers. The election returns also show that the Filipinos use their votes selectively. The common practice of ticket-splitting may well arise from differing judgments as to the favors that rival candidates would dispense, but it also reflects the presence of certain standards of public probity. A reputation for blatant graft combined with mediocre abilities is not a winning combination even with money to give away.

There is little to distinguish the two main parties from each other in composition or doctrine, but since the two-party system dates only from 1946, it is too early yet to tell whether the parties will come to differ radically in doctrine and social composition. In the struggles between the Congress and President Macapagal there have been signs of party allegiance and discipline becoming a more significant issue, at least to the Nacionalistas, who tried to prevent some of their members allying themselves with the Liberals. Not so long ago independence was the only acceptable political symbol, but today there is a greater variety of symbols and the national political discourse is carried on in terms of broad issues. Philippine politics is more than a projection onto the national scene of the relations between the cacique and the semiliterate peasants in an isolated barrio. It is also more than a single-minded pursuit of status, wealth, and power by the kin-affiliated individual. Today we have to take into account the political dynamics of class conflict and nationalism.

Nationalism and the Intellectuals

Modernization of a country requires an intellectual elite, the men and women who formulate the new values that stimulate and guide the process of change. The term "elite" is vague. In the Philippines it would obviously include Rizal, Senator Recto, and the theoreticians of the left, the Lava brothers—all men of outstanding intellectual achievement. It would include, as well, Aguinaldo, the self-taught warehouseman Bonifacio, and Taruc—men separated from the intelligentsia proper by a cultural gap but who can translate ideas into action. A definition of the intelligentsia for the Philippines must be broad enough to include al those who are the carriers of the new, as distinct from the traditional, values.

The present-day intellectual elite in the Philippines plays a role somewhere between that of intellectuals in the United States and those in the less-developed countries of Asia. This is because the United States was partly successful in imposing on the Philippines the ethos of an advanced industrialized democracy despite the absence of the essential industrial component. The intellectual shares with the businessman and the government official an ambivalent attitude toward the values of democracy; he is not completely divorced from the culture of the masses and he is relatively free to express his opinions. Only to a limited extent is he at variance with the dominant view of the nature of society; he does not expect to rule, or to be oppressed by the police. In contrast, intellectuals in many underdeveloped Asian countries are a distinct class and a social force of great political potential. Usually they are culturally divorced from the masses, having been educated abroad or in Western-type schools at home, and in many cases they are responsible for the direction of government.

The Filipino intellectual elite is large enough to staff the fields of education, government service, law, politics, journalism, and religion. This is one of the main sources of its strength. Over half of the key positions in the country are held by graduates of the University of the Philippines, but an increasing number of graduates of the best parochial schools are joining them. Many of the members of the intellectual elite are Masons or Protestants. The first two presidents were Protestants, and Magsaysay, though nominally Roman Catholic, was greatly influenced by the Protestant philanthropist Teodoro Yangco. The anticlerical tradition of the revolution is still strong with the intellectuals. By an Act of Congress in 1956 all schools are required to teach the life and works of Rizal despite the fact that his books are still on the Index.

The intellectuals are limited, however, in their opportunities for scholarly work, for scientific research, and for the writing of literature. It cannot be said that there is yet an independent, self-regenerative intellectual life in the Philippines. In training and outlook the educated Filipino is still dominated by American culture, even when he is fulminating against it; unlike some of his neighbors he has no substantial, pre-Western, intellectual traditions. Because first Spain and then the United States controlled military affairs, the Filipino intellectual class tends to be civilian in outlook, but it is not opposed to the use of violence nor averse to active participation in violence.

As there has been a system of public education for several generations, the educated Filipino is not as divorced from mass culture as was, say, the educated Russian before the Bolshevik revolution. But as only a modest amount of education is available for the majority of the population, the cultural gap is far from closed. And since education is one of the main channels of upward social mobility, the Filipino intellectual will tend to be a social conformist so long as society is able to provide adequate rewards and opportunities for his talents. If it cannot, there are explosive possibilities in the combination of radical intellectuals and organized peasants and workers.

The Filipino intellectual today is deeply concerned with the problem of nationalism, and in the long run it is he who will decide its character and content. Not surprisingly the debate on nationalism has gathered momentum since independence, as the Filipinos have had to decide their own policies in a rapidly changing world and make their own arrangements with other peoples, especially those in Asia, from whom they had been shielded for many years. Philippine nationalism is in a state of transition, and where the Filipino will go in his search for identity is far from clear.

The spirit of nationalism is a sense of tradition, of common purposes and values for which men are willing to make great sacrifices. Those who write history help to define these traditions and values; if their image of the past is accepted, they can do much to shape the future. In the Philippines today books may well make history. It is no accident that Filipino intellectuals are turning to the past in search of moral support, guidance, and polemical material. Hence the search for purely Philippine cultural patterns and material accomplishments and the claims that the cultural level of the inhabitants of the Philippines before the coming of the Spaniards was much higher than had been assumed. In the words of Benito Legarda:

The puerile idea, implicit in some modern writings, that the Filipinos were too busy rattling their chains in colonial darkness to do anything creative finds no support in the surviving examples of colonial art, many of which are quite excellent. . . . It should be part of our national education to teach our people to appreciate the handiwork of our ancestors, and to cherish it. For it is in doing so that we can best find our national identity, and thus know ourselves.[2]

This healthy view of the colonial period stands out in sharp contrast to that of the left wing intellectuals to whom colonialism is the root of all evil. For example, to the rhetorical question, What cancerous growth afflicts our national organism? Horacio Lava writes:

It was, and still is, the colonial institutions forced upon us from the early days of the Spanish and American colonization, and which did not terminate with the proclamation of independence, but instead lingered on, and in certain spheres, have fortified themselves even more. The features of colonial institutions are manifest in the colonial economic structure, the colonial political leadership, the colonial educational system, the colonial culture, the colonial military thinking, and the almost complete absence of national self-respect and dignity on the part of a large sector of our leadership.[3]

In pointing out that education is the key to a re-orientation of nationalism (and congratulating the Americans on understanding its importance), Mr. Lava continued, "With a colonial psychology already deeply rooted into our mental system, with an economic structure almost wholly colonial, with a political environment of subservience, with the pre-eminence of foreign culture in our midst, and with the predominance of foreign-inspired propaganda, the use of a foreign language as the medium of instruction in our schools could result only in imparting to our children's minds the sense of their inferiority and lack of national individuality." The Filipinization of schools and textbooks, of history and the social sciences, is actually underway, as it should be, but the Lava formula for nationalism is described by other Filipinos as a call for prejudice, hate, censorship, and thought control, rather than for love of country.

For his heroes the Filipino nationalist must turn to the last ten years of the nineteenth century, to the leaders of the revo-

[2] Benito Legarda, "Colonial Churches of the Ilocos," *Philippine Studies,* v. 8, no. 1, January 1960 (Published quarterly by the School of Law, Ateneo de Manila), pp. 121-158.

[3] Horacio Lava, "Colonialism in Our Classrooms," *The Manila Sunday Times Magazine,* March 1, 1959 (Manila Times Publishing Co., Inc.), pp. 18-20.

lution against Spanish rule and of the resistance to American conquest, to the writings of Rizal, to the memory of the short-lived republic proclaimed by General Aguinaldo, and to the so-called proletarian, Bonifacio. Until recently his short career has been overshadowed by the more famous Rizal and Aguinaldo, but now a revisionist school of historians is building Bonifacio up as the man of the masses, a hero of the people, a proletarian who understood the need for organization. The revised view of Bonifacio as the real hero of the revolution was developed by José Lava, one of the more sophisticated Filipino Communist intellectuals; it was elaborated by Luis Taruc in his apologia; it was the main theme of the historian, Agoncillo, in his book *The Revolt of the Masses.*[4] In an important speech to the National Writers Conference in 1958, Senator Recto dealt with this theme. Rizal he described as a realist, a man who saw what should be done but who cautioned against violence on the ground that it would not succeed, that the revolution would be drenched in the blood of his compatriots, and that ". . . an evil thing cannot be cured by another evil." Only an idealist could take up arms at this time, said Recto, and ". . . that idealist was Bonifacio, poverty-born, a man risen from the mass of the populace, the true poet of the revolution . . . Bonifacio was given to us by God." "Let us dream like Bonifacio," concluded Recto, "and let us continue to battle for the absolute redemption of our race from the new slavery . . ."[5] In the context of the speech this was a call to violence, or at least to action. Revisionism has not gone unchallenged. The counterattack has come mainly from Catholic historians and from the journals of the Roman Catholic Church. The battle of ideas is at least out in the open.

The theme that the Filipino is an alien in his own land runs through much of the contemporary literature. In its extreme form this view was expressed by Carmen Guerrero Nakpil, who claimed that Filipino culture is a hybrid of elements from in-

[4] Luis Taruc, *Born of the People* (New York: International Publishers, 1953), p. 44. Teodoro A. Agoncillo, *Revolt of the Masses: The Story of Bonifacio and the Katipunan* (Quezon City: University of the Philippines Press, 1956).

[5] Claro M. Recto, "The 1958 José Rizal Lecture," *Comment*, no. 8, First Quarter, 1959 (Manila: Regal Printing Co., Inc.), pp. 27-43.

congruous sources and held that "Nature punishes hybrids with sterility . . . It is all very well to enrich a matrix of culture with selective borrowings; or to perform some skilful grafting here and there; it is tragic to have almost no matrix and no roots to speak of." [6] In the cultural renaissance that is beginning rather timidly, she went on, "There seems to be a general interest in our national history and an effort to gain moral dignity as well as cultural integrity from its lessons . . . Nativism is only another symptom of the cultural nationalism which may yet engulf the country. It is only an extension of the political and economic nationalism of all modern Asia, and it draws its strength from historical necessity."

But Filipinos do not look entirely to their own past. "There are not a few among us, for instance," wrote Pura Santillan Castrence, head of the Cultural Affairs Division of the Department of Foreign Affairs, "who have looked with envious eyes at Communist China. Other Asians less dedicated to democracy must feel the envy still more than we do. In this hurrying struggle of Asia for nationalism, the primary concern appears to have become the eschewing of colonialism, the development of national strength and the ability to command the recognition of the world through self-sufficiency and prestige." [7] Others claim to find inspiration not in Asian nationalism but in the European intellectual tradition. According to Alfredo T. Morales, an American-trained educator, Filipinos are discontented with so-called American materialism and mediocrity in educational matters and they turn to Europe and also to India and China.[8] But he warned that over-anxiety to find something new to believe in and an impressive foreigner to call a new friend "may be just a survival of colonial mentality," a failure of self-confidence. He pointed

6 Carmen Guerrero Nakpil, "The Hybrid Character of Contemporary Filipino Culture," *Comment*, no. 5, First Quarter, 1958 (Manila: Regal Printing Co., Inc.), pp. 58-63.

7 Pura Santillan Castrence, "Nationalism: A Potent and Growing Force," *Silliman Journal*, v. 6, no. 1, First Quarter, 1959 (Dumaguete City, Philippines: Silliman University Press), pp. 18-27.

8 Alfredo T. Morales, "Westernization and the Revolutionary Social Outlook," *Comment*, no. 2, First Quarter, 1957 (Manila: Regal Printing Co., Inc.), pp. 3-9.

out the vast difference in social outlook between the Philippines on the one hand and Southeast Asia and the poorer countries of Europe on the other in respect to their treatment of the common man. Southeast Asia, with its lack of sanitation, the misery and cheapness of human life, and the humiliation of the human spirit, whatever its philosophies and ancient traditions, has no attractive substitute for "the Filipino concept of the welfare and dignity of the common man."

Most Filipino intellectuals would agree on one point, that the country is politically but not economically independent. As President Garcia told the Filipino writers, assembled in conference at Baguio in 1958, "We must now bend our efforts toward this new objective of economic freedom without which political freedom would be empty." The fight for independence is not over and the writer has the same role to play in the economic struggle as he formerly played in the political. The writer has an additional task: "I would ask you," said President Garcia, "to delve into our culture and glorify it. There is no dearth of subjects to write about. The blending of three main cultural streams —the Malay, the Latin, and the Anglo-Saxon—right here in our own country provides an inexhaustible wellspring for our writers to draw upon." [9] In the view of the President, a poet in the vernacular in his own right, the Filipino writer should consciously play his part in the unending task of nation building. But in what language should he write? Garcia pointed out that Rizal wrote his greatest works in Spanish, including his testament, *Last Farewell,* and that Palma used Spanish when writing the lyrics of the national anthem. Spanish and, later, English were the languages used in the fight for political independence, although the vernaculars had to be employed when the leaders wanted to reach the masses. It is possible to be patriotic in any language, but it is not difficult to understand the consuming interest of the Filipino intellectuals in the problem of a common language. Garcia himself admitted that the "national soul" can be truly expressed only in the autochthonous language of a people.

[9] Carlos P. Garcia, "The Filipino Writer and National Growth," *Comment,* no. 8, First Quarter, 1959 (Manila: Regal Printing Co., Inc.), pp. 26, 24-25.

But what shall it be? Of the 23 million inhabitants of the Philippines, less than one per cent speak English or Spanish as a first language; but as a result of American policy some 37 per cent speak English, in some degree, as a second language. English is still the language of instruction in most of the schools above the lowest grades. The nearest competitor is the national language, Tagalog, which became the second official language with the establishment of the Commonwealth. It is spoken by about the same number of people as is English. Most of the Philippine languages belong to the Malayo-Polynesian family, with the closest affinity to the various Indonesian languages. Social stratification and geographical isolation have perpetuated linguistic differences; even Tagalog has seven mutually intelligible subgroups.[10] Although the most recent studies classify the languages spoken in the Philippines into 75 main linguistic groups, the eight major language groups are spoken by nearly 90 per cent of the population.

It is with the members of these eight ethnolinguistic groups that the problem of language arises, for they are the typical Filipinos—the barrio dwellers of the lowlands, Catholic in religion, agriculturist by occupation, family-centered in social relationships, and extremely limited in their comprehension of the concept of nationalism. Except for the important inroads made by the religion of the Spaniards, the schools and economic policies of the Americans, the violence and exploitation of the Japanese, and the paramilitary organization of the Huks, this part of the Philippines still bears a close resemblance to the way of life of much of Malaysia. Language and politics are closely connected because the strong regional feelings in the Philippines follow, in the main, the contours of language groups. When the Filipino breaks out of this pattern, it is usually to move to the urban centers, especially Manila, where he brings to national politics or modern economic organizations the values to which he is accustomed—suspicion of government, reliance on kinship loyalties, and identification with his own region. Hence, it is not surprising that only a small percentage of Filipinos, limited mainly to the urban centers, think in national terms.

10 *HRAF Handbook,* cited, v. 1, p. 322.

Linguistic regionalism can be broken down only by the further spread of education, development of communications, increase in social mobility, growth of local government, and acceptance of a common means of communication—a national language. These conditions are all interrelated. Even in high quarters there is considerable opposition to the domination of Tagalog. President Garcia, who comes from the Visayas, pays lip service to the national language but suggests that perhaps the ultimate solution is a mixture of all the main Filipino languages. "Could all these [vernaculars] not be welded into a rich and beautiful national language further enriching it with the coinage of words for science and art?" [11] Nevertheless, Tagalog is spreading and rivalling English as a second language. It is far from being the national language in fact, but it is the only one of the vernaculars with an increasing percentage of speakers. It has several advantages in its favor, particularly its great prestige and practical usefulness as the language of Manila, the political, social, and economic center of the country. The motion picture industry and the vernacular press both use Tagalog to a very large extent, and other mass media, such as advertising, find its use profitable.

All schools have to teach the national language for a minimum of forty minutes a day in all elementary and secondary grades. Since Spanish was added as a third official language in 1952, this means that a Filipino from a non-Tagalog speaking area has to learn English, Tagalog, and Spanish. If he drops out of school in the fourth grade, as nearly three-quarters of the school children do, he is usually illiterate in all three.

Tagalog will probably outstrip English as a second language because it is easier for those outside the schools to learn, and the mass media are providing strong incentives to learn it. But in some ways the two languages are noncompetitive, at least for the immediate future. English is the formal language of government, the schools, business, many newspapers, and some literature, but it is not the informal language of the home, society, school, or business. Also, the general level of competence in English is going down. Under the American occupation English had to be spoken by children in the schoolyard as well as in the class-

[11] *Comment,* cited, no. 8, First Quarter, 1959, p. 23.

room, but this is no longer true. Spoken English is deteriorating in quality so rapidly that serious efforts are being made, with aid from the Rockefeller Foundation, to improve it by bringing teaching methods up to date. Although English will remain as a second language for the foreseeable future, it is still very much an open question whether Tagalog will ever become a true national language, replacing all other Filipino vernaculars. Either it will be a national second language or it may be the main strain in a new mixture of Filipino languages, as President Garcia has suggested.

The president of the Philippine Republic cannot make a radio address to the people today and expect to be heard or understood by the majority. Whichever language he uses, he cannot be understood by much more than one-third of the people, and there are not enough radios to bring the bulk of the population within the sound of his voice. Communication between political leaders and the people is more often than not through a second language. There are five million Filipinos, a not inconsiderable number, who do not speak any of the official languages—Tagalog, English, or Spanish. Under these conditions political life has a different quality and nationalism a slender base.

Language is important to nationalism for more than ethnolinguistic reasons. The level of literacy sets limits to political participation in elections and to the efficacy of written communication. About one-half of the adult population is illiterate and therefore unable to vote because it cannot pass the literacy test of writing the names of the candidates. In recent national elections less than 15 per cent of those eligible actually voted, participation being lowest in the rural areas. Language, in other words, can be a mark of class as well as of regional distinction, and the class distinctions may be the more significant to the nationalist movement. Regional subgroups, whether linguistic or religious (in the case of the Moros), present no obstacles to the concept of the nation-state that time and other factors cannot overcome. It is when language is a barrier to communication between the political and economic elite on the one hand and the common people on the other that it may present serious problems for national unity.

A relatively small number of people in the Philippines will decide the future of nationalism. Those who can comprehend such concepts as the national interest of the Philippine Republic are few in number and belong mainly to the small upper class—comparatively wealthy, college educated, fluent in the use of English, often better traveled abroad than at home, and generally fearful and contemptuous of the "typical" Filipino, the inhabitant of the barrio, the laborer, and the servant. A member of this class is often described as a man who tends to identify himself more easily with the West than with Asia, with Americans than with most Filipinos; he is ashamed of the pagan tribes and aloof from the Moslems. He is a ceremonial and ritualistic Roman Catholic, sometimes a devout one, and he takes anticommunism for granted. Samples of student opinion at the University of the Philippines indicate that he admires Americans and wants to be like them even though he believes Americans are race-conscious and consider themselves superior. The very closeness of the emotional and political relationship with Americans produces resentments, ambivalences, and openly hostile reactions that are more important today because the Filipino is now open to new cultural influences from Europe and Asia, new relationships with Americans, and a new need for national identification.

There are many Filipinos who have acquired the educational qualifications, at least on paper, for entry into the upper class but who lack economic opportunities which they consider adequate to their desired status. They have been referred to as the intellectual proletariat, an ambitious, restless, potentially revolutionary group. The elite is far from being homogeneous in its values; for one thing, it is vague about its concept of nationalism. Many members of Congress and many of the wealthy men outside it evade paying taxes, and their nationalism is often no more than a political device to achieve economic advantage—for example, to legislate against Chinese businessmen. Loyalty to kith and kin is still a primary value.

There is little agreement on the way in which the Philippine nation will grow, on the social content of nationalism, the relation between government and the governed, between the rich and the poor. This vagueness about the national image would be of no great consequence if there were no competing philosophies, no Communist program. But there are sufficient divisions within the composite ruling class to make it possible for the Communists, with their competing appeal to nationalism, to make serious headway. In the political power struggle the very concept of a Philippine national image will be used for purposes of manipulation because it is the most powerful political symbol in the country. He who captures Filipino nationalism captures the Philippines.

Chapter 9

Social Dynamics

The political potential of the various social classes in the Philippines has to be estimated with the help of history, analogy, and the statements of Filipinos themselves. This is a highly controversial and subjective area, but some sort of judgment has to be made unless policy is to be decided on the basis of unexamined assumption. The most important classes for our purposes are the peasantry, the workers, the middle class, and the oligarchy. The intellectuals, who are probably a part of the middle class rather than a separate group, are discussed separately in the preceding chapter because of their importance to the nationalist movement.

The peasantry is the most numerous and formidable of the social classes. It is dangerous to assume that the peasant is not a political force of any importance, for history is not kind to this view. Ever since the agrarian movements of the 1930s came under socialist and later Communist control there has been an irreversible change in the character of peasant protest. During and after World War II the Huks showed that they were able to set up an organization that could defy the traditional value system even in this sector of Philippine society, which is supposed to be the most difficult to change. The Huk organization cut across ethno-linguistic groups, demanded institutional loyalties, and linked itself to national and even international purposes.

There are several reasons why this was possible then and why the political potential of the countryside must not be overlooked today. In the first place, economic and social forces during the last few decades brought about far-reaching changes in the traditional relations between classes and modified the political dynamics of Philippine society in general. Contrary to the general assumption, these changes may well have gone as far in the rural areas as in the urban. Relations between landlord and tenant changed, largely as a result of the spread of a money economy. Because of the breakdown of the old reciprocal obligations and responsibilities between the two, the landlord class came to hate and fear the lower orders because it lost contact with them socially, and in some cases physically, as there are many absentee landlords. Paternalism gave place to class hatred. The more the landlord exploited the peasant without giving anything in return the fewer were the bonds of respect, deference, and obligation to be broken. Second, the value system of Philippine society is not of uniform intensity in all classes. The typical concepts of the family are strongest at the top and weakest at the bottom, where kin are too poor to help kin. Last, the Communists and their allies provided leadership to the peasantry which was more than equal to that of the landlords or the clergy. The achievement of the Communists in building up a military machine in the countryside on such a large scale and on such a relatively impersonal, rational basis was an extraordinary accomplishment. The Huks channeled into revolutionary enthusiasm the social energies released through this breakdown in the traditional relationships between landlord and tenant.

With the defeat of the Huks those energies lie dormant today, and there are many, including prominent Filipinos, who have already forgotten the threat from the organized peasantry in the early 1950s and even discount its danger to the republic at that time. But the revolutionary potential remains. In fact, anyone who can find the formula and provide the leadership to connect the aspirations of the peasantry with the concept of nationalism could sweep the country.[1] Without a doubt there can be large-scale political organization to include the peasantry; it has been done once, it can be done again. This is not to suggest that the importance of the peasant stems entirely from his revolutionary

[1] See Claude A. Buss, *The Arc of Crisis* (New York: Doubleday, 1961), pp. 149 ff.

potential. The tao is already more powerful today than he was ten years ago because of his increasing use of the ballot box. The election of 1961 showed that it is becoming increasingly more difficult to deliver his vote.

The workers are also rising in political influence. They are organized into a wide variety of unions—about 4,000, with a total membership ranging between 200,000 and 400,000. Although essentially of the middle class, the labor leaders vary a great deal in political outlook and motivation. They include leaders of the Hoffa type, several real and some crypto-Communists, a Jesuit priest who works on the waterfront and another who organizes sugar workers, some honest professionals, and many political opportunists. The chances for the growth of honest unions are hard to evaluate. What is certain is that the struggle for control of labor among the various forces at work within the union leadership is going to get more and more violent. Officially the United States has been involved in the struggle through the activities of the labor division of its economic aid mission, which maintains close contact with the unions and sponsors a training center for union leaders. At the same time Mr. Harry Bridges and his International Longshoremen's & Warehousemen's Union are quite active and have excellent contacts in the Philippine unions.

The political role of the labor movement in the election of 1961 shows that the days of nonpolitical unionism, if they ever existed, are over. The major federations of labor all supported Garcia against Macapagal, the reasons for this being largely political. Some union leaders, it is true, were bought off in various ways by President Garcia, but others supported and promoted a political organization known as the National Progress Movement (NPM) whose leftist political objectives became so clear that the Roman Catholic hierarchy denounced them, and Garcia himself felt it expedient to do the same. Garcia's failure to exploit the left wing to get elected is not so important as the fact that the left wing could deliver union support in such impressive amounts.

For the United States the moral is clear. The concept of the nonpolitical union which our government agencies must officially support is completely inappropriate in the Philippines because it is neither possible nor desirable. Labor unions in the Philippines have a tremendous task to do for the worker in addition to collective bargaining for higher wages. The unions are in a position to take the lead in providing the worker with facilities to improve his formal education and in arousing his interest in social welfare, insurance, health, and old age pensions. Union leaders can help to raise the level of social consciousness by giving the worker a sense of how he can participate in a democracy. Philippine unions have a tremendous social responsibility to the worker that they are far from accepting, let alone fulfilling.

The Role of the Middle Class

In the urban areas, new town and old country live side by side. Here are the absentee landlords at one end of the scale, and at the other end the wretched squatters who put their shacks up in open spaces, often next to the finest buildings; and here are the slums of the workers, so recently from the countryside. What then of the middle class? There is no question but that a middle class of Filipino businessmen, intellectuals, professional specialists, educators, bureaucrats, and politicians has emerged over the years in response to the needs of a free economy and a democratic type of government. The channel to this class is by way of education, business, or political favoritism. The middle class is big enough to maintain a flourishing Chamber of Commerce and several service clubs, but compared with other classes in society it is very small. Why is this class so small? It is usually argued that this is because the Chinese, Spaniards, and Americans perform the tasks of a true middle class, leaving no room for the Filipinos. This is a description of the results, not of the causes. The blame is sometimes put on the Filipino value system, which inhibits cooperative ventures outside the kin group and encourages nepotism. There is much truth in this view, although with comparable values the Chinese have produced wealthy merchants. But it is perhaps wiser to see the absence of a strong middle class as a by-product of the revolution that never happened, the agrarian revolution. Nor is it easy to see how a middle class can grow today unless there is a fundamental change in the social relations, the class structure, and the technology of agriculture, resulting in an increase in peasant purchasing power.

So long as politics is the chief, perhaps the only, path to real wealth and power, so long will there be serious limits to the growth of a Filipino middle class. The obstacles are not lack of ability, capital, resources, or knowledge of the opportunities and the national needs. The obstacles lie in the attitude of the oligarchy toward the investment of capital, toward politics and government and the worth of their own people. The Filipinos are as acquisitive as people in other countries; but since their traditional social values have no place for the spirit of capitalism, members of the Filipino middle class have the difficult task not only of competing with Chinese and American businessmen but also of securing status and recognition in their own society.

The small middle class is one of the few potential sources of constructive political dynamism in the Philippines. President Macapagal has gone out of his way to give honor to Filipino businessmen as individuals and as a class, and it is very much to the interest of the United States to do so, too. As the history of Europe shows, the greatest need of a growing middle class in a hostile environment is for moral, in other words, ideological support. The Filipinos can hardly be expected to adopt the capitalist virtues wholesale or to subscribe to the Protestant ethic, but they have to work out a social and moral philosophy that can give men the necessary courage and direction. Though it may not be possible to avoid some of the ugly features of the rise of capitalism in the West, the Filipinos do begin with many advantages. They can, if they wish, take advantage of developments in the theory of management, in labor relations, and in technology that have taken place in Western Europe and the United States. They can also, if they wish, study the relationship between industrialization and agrarian reform either in the economic history books or in the countries around them, such as Taiwan and Japan, for the middle class cannot grow to any marked extent unless it is successful in helping to bring about agrarian reform by peaceful means. If violence breaks out, there are others more skilled in exploiting it than are members of the middle class.

The interdependence of agrarian reform and industrialization varies from country to country, but some general considerations might be said to apply to all cases except the Communist. Agrarian reform is necessary in all Asian countries to raise the purchasing power of the peasantry so that there will be a market for industrial products, to produce a surplus of food and other agricultural products, and to release workers for the industrial sector. In order to do this, changes are necessary on several fronts at the same time. The conditions of land tenure must be changed so that the tenant receives a larger share of the crop and has legal security of contract, and so that both tenant and landlord have incentives to apply more capital to production. The structure of credit must be changed so that the tenant is not caught up in usury and can borrow money at rates that make it possible to invest in tools and equipment. Markets must be opened up by building roads and providing other facilities so that surplus production can be sold. There must be a rise in literacy so that new techniques can be understood and applied, and so that the peasant can cooperate in local government and protect himself against those who would use his ignorance against him. Above all, there must be a systematic application of capital, science, and technology to agriculture so that more can be produced per acre. This usually leads to a decrease in rural and an increase in urban population.

Examples of agrarian reform are at hand for the Philippines to observe. In the Middle East, for instance, it has been pointed out that however disagreeable to us were the revolutions in Egypt and Iraq, "an analysis of Nasser's and Kassem's agrarian reforms reveals beyond doubt that the one was as little fascist as the other was Communist in design. Both aimed in their own imperfect way at creating a new vested interest without which a class of entrepreneurs, civil servants, industrial managers cannot grow." [2] Castro's agrarian revolution, in contrast, was aimed at collectivization, on the Communist model. In one way or an-

---

[2] W. K. "The Agrarian Question," *Survey: A Journal of Soviet and East European Studies,* no. 43, August 1962 (London), p. 43.

other the conditions of land tenure have to be modernized before there can be large-scale industrialization. The Communists understand this and quite logically oppose any agrarian reform not under their control that looks as if it might be successful. But where reforms are carried out effectively "in anticipation of the development of individual initiative and to encourage the growth of a responsible governing class, there will be no need to fear the attraction of the Soviet model." [3]

The middle class in the Philippines can move in two directions. It can share, as it is doing today, in the rewards of the technologically advanced sector of the economy and ignore the technologically backward agricultural sector. In following this course it may be tempted to use political connections in order to acquire capital and to neutralize competitors, particularly aliens. Under these conditions a few individuals will accumulate vast fortunes, but the middle class, as a class, will not grow a great deal in wealth or in power. The other direction in which the middle class can move is to take the lead in arousing the latent energies of the people to harness these energies to the economic revolution. This would call for a conscious and deliberate effort to form an alliance with the peasants and workers and with the army. Only in this way can the agrarian changes be brought about that will make further industrialization possible.

The Macapagal strategy calls for the voting support of the peasantry and workers, but this is not the same thing as an active alliance. Nor is it clear that the economic program, which provides for heavy investment in the technologically advanced sector of the economy, gives sufficient emphasis to the agrarian problem to avoid the pitfalls prepared by the Communists, who stress industrialization presumably in the expectation that it alone will not produce the desired results.

The philosophy that lies behind Macapagal's Five-Year Integrated Socio-Economic Program for the Philippines, which he presented to the Congress in January 1962, is essentially conservative and respectably middle class. According to the plan, which was prepared under the Garcia administration, the task of economic development belongs principally to private enterprise

[3] Same, p. 43.

and not to government, to Filipinos and not to foreigners, although foreign assistance is welcome in certain specific areas. The role of government is to assist and to create a favorable environment for private business, and to do this the government must have integrity. Excessive economic power in the hands of the government, according to Macapagal, is the root of corruption, and for that reason exchange controls had to go shortly after the new administration came into office. Macapagal emerges as a leader with a mixture of Hamiltonian views of the role of government and a Jeffersonian concern for the welfare and rights of the common man. In the Philippine setting these views and this program are revolutionary. The question is whether Macapagal can enforce his program even if he can count on the support of the whole middle class, broadly defined, or whether he will need strong allies in action as well as at the ballot box.

There is no convincing evidence that President Macapagal understands the agrarian problem as distinct from the rural vote. If he decides to steer the middle class in the direction of a real alliance with the peasantry, then Macapagal will need men and women from the middle class, including intellectuals, who are willing to lead, organize, and live with the peasants in the barrios. They must be well trained and dedicated, as are the Communist cadres who will be their chief opposition.

Already there is much for them to work with. Government and private institutions are reaching out to the peasant in a variety of ways. There are active programs to promote community development, such as the office of the Presidential Assistant on Community Development (PACD), run by the government, and the Philippine Rural Reconstruction Movement (PRRM), run by a private organization. Much is being done to apply science to agriculture through the universities and the newly established Rice Institute at Los Banos. The Court of Agrarian Relations could do much more to settle disputes between landlord and tenant. There are government programs in public health and social welfare. Army engineers construct feeder roads, clear land, and build schools. Many able Filipino college graduates are devoting themselves to working with the peasantry. Most encouraging of all, there is in many of these efforts a self-conscious

attempt to get the peasant to take the initiative. Economic mo-
bilization, as Raul Manglapus once put it, requires an active
and eager population, one that progress has not passed by.[4]

On the surface the middle class appears to be reaching out
toward the peasant, and given all the time in the world, these
efforts would bear fruit. If the Barrio Council legislation, for
example, leads to widespread participation in local government,
many things could change very rapidly for the better. But time
is short, partly because of the inadequacy and imbalance of the
total effort, partly because the opposition from the traditional
order is still unbroken, and partly because the Communist opposition is not likely to permit an orderly and leisurely solution
of the problems of the peasant. The middle class needs to make
a greater effort. To reiterate, it has to make strong allies of the
peasantry and the intellectual, the one to force the pace in the
barrios, the other to control the intellectual climate, and both
to hold the line against the old guard in the oligarchy.

The well-established landed families, who dominated politics
from the start are now declining in influence and are somewhat
on the defensive. Their wealth comes from sugar, copra, land
rent, and the full exploitation of political influence. Culturally
they tend to be somewhat pro-Spanish and to have close ties with
the Roman Catholic hierarchy, which are both acceptable ways
of being anti-American.

The big processing industries, such as sugar and copra, are
deceptively modern in that they use capital and sell in foreign
markets. But the crops are grown on small lots rather than on
large plantations. The traditional patterns of landlord and tenant relations have therefore tended to persist with paternalistic
authoritarianism on the one side and ignorant dependence on
the other. A variety of factors, including trade unionism, has
changed this relationship, and as the election of 1961 showed, the
sugar bloc cannot deliver the vote any more. The big old family
dynasties no longer have the magic and the power, but they still
have the money.

Some of the younger members of the upper class are using their

---

[4] Raul Manglapus, "New Dimension for the Barrio," *Comment*, no. 11,
Second Quarter, 1960 (Manila: Regal Printing Co., Inc.), p. 16-17.

money in business ventures and may well prove to be the most dynamic leaders of the middle class. Filipinos refer to them as the "young bucks." In spite of their education in the best parochial schools of the Philippines and the United States they tend toward hedonism in outlook and behavior. Of this urban high society it has been said that honors, wealth, and position obtained through immoral or illegal means are matters of gossip and scandal but not of social ostracism. To some members of this class, Catholicism is beginning to serve as the basis of a caste system.[5] Although there is some question as to the quality of their Catholicism, this group differs from the main body of intellectuals to whom association with any Roman Catholic organization is considered to be incompatible with the intellectual life. This wealthy, well-connected, headstrong urban elite may well provide everything from the economic dynamism of the robber-baron type to political statesmanship of a high order. It is a bridge connecting the oligarchy, the Catholic church, and the middle class.

The Political Role of the Military

The character of the Philippine military establishment is intimately connected with the quality of nationalism, with the working of political institutions, with the growth of the economy, and with the mood and direction of foreign policy as well. The United States has ties with the army that are closer perhaps than those with any other institution in the Philippines. The relationship is a long one, ever since the United States established a Philippine Constabulary in 1901 and used it in the suppression of Aguinaldo's forces.

Modeled on the American concept of an army, the Philippine military forces were to some extent a channel for upward social mobility. Except for the church, the military establishment was the one national organization that demanded of Filipinos institutional loyalties and could enforce a code of honor. Though possible, it was more difficult in the army than in other organiza-

---

[5] Maria Kalaw Katigbak, "The Filipino and His Faith," *Progress Magazine 1959* (Manila Times Publishing Co., Inc.), p. 220.

tions to resolve conflicts between kinship and institutional values in favor of the family. In the early days of American rule William Howard Taft had demonstrated that the military is subordinate to the civil authority. This lesson was inculcated in the Philippine army so successfully that after independence the Philippine Republic stood in less danger of a military *coup d'état* than any other country in Southeast Asia. Of all the American contributions to the Philippine value system, that of the military establishment was perhaps decisive.

American influence continued to be important both during and after World War II. When hostilities ceased in August 1945 the Philippine army had been rebuilt, through the incorporation of guerrilla units, to a quarter of a million men, some of whom had been expected to take part in the invasion of Japan. The United States demobilized this force down to about 35,000 men before turning it over to the Republic of the Philippines in July 1946, together with certain army and navy bases and some military equipment and supplies. At the same time the Philippine Constabulary was reactivated and put under the Department of the Interior, where it had been before the war. The army transferred 12,000 officers and men to the constabulary, which was built up to a total of about 20,000 men by early 1948 and given the task of restoring law and order.

The fact that American and Philippine forces were inadequate to prevent the Japanese invasion was due to serious shortcomings in American policy, which have to be weighed against the long-range contribution to the social and political institutions of the country. When independence was decided upon in 1934, the Philippines was in no way capable of defending itself, and remarkably little thought had been given to the matter. The United States had borne the cost and responsibility for defense while the Philippine Constabulary maintained domestic law and order. As few things are more important to a sense of national self-respect than complete control over and responsibility for national defense, it is clear that the Filipinos have a case against American preparations for Philippine independence. The case is that political independence, as originally planned, would leave the Philippines economically crippled and militarily impotent.[6]

The mission of the armed forces today is to guarantee internal order, particularly against the threat of armed Communist subversion; to provide for the defense of the Philippines in cooperation with the United States; and to support the international role that Philippine diplomacy has undertaken through SEATO and the United Nations. To carry out these obligations a force of about 50,000 officers and men, including the constabulary, is obviously not excessive, especially in comparison with armies of about one half-million each in Taiwan and South Korea. But the support even of this small force cuts heavily into the budget and is under constant criticism in the Congress and press. Charges are often made that it is too big for peace and useless for war, top-heavy with officers, far too expensive, a drain on resources that should be used for economic growth. Opponents of the party in power charge that the incumbents can use it to keep themselves in office. Admittedly the army was essential at the time of the Huk campaigns, but now that the Huk danger has been eliminated as a military threat, it is claimed that this justification for increased appropriations no longer exists. In spite of the criticism, the armed forces receive increased appropriations every year. In 1959, for example, the government allocated to them P.190 million, compared with P.240 million for education and P.54 million for health. In 1960 the figures were P.211 million for defense, P.306 million for education, and P.69 million for health.

President Magsaysay gave to these forces a sense of mission, a social purpose, and a new moral stature. He used military men freely for special tasks that would normally have been in the hands of civilians. He left behind him the powerful tradition that the members of the armed forces are dedicated to the service of their country and can be trusted to handle the major problems of communism, graft, and corruption. Although there are opportunists who are able to take advantage of this tradition, the members of the armed forces, at least in the public eye, have certain advantages over politicians, most of whom are considered

[6] *Hearings before the Joint Preparatory Committee on Philippine Affairs, Manila, September 21, 1937,* Dept. of State Conference Series, 36, v. 2, 1938 (Washington: GPO, 1938), pp. 615-618.

to be corrupt and self-seeking. The military men are associated with the successful struggle against Communist insurrection after World War II. It was on this issue of anticommunism that former Chief of Staff Jesus Vargas ran for office as a member of the Grand Alliance in the election of 1959 with the slogan "A vote for the Nacionalista Party is a vote for Communism," and the need for a peaceful revolution "along the tradition exemplified by the late President Magsaysay." [7] The mantle of Magsaysay is a significant if elusive symbol because the army handled the Huk problem not only with military force but also with a social and political program.

The fact that retired military men go into politics—rather than standing aloof and contemptuous of the democratic political process as they do in some countries—means that there is not, at present, a deep division between politicians and military men, for they share roughly the same value system. They do not represent a separate professional military class with its own traditions and way of life, as in prewar Germany or Japan. The officers and men of the Philippines armed forces are drawn from the general population, to which they return; the officers trained at the Philippine Military Academy are brought up in the tradition of the supremacy of civil authority. The problem in the Philippines is not so much one of the military taking over the government by *coup d'état* as of keeping the armed forces free from gross political interference by Congress and the local authorities.

As the struggle between old and new values is perhaps the most intense in the officer corps of the armed forces, this is a group that is likely to produce leaders and programs for the new Philippines. For this reason it is important that the officers are not a caste apart and that there is considerable lateral social mobility between politics, the army, and business. Though not a graduate of the military academy, Magsaysay had had guerrilla experience during the Japanese occupation, had led the army in the fight with the Huks, and had come to the presidency by way

[7] *Philippines Free Press,* November 14, 1959 (Manila: Philippines Free Press, Inc.). Hereafter cited as *Free Press.*

of the office of Secretary of Defense. General Vargas entered politics as soon as he ceased to be chief of staff, and other retired officers have become senators, congressmen, mayors, or special assistants to the president. Although there are many dedicated officers in the Philippine army who wish no other career, for many of them their military career runs parallel to a career in politics, a phenomenon that is due in part to the direct intervention of politicians in the promotions and assignments of army officers.

One obvious consequence of the part played by politicians in the army is that it is top-heavy with officers. Senator Tañada said that in May 1960 there were 5,187 officers, 8,758 privates, and 32,531 corporals, sergeants, and other noncommissioned grades. There were almost as many lieutenant colonels (417) as buck privates (534). Senator Tañada added that "All too often, 'political padrinos' save reserve officers from going on inactive duty, and more than one-half of the officer corps is made up of reserve officers, inactive but kept on the payroll, for whom membership in the armed forces provides a sinecure." [8] Salaries for personnel make up the largest portion of the military budget; for example, salary expenditures were ₱.113 million in the total 1958 budget of less than ₱.200 million. This is partly explained by the fact that the United States provided much of the equipment. In the five-year period 1955-60 the United States transferred to the Philippine government over $219 million in military assistance, including conventional weapons of all kinds, vehicles, aircraft, naval vessels, supplies, and equipment.[9]

The policy of the armed forces, which requires its officers to retire after thirty years of service (including the period of cadetship at the military academy), besides being expensive, discourages the professional soldier. He is discouraged even more by the direct interference of politicians in the internal affairs of the armed forces. A statement by navy Captain Carlos L. Albert, a graduate of the U.S. Naval Academy, when he resigned after twenty-four years of service on the ground that he could not stand the political interference, is worth quoting in part:

Since the liberation, the influence of politicians in the armed forces has been steadily growing. I do not question the fact that the highest policy of the land must be made by the elected civilian leaders but when our elected officials have a direct hand in the assignment, promotion and discipline of individual officers and enlisted men, a dangerous situation is created. It is bad enough when assignments cannot be made if some politicians object—it is worse when the politicians insist that such and such a person be assigned to such and such a position. Promotion lists are badly mangled by the time they are final.

For some years now we have seen the spectacle of opportunistic officers who sacrificed their dignity by approaching politicians but the truth is that these approaches would not have been made if it were not a well-known fact in the armed forces that a political sponsor can get you a choice assignment or get you included in the promotion list. This is not to say that there are not promotions or assignments made purely on merit basis but the extent to which politicians have intervened in the internal affairs of the armed forces has been widespread.[10]

Most regulars retire around the age of fifty; but reserve officers, who usually get their commissions later than the regulars, may remain in service until the age of sixty if they have not previously completed thirty years of service time. As the reserve officers comprise about half the officer corps and retirement for the regulars is comparatively early, and as political pressures are exerted to promote friends and relatives, it is natural that the regular officers should be tempted to turn to political means to hasten their own promotion before retirement or to extend their period of service beyond the statutory limit. (President Garcia extended the term of Lt. General Manuel F. Cabal, Chief of Staff, for example, from 1959 to 1962.)

Divisions within the armed forces seem to follow along much the same lines as those in civil life. There are personal cliques and rivalries, struggles over promotion and "soft" assignments, and bitter quarrels over opportunities for making money. A struggle between Alejo Santos, Secretary of Defense, and General Isagani Campo, head of the constabulary, involved President Gar-

[10] *Free Press*, August 1, 1959.

cia himself. During the course of the dispute Campo, in order to clear his name of certain charges, felt compelled to reveal the secret methods used by the constabulary to counter subversion, while Santos, who was campaigning openly for Garcia, was ordered by the court of first instance not to engage in partisan politics. The case went to the Supreme Court on the motion of the government. The Supreme Court approved of Santos' electioneering on the grounds that his was a political, appointive office.

The constabulary, which has a national responsibility for the enforcement of law and order, especially during elections, is bound to step on the toes of the Secretary of Defense, a political appointee loyal to the party that puts him in office. The point of greatest friction is where the national constabulary has to control the local police, usually the creatures of local bosses whose political connections lead to the Congress and Malancañang. The constabulary, therefore, cannot do a better job than the politicians will permit it to do—this means, in no small measure, the president.

If politics influences the military, the reverse is equally true. The Philippine Constabulary has investigating functions and responsibility for enforcement of the election laws. Here again the name of Magsaysay is a legend because of the contribution he made, as Secretary of Defense, in ensuring the clean elections of 1951, in which the Nacionalistas gained congressional and provincial seats that had been held by the Liberals, the party in power. Since the task of the Philippine Constabulary in elections is of high political import, its chief can be in a very difficult position. In the 1959 elections, for example, Brigadier General Campo ordered the disarming of the auxiliary anti-Huk fighters, the Civilian Commando Units, which had never been completely disbanded since their formation more than a decade earlier in the struggle with the Huks. This was a political move because it was generally assumed that these units would help the administration in the election. In some areas the constabulary took over jurisdiction from the local police during the election. In Cavite, a sensitive province, the constabulary provided security measures for all political meetings after several local officers had been murdered and an attempt had been made on the life of a former governor. In such situations the army and constabulary can obviously be used either to help ensure a clean election or to favor one party over another; they are certain to be involved.

In the 1949 election, the worst since the war, the Liberals used the army to put themselves back into power. In 1951 Magsaysay kept the elections so clean that his own party, the Liberals, lost to the Nacionalistas. In 1953 the Liberals again tried to use the army to help their party, but this time they failed and Magsaysay, now a Nacionalista, was elected. The Secretary of Defense at that time, Oscar Castello, a Quirino appointment, was later imprisoned on the charge of murder. In 1959 the Commission on Elections tried to reduce constabulary participation as much as possible in order to create the impression that voting was a purely civilian affair, but the level of pre-election violence was too high to permit this. It was necessary for some 9,000 constabulary troops to take over control of the police forces in sixty-six municipalities, where they provided protection to political candidates of all parties. All other forms of personal protection were prohibited. Constabulary officers assigned to election work were deputized to the Commission on Elections, which actually paid for their service—a device for emphasizing civil control over the voting process.

The use of the armed forces in elections has actually decreased steadily over the years. In 1951, when the constabulary came under the control of the Secretary of Defense, practically all members of the armed forces were deputized and 5,000 ROTC cadets were impressed into service. By 1959 only about two-thirds of the constabulary were deputized. The 1961 elections were in many ways cleaner and better organized than any previous ones. The Commission on Elections reduced opportunities for connivance at the precinct level by arranging for precinct returns to be given to both party appointees on the precinct election boards. A remarkable movement known as Operation Quick Count (OQC) organized voluntary help all over the country to report the returns immediately. The Commission on Elections, using mail and telegraph, took two or three days, whereas OQC brought in the returns within twenty hours of the closing of the polls, considerably reducing the opportunities for manipulation of returns. On the other hand pre-election casualties were 35 dead and 34 wounded, much higher than in 1957 or 1959.[11] The trend to lessen dependence on the armed forces can proceed only as fast as the local police can be depended upon to preserve the peace and to behave in a nonpartisan manner. This will take time. But today it is much more difficult than it was ten years ago for the party in power to use the armed forces to influence the vote in its favor.

Other investigating functions of the constabulary are of considerable political importance since the power to investigate and prosecute can be and often is used in the political warfare among agencies and individuals. Its Criminal Investigation Service co-operates with the Bureau of Internal Revenue in tracking down tax evaders, smugglers, and "economic saboteurs," often getting its leads from the National Intelligence Coordinating Agency.

The higher ranking members of the armed forces can, if they are so inclined, use their military positions to become wealthy men. In 1956 eight generals set up a business organization known as the World War II Veterans Enterprises, Inc. (WAR-VETS), ostensibly to find jobs for veterans, but in practice to handle government contracts.[12] According to the findings of a Justice Department probe, the organization had the approval of President Magsaysay, after whose death it was abandoned. It was later re-created to handle a trust fund for veterans as stipulated in the Reparations Agreement with Japan. Under the reparations law, private businesses in the Philippines could contract for the services of Japanese technicians, and payments for these services would be put into a trust fund for the benefit of World War II veterans and their dependents. WARVETS offered to import ₱.8 million worth of Japanese reparations goods, add

[11] Maximo V. Soliven, "The Elections: 1961," *Philippine Studies*, v. 10, no. 1, January 1962 (Published quarterly by the School of Law, Ateneo de Manila), pp. 3-31. See also David Wurfel, "The Philippine Elections: Support for Democracy," *Asian Survey*, v. 2, no. 3, May 1962, pp. 25-37.

[12] *Free Press*, March 29, 1958. (Among the eight generals were an incumbent Chief of Staff, Lt. Gen. Alfonso Arellano; a former Chief of Staff, Major Calixto Duque; three former constabulary chiefs, Alberto Ramos, Florencio Selga, Guillermo Francisco; and a former Secretary of National Defense turned senator, Eulogio Balao. In less than a year, WARVETS was handling $8 million worth of business on a paid-up capital of ₱.25,000.)

a 15 per cent profit on the sale of the goods in the Philippines, and pay the profit into the trust fund (which would be used to underwrite the "unification of all veterans"). It also offered to send a mission to the United States to work for more veterans' rights and more aid, build a headquarters for veterans, and invest in job-creating industries which would employ veterans. With the approval of President Garcia and also, it was claimed, of the National Economic Council, the WARVETS got going again in August 1957.[13] The Department of Justice recommended that the reparations award to WARVETS be revoked for violation of the terms of its agreement with the government, but the recommendation went unheeded.[14] Whatever the personal financial advantage to the generals concerned, it is clear that the special provisions of the 1958 appropriation act governing the status of military personnel in civilian positions were not observed. According to this act, military personnel "who accept any civilian position in the government or employment in any government owned or controlled corporation or enterprise for a period of more than a year shall be considered resigned or retired or returned to military duty status in cases of regular military personnel, and considered reverted to inactive reserve status in cases of reserve military personnel." [15] This applied particularly to the Army Chief of Staff, Lt. General Alfonso Arellano. At least for some, the armed forces provide a route to wealth, and wealth is the path to power.

It is difficult to measure the influence of the military establishment as a political power in its own right, but there are many indications, besides the obvious control of patronage, of its potentialities. Secretary of Defense Santos campaigned openly with the approval of the President and also made efforts to establish a huge private army of so-called peso-a-year agents for intelligence work. Though vigorously resisted in Congress, the idea received support in several important quarters. The country abounds in veterans' organizations of various sorts set up to fight the Huks and "cattle rustlers." Often under the control of the constabulary

[13] *Free Press*, April 19, 1958.
[14] *Free Press*, July 19, 1958.
[15] Same.

or the local police, the organizations can obviously be used for purposes of political support of the incumbent administration or on occasion for political intimidation. The administration of veterans' benefits is a source of political and financial gain that the army cannot be expected to surrender, since the adjutant general's office examines all claims for army back pay, a rewarding source of patronage. The Council of Elders, composed of eight former chiefs of the constabulary, is a political body that the president uses on occasion to approve high policy decisions, such as the request for missile bases, when he wishes to avoid further discussion. In all its political activities, the stock in trade of the military is the fight against communism, and this powerful weapon is used to back up requests for increased appropriations, to justify the work of veterans' organizations, to further the political fortunes of officers who go directly into politics, and, through the power of investigation, to embarrass critics and opponents.

The character and structure of the Philippine military establishment is of very great importance to the United States. If our long-range interest is to make a success of an independent Philippine Republic, then the Philippines must have a modern military establishment satisfactory to its national self-esteem, able to contribute to collective regional defense, sufficiently well balanced to be useful should U.S. protective forces be withdrawn or heavily involved elsewhere, and not too great a burden on the national budget. The expected increase in nationalist sentiment in the Philippines, which has been felt in the negotiations for the revision of economic arrangements and base agreements, both helps and hinders the work of JUSMAG, the body responsible for joint military planning. The Filipinos are particularly pleased with the Philippine-United States Mutual Defense Board, established in May 1958 to supervise the implementation of three bilateral military treaties—the Mutual Defense Pact, the Military Assistance Agreement, and the Military Bases Agreement. In addition to ironing out some of the security and boundary problems connected with the American bases, "the first serious attempts at honest-to-goodness mutual defense planning came with the advent of the board," according to General

Cabal.[16] The Filipinos have demanded more modern weapons, such as fast jets and sidewinder missiles, both of which have been provided. They press for nuclear missile bases and exhibit considerable sensitivity over inequality of housing for American and Filipino officers.[17] They also exert pressure on the issue of jurisdiction over the bases. These forms of nationalism were to be expected and can be handled more or less amicably. But it is not here that the main issues arise for U.S. policy. Much more important is the political direction that the armed forces of the Philippines may take and the influence they bring to bear on domestic and foreign policy.

So long as the intense struggle for promotion is influenced by politics, the danger is always present that some elements in the armed forces may turn to radical solutions to satisfy their ambitions. There have been occasional accusations that army officers have planned to take over the government by *coup d'état,* but these seem to have been more or less irresponsible claims in the complicated game of personal political warfare. However, as the case of Captain Albert shows, there are signs of growing dissatisfaction among the professional officers over the interference of politicians with the armed forces, and this could grow into a political movement if the appropriate philosophy were provided. But political systems are rarely produced by army men; the military radicals of the left and the right get their ideas from the world around them. Today the Filipino officer lives in a very different intellectual climate from that of even ten years ago, certainly from that of preindependence days. He is aware, as never before, of the political and social influence of the institution to which he belongs; in fact, the status of his profession in the country was enhanced by independence far more than that of any other. The removal of direct American military responsibility and control exposed the military establishment to the forces of Philippine politics right after World War II at a time when

[16] Manuel F. Cabal, "Philippine Security: Its Strength and Its Needs," *Fookien Times Yearbook, 1960,* p. 61.

[17] Filemon V. Tutay, "Controversial Housing Project," *Free Press,* September 12, 1959, pp. 7, 67. (A discussion of JUSMAG'S refusal to move into new housing provided under the military arrangement, in view of the criticism directed to the "royal treatment" of JUSMAG personnel.)

it was least ready to cope with the new situation. Practically submerged in the political cross currents, the military were in no shape to handle the Huks. It took the inspired cooperation from the American military, combined with the political gifts of Magsaysay, to make it possible for the armed forces of the Philippines to take the field successfully against the Huks.

The importance of the Huk episode is twofold: the United States helped restore self-respect to the Philippine military profession, and the cooperation between the American and Filipino military brought about the one change in the republic that was essential to its survival as part of the non-Communist world. The Filipino military leaders, in other words, were the one group in the country capable of providing political dynamism because they combined power, authority, and flexibility; and the army's institutional self-interest and the needs of the country went hand in hand. At the time no other group—neither the church, the landed aristocracy, nor the politicians in Congress—was able to provide the necessary political dynamism even to use the military units that then existed. Out of this experience came new military doctrines, of great interest to other countries in Southeast Asia, on how to fight armed Communist insurrection in an agrarian country. Some of these doctrines are potentially of prime importance to the future of Philippine political development because they feed one of the most powerful political traditions in the country today.

The army is the residual legatee of the Magsaysay myth. Where the politicians failed, runs the myth, the army and the constabulary succeeded in crushing the Communists; then they put their man in as president to complete the job of cleaning up graft and corruption, bringing the government to the people, and carrying out agrarian reform—a program of responsibility in government and of social justice for the common people. Since the destruction of Huk military power, the social and political program that made the accomplishment possible has to a large extent fallen by the wayside. The sense of urgency is no longer there and Magsaysay is dead.

The army officers are in a difficult position, for their proud claim of having crushed the Communists is turned against them at appropriation time. Politicians who are violently opposed to the social program blandly argue that increased appropriations for the military would cut into the more effective method of fighting communism by attacking poverty and ignorance, which they have little intention of doing. The Communists have also made things more difficult for the army by changing their tactics to infiltration of the labor unions, the mass media, and the educational system. It is one thing for an army to win over the peasant, but it is quite another for it to win over the intellectual. It is one thing to point to a body killed by a Huk, but another to identify an idea distorted by a columnist for a respectable metropolitan newspaper. The new situation is frustrating. This frustration results in fierce interservice rivalry to bring in the remaining Huk leaders and aggressive efforts on the part of some officers to get into political life on the anti-Communist issue. But military men rarely have the political gifts and the charismatic qualities that are needed for success in politics; they have to have allies, as they once had in Magsaysay.

The role of the army depends in large measure on what happens to the rest of the country. If Communist subversion again becomes an immediate problem, the armed forces will consider it their mission to do again what was done before. And if the higher officers do not accept the challenge, then idealistic young officers could easily persuade themselves that the patriots should remove those who stand in the way, whether they be civilian or military officials. They now have what they did not have before: the example of the armed forces in other Asian countries, such as Korea, Burma, Pakistan—the solution of the radical right. But the myth could just as easily be appropriated by the radical left if the left could put its program in such a way as to gain ground in the armed forces. Strangely enough, however, it is the United States army that has what is perhaps the closest relationship with the Philippine armed forces in these matters. This is because the countersubversion doctrines of the U.S. armed forces, which have recently been much emphasized in the fighting in Laos and Viet-Nam, derive from the campaign against the Huks. These doctrines are based on the premise that the armed forces have a political role to play in their relations with the peasantry. As actions speak louder than words with the peasant, good relations can be established between government and people only if the government demonstrates a real interest in their welfare. The Philippine army showed that this could be done by building roads and schools, by digging wells and irrigation ditches, by opening up new land, thus demonstrating a practical interest in the peasants. By policing the elections of 1951, the army also proved that the government could be changed if the people used the ballot box. With a clear understanding of the strategy and tactics of the Communists, gained during the Huk campaigns, the rich experience of the Philippine army is now part of the free world's body of doctrine on countersubversion or, as it is now called, counterinsurgency.

On the American side this subject is considered of the highest priority. For counterinsurgency operations, which are under the general direction of Brigadier General Edward G. Lansdale, Deputy Assistant to the Secretary of Defense, there are new doctrines, new staffs in the Pentagon, new command structures in the field, special units, and new courses on the subject in U.S. military schools and colleges. General Lansdale was one of the American officers who was in the Philippines during the Huk campaign. The American and Philippine armed forces have shared many experiences together in the field, but their joint effort in developing the doctrines of counterinsurgency is perhaps the most significant bond of all. Both sides understand that in the type of warfare that prevails in Southeast Asia today, the objective is not the control of territory but the winning of the loyalty and support of the people. To win the people means, for most governments in Southeast Asia today as it did for the Philippine government in 1950, a social and political revolution. This is why the armed forces in some of the countries of Asia are more alert to the needs of the people than are the politicians. They know that they cannot fight successfully against Communist guerrilla operations without having the people on their side. While it is unlikely, though not impossible, that conditions in the Philippines will revert to those of 1950, the fact that the army knows the doctrines of counterinsurrection will mean that if political dynamism does not come from the middle class, it could, if things are bad enough, come from the army.

The course of wisdom, however, is for the middle class to make an active ally of the army, supporting and extending its present activities in civil affairs, such as engineering projects, land clearing, communications, and enforcement of election laws. President Macapagal wisely increased the pay of members of the armed forces soon after coming into office, but this is not where the main problems arise. Experience in pre-Communist China shows that the greatest danger is the alienation of the intellectuals from the military and from the government. The Filipinos have an advantage, for in China the military were brought up on the German-Japanese value systems and the intellectuals on the English-American. Once the nationalist movement had become a government, it was difficult to build a bridge between them. In the Philippines, certainly since 1898, all classes have been exposed to the same value system. There are no violent contrasts in values between the army officers, the government officials, the professional classes, the politicians, and the intellectual leaders. The only competing value system is that of the Communists.

Chapter 10

Partnership in
Economic Growth

In his State of the Nation address of January 22, 1962, President Macapagal signalled the close of a decade of economic development. "We must recognize," he said, "that the country has fully exhausted the potentialities for growth offered by the complement of policies ruling over the decade of the 1950s. Over the past three years from 1958 to 1960 the growth rate of real gross national product declined, and it has become obvious that the impetus has worked itself out." [1] For these and other reasons, the President went on, it was essential for the government to formulate and adopt an integrated economic program, for without it, "all economic development efforts will be haphazard, sterile, and ineffectual." He traced the sluggishness of economic development in the preceding few years to the absence of a "concrete economic blueprint" laying down public policy. Macapagal put before the Congress a Five-Year Integrated Socio-Economic Program, by which the power of the government was to be used to make possible the fullest and most purposeful development of free enterprise and initiative.

A decade of exchange controls had come to an end, and so, in a sense, had a decade of American economic assistance. The State of the Nation address implied very clearly that Filipinos

---

[1] "Five-Year Integrated Socio-Economic Program," President Diosdado Macapagal, Address on the State of the Nation to the Fifth Congress of the Republic of the Philippines, January 22, 1962. *Manila Chronicle,* January 23, 1962, pp. 5-6.

were going to take charge of their own economy and that they knew what they wanted to do. The change from the early 1950s, when U.S. influence was predominant in almost every sphere, to the early 1960s, when the Philippine government was showing so many signs of self-reliance and independence, came about step by step as a result of the friction between Philippine and American policies—the friction of enforced partnership. During this period, the Philippines forced the United States to modify the economic assistance program, secured a revision of the trade agreements of 1946, and began to take hold of the control and direction of its own economic life.

Economic Assistance

The story of U.S. economic assistance has three important aspects that bear on relations with the Philippines. First, there are the philosophy, scope, and method of granting aid, all of which have been matters of considerable dispute and now are up for rigorous review. Second, there are the efforts to encourage a radical land reform, which met with minimal success and maximum acrimony but are still of high priority. Third, there are the deliberate efforts to promote free labor unions, which are continuing and have a long way to go before they can be considered really successful. In addition, there is the contribution that economic assistance has made to the emergence of a Philippine economic policy and the problems of adjustment that this implies for the United States.

When the United States and the Philippines made their economic and military agreements in the early 1950s, they assumed a pattern of mutual dependence as close, almost, as that of the colonial period. But there was a difference. The United States, for reasons of its own, still needed the cooperation of the Philippines but could no longer demand it. The Philippines, newly independent, would normally have wished to go it alone but was in no position to do so. It would have been easier for the new relationship to mature if the pressure of world events and the legacy of the American occupation had not forced the two countries back together so quickly after the granting of independence. The Filipinos have had to assert their independence, as it were, without leaving home. With the passage of time, new men have come into power in Washintgon and in Manila who lack experience of the colonial period and are therefore more aware of the responsibilities and opportunities of an independent Philippine Republic. Filipinos have come to power who are able to accept with dignity the facts of cooperation.

To turn first to the purpose and method of granting aid. The U.S. economic assistance program, which began with the Quirino-Foster agreement of 1950, was part of the general program of economic aid extended first to Europe and then to Asia. In Europe economic assistance preceded military aid, but in Asia the two came together. Whatever the political and economic reasons for the aid, which were quite sufficient in themselves, the program was justified in Congress in terms of the cold war. Put in the simplest terms, there were three concepts behind the Mutual Security Act of 1951. The first is that as communism is a threat to both the external and internal security of all countries, especially the new nations, the threat has to be met by military measures to prevent further open aggression and by political and economic measures to prevent internal subversion. Second, it was assumed that defense against open Communist aggression is a collective responsibility which all should recognize and in which all should share; hence, the concept of mutual security. Third, the economic assistance as part of the mutual security program is of direct value to the economy of the United States.

The importance of this last concept was made clear in 1959 by Secretary of State Dulles in a statement to the Senate Committee on Foreign Relations. He made four main points: many of the nations we are assisting provide commodities essential to our economy; the cost of assistance will be repaid many times over by the increase in general free world trade; the aid helps U.S. production and employment as three-fourths of the money is spent in the United States; the cost, excluding military assistance, is very small, less than one per cent of the gross national product.[2]

---

[2] *Effects of Foreign Aid Program on U.S. Economy*, Hearings before Senate Committee on Foreign Relations, 86th Cong., 1st sess., March 11, 1959 (Washington: GPO, 1959), pp. 32-33; 80-81.

Foreign aid makes possible the employment of about 600,000 men and women in American fields and factories.[3] Economic assistance, in other words, is directly related to the growth of the American economy; it is not, as the Filipinos are well aware, a philanthropic enterprise or a form of international slumming.

The economic assistance program was a greater departure from earlier practice than is generally realized. The main innovation was the assumption that democratic political institutions require democratic economic foundations and can best survive if certain conditions are met. These were that the private sector of the economy should dominate the public, the role of the government should be limited to assuring the optimum climate for private enterprise, foreign wealth should be distributed in a reasonably equitable manner among the major social classes, and public administration should be efficient and honest enough to make the system work. Economic assistance became more than a relief measure; it became an instrument that could be used to bring about social and institutional changes.

Since the Bell Mission, therefore, U.S. policy has been directed toward persuading, leading, and on occasion compelling the Philippine government to exercise the sort of leadership that would result in a free economy, a more equitable distribution of wealth, and democratic political institutions. What was new was the assumption, written into the Mutual Security Act, that these three go together. Political democracy without social and economic revolution does not provide the dynamism for a working democracy. Hence the unfinished revolution in the Philippines.

The most thoughtful of recent foreign evaluations of the American role in the Philippines makes the same point, though in a different way. The French writer, Georges Fischer, criticized the American approach as being too legalistic and therefore doomed to failure because it ignored the social setting of the new institutions.[4] Fischer argued that the Philippine social structure is static and frozen, like those of many other underdeveloped coun-

[3] See "Foreign Aid and the Domestic Economy," *Economic Review*, December 1958, a publication of the AFL-CIO.

[4] Georges Fischer, *Un Cas de décolonization* (Paris: Librairie Générale de Droit et de Jurisprudence, 1960), pp. 273 ff.

tries; that change cannot come from internal forces, as in the West, but has to come about from above and usually through the intervention of the state; and that the policies of the United States have reinforced the static conditions and stifled the possibility of this intervention by the state. The most striking features of the American colonial regime, according to Fischer, were that the Philippine economy was oriented to serve the interests of an influential group in the United States and that there was an alliance between the dominant American political and economic interests and the small Filipino elite which benefited from the colonial connection. This alliance, Fischer asserts, survived the granting of independence because the United States took steps to assure its continuity. According to this view, the United States gives to the new elite a legitimacy founded on the forms and mechanisms of Western democracy and so confirms the inequality that was at the base of the colonial relationship; the frictions between the Filipino elite and the American interests will never be deep enough to founder the alliance. The United States not only robbed Philippine independence of its dynamism but also helped to maintain structures unadapted to the needs of development.

Fischer does not explain the nationalist movement in the Philippines, or the struggle against the Japanese occupation. He neglects the fact that political democracy, especially during the first part of the twentieth century, was the most dynamic force in the world and that it was exported to the Philippines, not as a set of legal arrangements to bolster the position of a native elite, but as an absolute value, the key to human dignity, political stability, and social and economic progress. It is a serious indictment of American colonial policy in the Philippines that little was done to improve the lot of the average Filipino and that the Philippine economy was tied to the American to the advantage of the few. But one of several competing American interests, the agricultural, was strong enough to help force rather than hinder the pace of independence; and there were several competing interests among the Filipino elite as well.

Nor do political independence and democratic institutions lack dynamic qualities, as Fischer himself points out. In the Philippines they stood the test of war and occupation. It is tempting to reflect how much easier it would be to build democracy in the Philippines today if certain measures, especially with respect to the land, had been carried out when the United States had the power to do so, but all policies have to be viewed in the light of the times that produced them. Only recently, and mainly because of the newly independent Asian countries, has there grown up in the free world a slender body of theory on the subject of economic growth in underdeveloped areas.

In applying the new policy it was the quality rather than the quantity of aid that mattered. But the Filipinos have always been critical of both. American aid to the free nations of Asia in the first ten years after World War II amounted to ten billion dollars. Much of it went to provide food and other necessities to people recovering from the destruction and devastation of war; some of it was for military purposes and some for strictly economic development. Well over $2.35 billion went to the Philippines in both direct and indirect assistance. The figure includes cash disbursements under the Philippine Rehabilitation Act for war damages ($509.5 million), transfer of surplus property ($100 million, original cost over one billion), U.S. army civilian relief ($48 million), contribution to UNRRA programs in the Philippines ($7.7 million), ICA grants ($127.1 million), various other grants amounting to $36.7 million, loans and credits ($216.5 million—first under the ECA and then ICA, as well as from the Reconstruction Finance Corporation and the Export-Import Bank), Veterans Benefits and War Claims ($1,002.3 million as of the end of 1956), and military aid of $169.3 million. The figure also includes disbursements for the redemption of guerrilla currency, USAFFE back pay, and numerous other smaller payments. It includes the aid granted under the Economic Development Program launched in 1951 under the Quirino-Foster agreement, with the various sums being spent as follows: industry and mining ($38.9 million), transportation ($25.7 million), rural and agricultural development ($33.0 million), health, public administration, public works, education and labor ($38.6 million), and imports of industrial machinery to generate pesos ($5 million).

Since 1956 the amount of economic aid given to the Philippines has tended to go down and to compare unfavorably with that given to its Asian neighbors, Cambodia, Laos, Korea, Formosa, and South Viet-Nam. The amount spent in the five years from 1951 to 1956 was considerably less than the $250 million suggested for this period in the Bell Report. At the same time a large amount of direct military aid in the form of equipment, ammunition, and training, the actual value of which cannot be made public, was made available by the United States. It has been estimated that between the end of the war and 1955 the United States spent $1,039,000,000 on military expenses connected with its air, army, and naval bases in the Philippines.[5] The amount spent on economic aid proper is not impressive compared with this, and the whole program and approach have come under severe criticism.

The Philippine government always wanted more control than it was granted. In view of past and current criticism of the economic aid program it may be wise to keep its operational philosophy in mind. This philosophy has four main aspects. In the first place, the program involves a partnership that combines in productive union the technical know-how and capital resources of the United States with the natural resources and labor supply of the Philippines. The Philippines is not given grants to do with as it will, nor does the United States undertake, at the invitation of the Philippine government or as a gift, to construct steel plants or state farms and turn them over upon completion to Filipino management and ownership. The United States insists on joint discussion of which projects are to be supported, on joint financing, and, in effect, on joint agreement as to the character and direction of the economy. This involves a very high degree of direct and indirect influence on Philippine economic efforts.

Second, economic growth in the Philippines must proceed along certain specified lines. Many grants of ECA funds for particular projects were made contingent upon well-defined steps to be taken by the Philippine government. The money was used as

---

[5] Amry Vandenbosch and Richard A. Butwell, *Southeast Asia Among the World Powers* (Lexington: University of Kentucky Press, 1957), p. 105.

much as possible for capital investment and economic development.

Third, economic assistance is used to promote industrialization, but a sound program of industrial development must be gradual and evolutionary, "not a dramatic, revolutionary development overnight." [6] Increased efficiency in agriculture, therefore, must precede industrialization and the specialization of labor; agricultural production must provide for home consumption and for exports, as exports are essential to secure venture capital and credit for industrial development. At the same time the United States promotes the diversification of the Philippine economy through its sound industrial development "in the interests of mutual security." This requires a stable medium of exchange and an honest, efficient public administration.

Fourth, economic assistance is used to help bring about the essential condition for economic improvement: a socially responsible and honest leadership. Some of the conditions laid down in the Bell Report, to which the Philippine government agreed, were that public administration be improved and reorganized and civil servants receive higher salaries, and that the United States send a technical mission to assist in carrying out agricultural and industrial development, fiscal controls, improvement of public administration, and labor and social welfare programs.

Whether the purposes are commendable or not, cooperation can take place only in areas where the goals of the Philippine and United States governments are in real or apparent agreement. The role of the ECA was to work with Filipino officials from the initiation of plans to their operation but not to be an operating body itself. It was to provide the technical assistance needed to initiate legislative or administrative measures, to help in planning and to advise in the operation of the project, to provide some of the financial means whereby needed materials could be imported, and to provide control over the use of U.S. funds as required by law. The Philippine government was first represented by the Philippine Council for United States Aid (PHILCUSA). Planning of projects and formulation of detailed

[6] *Congressional Record*, v. 98, pt. 3, April 8, 1952, p. 3710.

budgets was done through three-way cooperation among ECA, PHILCUSA, and the appropriate Philippine agency or bureau. In 1955 the Philippine government merged PHILCUSA into the National Economic Council whose office of Foreign Aid Co-ordination took over the functions indicated by its title. Such a relationship obviously assumes a high degree of mutual confidence between the two countries, a large measure of agreement on what has to be done, and a real capacity for intimate teamwork. The United States is informed of practically every aspect of Philippine politics, planning, and economic life—an unusual privilege.

The most far-reaching recommendations made by the ECA during its first few years concerned land reform and labor unions. Of the two reports in which the recommendations on land reform were laid down, Robert Hardie's *Philippine Land Tenure Reform* proved to be a highly controversial document. Published in an election year, it was called by President Quirino "unfortunate" and an "exaggeration" of existing conditions.[7] Other high officials attacked the report as Communist-inspired, implying that ECA officials should be screened for Communist sympathies, or denounced it as containing implied threats of intervention by the United States if the Philippine government did not follow the recommendations.[8]

The general argument of the Hardie report is the familiar one that the "pernicious land tenure system which thwarts all efforts for technological improvement in agriculture" is one of the chief obstacles to economic progress.[9] The Philippine government, he claimed, professed an interest in protecting tenants and helping those on landed estates to become owner-operators, but when laws were passed they were made ineffective by legal ambiguities, lax enforcement, and failure on the part of the Philippine Congress to provide funds to achieve their stated aims.

[7] *Philippines Free Press,* January 3, 1953 (Manila: Philippines Free Press, Inc.), p. 52. Hereafter cited as *Free Press.*

[8] Albert Ravenholt, "Philippine Land Reform," *American Universities Field Staff Reports Service,* v. 1, no. 3, February 1953, pp. 1-8.

[9] Robert S. Hardie, *Philippine Land Tenure Reform: Analysis and Recommendation* (Manila: U.S. Special Technical and Economic Mission to the Philippines, October 23, 1951), p. 5.

Resettlement is not an effective way of solving land tenure problems, and Hardie also considered the purchase of landed estates by the government for resale to tenants an inadequate solution. So long as there are high rents, insecurity of tenure, inadequate credit, lack of transportation, and widespread tenancy there will be peasant discontent and revolt.

The improvement of the land tenure system, according to Hardie, was essential for political stability; for the improvement of agricultural production; for industrialization, as rentier wealth lies dormant in land; and for fiscal management, as tax burdens mount with increasing costs for maintaining law and order. Remedial action must be sweeping and fundamental. The Philippine government should set up a Land Tenure Authority with power to reduce tenancy, enforce fair tenancy practices where necessary, and encourage owner-operator farms. It should purchase agricultural lands, clear up disputed titles, transfer by sale clear titles to *bona fide* cultivators, and determine prices for land and methods of payment. It should pass new laws pertaining to contracts, to the adjudication of landlord-tenant disputes, to land title clearance, to inheritances, to wages of farm labor, and other matters.

The Hardie report recommended for the Philippines what the United States had already accomplished in Japan and what the government of Chiang Kai-shek was doing on Taiwan. In the one case, however, the United States had supreme authority; in the other the Chinese rulers were not the landowning class on Taiwan, and they had received a brutal lesson from the earlier failure to carry out land reform on the mainland. In the Philippines the officials of the United States were recommending that the Filipino elite, holding political and economic power based largely on land ownership, should undermine its own economic, social, and political position.

The conflict between the United States and the Philippines over the land question came to a head within a year of the establishment of the ECA mission in Manila and went deeper than almost any other dispute. For several years land reform was urged on the Philippine government, not entirely without success, by both the ECA and the State Department.[10] During the Magsaysay administration some important steps were taken along the lines suggested in various reports of the ECA and other agencies, but the momentum for radical changes was held in check by the landlord interests represented in the Philippine Congress and to some extent by lack of enthusiasm on the part of U.S. agencies in the Philippines. By 1954 many American advisers, possibly reflecting more cautious attitudes in Washington, no longer supported the opinions expressed in the Hardie report.[11] Mr. John B. Hollister, Foreign Aid Director (1955-57), made a statement in Manila to the effect that the United States would not put further pressure on the Philippine government to bring about fundamental agrarian changes. Nevertheless, the Magsaysay administration passed a Land Reform Act in 1955. Whatever the limitations put on the act and whatever the obstacles to its implementation, land reform had become an issue in Philippine politics and therefore in U.S.-Philippine relations.

American pressure to promote land reform was matched by a corresponding insistence on the importance of free trade unions. In the Philippine setting the pressure to establish and accept unions was as radical a measure as the land reform proposals. Some of the assumptions behind the policy were expressed by Valergy Burati, Director of the Labor Division of the U.S. Special Technical and Economic Mission in Manila in January 1952. He argued that as mechanization extends to the farm, the distinction between industry and agriculture will become more and more elusive, because human toil is the same whether in farm or factory. The organization of labor is a prerequisite for industrial democracy, and the labor union is the means by which the worker assures himself a fair share of the fruits of his labor. By raising the purchasing power of the consumer, the labor union

[10] When attempts were made to suppress the Hardie report, Ambassador Raymond A. Spruance took a hand in promoting its dissemination. On his retirement in 1955, he told the Philippine press that "sensible land reform is essential for progress and orderly development." Interested in more than tenancy reform, Spruance urged reform of the whole social structure, built on land ownership, to be carried out partly by new assessments and taxation to force the sale of presently unproductive property.

[11] See *Congressional Record*, v. 100, pt. 19, May 19, 1954, pp. A-3679-3680.

contributes to developing a sound economy; and it reduces class conflict. "A part of the program of the ECA in the Philippines is to give advice and assistance in the formation of free labor unions, and to help develop harmonious relations and collective bargaining between labor and management. In sponsoring free labor unions ECA is acting under the direct mandate of the Congress of the United States," which declared it to be the policy of the United States to encourage free enterprise in those countries receiving American aid and "to encourage where suitable the development and strengthening of the free labor movements as the collective bargaining agencies of labor within such countries." [12] Here was a direct application to another society of the American concept of labor organization, a concept that had become acceptable in the United States only during the last few decades and after long periods of industrial conflict.

The ECA efforts were not without results. An Industrial Peace Act, passed by the Philippine Congress in May 1953, revised existing labor legislation by shifting the emphasis from judicial arbitration to collective bargaining. This move fitted in with ECA objectives and, according to most observers, inaugurated a nonpolitical period in the development of Philippine trade unions. This "Magna Charta" of Philippine labor owes much of its phrasing and many of its provisions to American examples that were not derived from Philippine conditions. Nevertheless, the borrowed garb seems to fit much better than might have been expected. According to Wurfel, nonpolitical trade unionism in the Philippine pattern has grown up out of the early granting of an extensive franchise, a predominantly private-enterprise economy together with a liberal labor policy in government corporations, considerable upward social mobility based on a history of job opportunity, a relatively late introduction of Marxism, and an easily won independence.[13] This combination of factors is not a stable one. It is even open to question whether at this stage in Philippine development nonpolitical trade union-

[12] Same, v. 98, pt. 3, April 8, 1952, pp. 3709-3710.
[13] David Wurfel, *Some Notes on the Political Role of Labor Movements: A Philippine Case Study* (Tokyo: International Christian University, 1960), pp. 273-278, 280.

ism is possible or desirable. So long as there is Communist influence in the movement—of which there is ample evidence—there will be a need for politically sophisticated trade union leaders. Such leaders will not be able to guide and control their unions in the struggle with the Communists unless their followers are politically indoctrinated.

Revision of the Trade Agreement

In 1954 the United States made important concessions to the Philippine government on the question of trade arrangements. A letter from President Quirino to President Eisenhower requested a re-examination of the Trade Agreement of 1946 as an urgent matter. Three months of negotiation led to the signing of the Philippines Trade Agreement Revision Act of 1955, known as the Laurel-Langley Agreement, which became effective in 1956. The United States accepted the view that the weaker partner was entitled to special treatment and needed to protect its infant industries and increase its revenues through higher tariffs. It also accepted some of the Philippine demands for full reciprocity, for unfettered control over the national currency, and for the elimination of residual American controls over the Philippine economy. Not that the Filipinos got all that they wanted; they would have preferred to have Philippine exports to the United States continue free from tariffs until 1970, while two-thirds of the American imports to the Philippines would become subject at once to the full Philippine duties. The Philippine negotiators had to compromise on this issue largely because of the influence of American tobacco interests.

The three months of negotiation were not easy. In hearings before the House Ways and Means Committee the State Department emphasized that, unless those provisions of the 1946 Trade Agreement that were incompatible with Philippine sovereignty were removed, the Philippine government would denounce it and there might be a serious rift.[14] The greatest difficulties revolved around the first article, which defined the conditions of trade, tariff rates, and the question of parity.

[14] *Congressional Record,* v. 100, pt. 7, June 23, 1954, pp. 8766-8767.

The new agreement gave the Philippine government control over its own currency, thus permitting it to alter the exchange rate between dollar and peso if it so willed. It also eliminated most of the absolute quotas and the quota allocation limitations on Philippine articles subject to quotas entering the United States. It made reciprocal the enjoyment of parity rights by citizens of either country in the territory of the other, and likewise gave them the reciprocal right to engage in business activities. It permitted each side to impose quantitative restrictions on the importation of products from the other country. The agreement permitted exceptions to tariff and quota rules in the security interest of both countries. Tariff preferences for U.S. goods entering the Philippines were increased. It eliminated the prohibition against imposition of Philippine export taxes; it provided for the elimination of the Philippine foreign exchange tax and of the dual rate of exchange that went with it by substituting an import levy to be progressively reduced until eliminated. Finally, it permitted the Philippines to ask the U.S. Congress for a possible increase in the sugar quota when other nations were permitted to do so, and increased duty-free quotas in the United States.

The advantages of the agreement for the Philippines, Ambassador Carlos P. Romulo wrote, were the removal of controls over the Philippine economy, the extension of U.S. trade concessions for an eighteen-year period of transition from mutual free trade to normal international trade, and the recognition that the Philippines was at last free to manage its own "political, social, and economic affairs." [15] The United States, he said, had tacitly recognized the demonstrated ability of the Filipinos to govern themselves wisely and democratically.

The Philippines did not get an increase in the absolute size of its sugar quota at the time, and this, combined with the pressure from American tobacco interests, led to strong anti-American statements in the Philippine Congress. The best known of these, quoted in full in the U.S. *Congressional Record*, was made by

[15] A. V. H. Hartendorp, ed., "The Executive Agreement on Revised Philippine-American Trade Relations, Signed September 7," *American Chamber of Commerce Journal*, v. 31, no. 9, September 1955 (Manila: Published monthly by the American Chamber of Commerce of the Philippines), p. 375.

Representative Pedro Lopez, whose remarkable speech touched on every issue from Bataan to Moscow. It's main theme was that there had been a change of mood in the Philippines ". . . a swing from the former extreme of admiration, hero worship, and idolatry to the new extreme of disenchantment, disillusionment, and even hostility." According to Representative Lopez, expediency guides U.S. policy—witness the amount of money given to Japan as compared with that given to the Philippines, witness the efforts of American tobacco interests to ram their "huge excess of Virginia leaf tobacco worth millions into Filipino throats . . . Unquestionably Moscow and Peking owe the tobacco boys a medal for invaluable service rendered to the Communist cause." [16] The attack on the United States may have been an indirect way of embarrassing President Magsaysay in his land reform program.

One of the most important changes in American policy was the agreement to permit the Philippines to put higher tariffs on American goods than the United States put on Philippine goods. Certain American enterprises in the Philippines stood to gain from these arrangements, and the revised tariffs favored American products for Philippine industrialization. Moreover, the new agreement actually did assist the Philippines in increasing its revenues from the tariff and in diversifying its economy. Even the most critical commentators have admitted that the new agreement represented a change in the direction of assuming that the weaker partner should be deliberately favored.[17] With the means to protect the growing industries, it was now possible for the first time to construct an economy in the Philippines that would give some substance to political independence.

The Problem of Private Investments

The United States has always emphasized the primary role of private enterprise in economic affairs. During the Common-

---

[16] *Congressional Record*, v. 102, pt. 5, April 23, 1956, pp. 6721-6723. See also *Sugar Act Extension, 1957*, Hearings before House Committee on Finance, 85th Cong., 1st sess., January 16, 1957 (Washington: GPO, 1957), p. 305.

[17] Fischer, cited, p. 243. See also *London Economist*, July 30, 1955.

wealth period and immediately after World War II, this had meant, in practice, continuous efforts to protect the economic interests of American residents in the Philippines and the investments that American individuals and corporations had made there. Such a policy requires no justification insofar as it is an expression of the fundamental assumptions of a free society.

There is good evidence to support Frank Golay's view that the Philippine people have made the decision to organize their economy on the basis of private initiative and that their entrepreneurial type of economy is largely a legacy of American rule.[18] So far so good. Yet several questions must be raised about this policy in practice. What is the impact on Philippine economic growth of the special privileges on which the United States has insisted for its citizens? Has the emphasis on private initiative and investment been a substitute for a comprehensive program of economic development? It has to be admitted that the United States set up for its citizens monopolistic advantages not only with respect to other countries, but also with respect to the Filipinos themselves. The Trade Agreement Revision Act of 1956 was an important but not a final step toward removing these special advantages. Even then, the United States made it clear that the Trade Agreement would not go into effect until the Philippines agreed to implement Public Law 419 of the Eighty-third Congress of the United States regarding the establishment of treaty merchant status for aliens of the two countries. Thus, as part of the Laurel-Langley Agreement, Filipinos were compelled to adopt as their own a law already passed by the American Congress. This was necessary, the argument runs, because there was still no treaty of commerce and navigation between the two countries, and the immigration arrangements made in 1946 were due to run out very shortly. There was a real need for an agreement on the entry of American traders, and it had to be reciprocal; if other countries wished to make parallel arrangements, they were free to do so. All this may have been true, but it is also clear that the United States used pressure to secure advantageous

[18] Frank H. Golay, "Entrepreneurship and Economic Development in the Philippines," *Far Eastern Survey for the Institute of Pacific Relations,* v. 29, no. 6, June 1960, pp. 81-86.

terms for its nationals, for in practice the reciprocity has not meant a great deal to the Filipinos.

Because there were many Americans doing business in the Philippines, "national treatment" had consequences of direct concern to a new and weak country. Through their own Chamber of Commerce in the Philippines and through the Embassy, Americans can bring pressure to bear on a weak government and, in some instances, this pressure may well make it more difficult for that government to carry out reforms. More serious, there is sure to develop an alliance between foreign interests and certain domestic interests—commercial, producing, or financial—and enmity with others, thus splitting the Filipino middle class. Neither are foreign investments likely to pour into the fields of primary importance for economic growth, nor are powerful foreign interests likely to make it easier for the government to impose the controls necessary to improve its position in international trade.[19]

American businessmen have always argued that "national treatment" is necessary to help create a proper climate for investment. To some extent the issue has become a political football in the Philippines, and it naturally looms large in Communist propaganda, which depicts the foreign investor as a ruthless exploiter. The facts seem to be that investment in the Philippines is not as great as might have been expected in view of the degree of influence enjoyed by Americans over Philippine affairs.

The total value of American investments (excluding those of Americans resident in the Philippines) was $90.7 million in 1940, $149.2 million in 1950, $188 million in 1953, and $226 million in 1956.[20] While investments in the Philippines amounted in 1953 to 40 per cent of similar U.S. investments in the Far East, they were considerably less than those in Cuba, Mexico, or Peru, where there were no special arrangements such as prevailed in the Philippines. Including reinvestments, it appears that the Philippines received a net U.S. investment of $275 mil-

[19] Frank H. Golay, "The Philippine Monetary Policy Debate," *Pacific Affairs*, v. 29, no. 3, September 1956, pp. 253-264. See also Fischer, cited, p. 296.
[20] Fischer, cited, p. 298.

lion between 1950-56.[21] This was about 10 per cent of domestic Philippine investment. But during the same period the U.S. government spent $270 million in the Philippines—an interesting commentary on the hope that private capital will predominate in Philippine economic development. Each year since the end of World War II, revenues from foreign investments transferred from the Philippines to the United States have exceeded the new U.S. investments. Much of the figure given is for reinvestment and its seems that, on balance, since 1953 the Philippines has not received more than $20 to $25 million of new American private capital a year. Most American investments are in the Manila area and are not in new industries.[22]

The policy of economic liberalism, favorable to the interests of the private sector, has strong support in the Philippines. The question posed by Fischer is whether this has not limited the role of the state to such an extent that it is not strong enough to make the profound and rapid changes required by the situation. Rapid change, it is often argued, is more likely to be acceptable in underdeveloped countries than gradual change, and rapid change requires strong intervention by the state. Hence the proposition advanced by Fischer that American influence helps to maintain institutions and attitudes that are prejudicial to the economic future of the Philippines.

It is clear that in American policy today there are two main approaches to the Philippine economy. There is the long-established policy of supporting private enterprise and protecting foreign investments. And there is the newer policy of strengthening the role, as well as the operating structure, of the government in economic affairs. While Americans participate in the planning activities of the Philippine government and actively pro-

[21] Same.

[22] Same, p. 300. See also *Manila Bulletin*, March 13, 1962, p. 1. Senator Tañada revealed what he called "Startling facts in Philippine economic history: (1) In more than four decades of American sovereignty over the Philippines, less than 300 million dollars in investments entered the country despite the almost unlimited privileges and advantages to American capital. (2) Despite the extraordinary privileges granted American investors under the Bell Trade Act and the Parity Amendment, *only a little* over 17 million dollars came as investment money from 1950 to 1961."

mote long-range state planning for economic growth, the United States insists, by legislation and other means, that the objectives of planning shall be to promote private enterprise and encourage foreign investments. In theory there is nothing contradictory about these two approaches, in that they stem from the traditional liberal view of the state.

The problem in the Philippines is that we have succeeded in securing the formal acceptance of the purest form of free market capitalism, but we have not succeeded in establishing a state strong enough to tax, coerce, and provide the social services that make capitalism possible. In order to create state power of this sort the majority of Filipinos must accept the view that the state is there to serve, not private purposes, but the public interest. The middle class is the only one whose immediate economic interests may coincide to some degree with the national interest. There is, therefore, a tendency among American businessmen and officials to hope that the political dynamism necessary to build the institutions of the modern liberal-democratic state will come from the middle class, and that the middle class will determine the character of Philippine nationalism.

Emergence of a Philippine Policy

Partnership in a joint program of economic development requires a large measure of understanding and flexibility on both sides. Fortunately, Filipinos have an unusual understanding of the American political process and the American mentality, for otherwise many of the disputes of the last ten years might well have led to a break. It is remarkable that the two countries have adjusted as well as they have in this transition period when the Filipinos are sorting out their ideas about their political future and finding their way as an independent nation, for while the Filipinos are playing a cooperative role they are also increasingly aggressive and independent.

In 1951 the Filipinos had little choice about the terms of cooperation. The country was still in a state of economic and political crisis. Nothing but a deep sense of urgency and the great influence of President Quirino induced the Philippine Congress to pass the legislation necessary to implement the recommendations of the Bell Mission. President Quirino assigned highly capable men to the Philippine Council for United States Aid (PHILCUSA) and to its successor, the National Economic Council (NEC). These measures helped account for the high level of successful cooperation achieved between the two governments, for few other undertakings are as complex, demanding, and frustrating as teamwork between a large and powerful country and a small, weak one in matters as important as economic and military policies.

There have been serious problems, however. The Philippines, for example, did not make full use of the commodities available under Public Law 480 until 1957, although the law had been passed in 1954. Under PL 480 American agricultural products are exported to other countries, and the payment in local currency is held in a special fund that can be used by agreement between the two governments to finance projects for economic development. It has been suggested that the delay was due, to some extent, to the reluctance of the Philippines to include Virginia tobacco in the agricultural products to be imported under the act. There was certainly a noisy and brutal conflict over the tobacco question in Manila as well as in Washington, especially in 1956.[23] When the first PL 480 agreement was eventually signed by the two countries on June 25, 1957, rice, cotton, dairy products, meat products, and inedible tallow were included, but not tobacco. Southern legislators in the U.S. Congress were outspoken about the problems they faced with their constituents. They invariably saw a connection between the sugar quotas of Cuba and the Philippines and the sale of southern agricultural products to these countries. Senator Fulbright put the matter very simply in his comments on the Sugar Act Extension measure of 1956 when he pointed out that Cuban purchases of U.S. goods vary directly with the amount of Cuban sugar sold to the United States.[24]

Some legislators from the South were both direct and threaten-

[23] Frank H. Golay, *Public Policy and National Economic Development* (Ithaca: Cornell University Press, 1960), p. 302.
[24] *Congressional Record*, v. 102, pt. 2, February 7, 1956, pp. 2209-2210.

ing in their remarks: "Should the Philippine Government attempt to eliminate the Philippines as a potential market for United States leaf tobacco, the tobacco interests in this country will consider it necessary to oppose any proposal by the Philippine Government to change the existing trade agreement . . . There is additional legislation in which the Philippine Government, as well as Philippine citizens, are interested." [25] In the hearings on the Trade Revision Act of 1955 the General Counsel of the U.S. Tobacco Association stated that the committee as a whole was worried about the right of the Philippines to control their imports of American goods, "and most of the questioning is around this problem." [26] In the hearings on the Sugar Act Extension before the Senate Committee on Finance, Senator Barkley shifted the argument to what he termed "the Philippine discrimination against tobacco." In reply, John A. O'Donnel referred to the Bell Mission's report, which had recommended the development of a domestic tobacco industry and the limitation of nonessential imports. He also recalled that President Magsaysay had reluctantly agreed to import eight million tons of tobacco—"And I know that the President did this at a considerable political risk to himself and his party. The power of the tobacco interests over there might be likened to the twenty-two best states in the United States insofar as the island of Luzon is concerned. And they are very strong." [27] The Filipinos had a good case for the right to regulate their own imports, as several U.S. senators pointed out, but by the same token the United States had every right to limit imports from the Philippines.

In this critical period in the economic relations between the two countries, feelings ran so high that one Filipino legislator suggested that the aid mission be withdrawn and the Philippines hire and select their own advisers. Alfredo Montelibano, who as chairman of the NEC was in charge of Philippine economic planning as well as of cooperation with the United States, said, "It

[25] Same, v. 100, pt. 7, June 23, 1954, pp. 8766-8767.
[26] *Philippine Trade Revision Act of 1955,* Hearings before House Committee on Ways and Means, 84th Cong. 1st sess., July 20, 1955 (Washington: GPO, 1955), pp. 114-118.
[27] *Sugar Act Extension, 1957,* Hearings, cited, pp. 299-301.

is wrong to believe that the American policy towards the Philippines is dictated primarily by considerations of friendship. American policy in the Philippines is dictated by expediency and convenience." As evidence he cited the distribution of American foreign aid, pointing out that the common enemy during the war was now actually receiving more than the Philippines. He went on to complain of still unpaid legal claims against the United States, such as $24 million for the 1933 gold devaluation, $155 million for the balance of war-damage claims, which, with outstanding claims by veterans, totalled around $860 million. Many Filipinos, he said, were better qualified than the Americans sent under the technical assistance program; ". . . our foreign policy must be revised to advance our national self-interest . . . any foreign aid should be and must be administered by Filipinos." [28]

Filipinos, whatever the vested interests they represented (in the case of Montelibano it was the sugar bloc), were insisting more and more on the right to make their own blueprints for economic development, and the United States, in spite of conflicting interests in Congress, adjusted itself, with timely flexibility, to the new mood. By 1957 the Philippines entered into arrangements for the use of Public Law 480 to a degree that may even reflect an unwise dependence on American agricultural commodities for the growth of local industries. [29]

After coming to power in 1954 the Nacionalista Party gradually made it clear that foreign aid was to be used mainly for purposes of industrialization. The original objectives of the economic aid program had been defined by the dominant Liberal party in 1951, in Republic Act 604, as the good of the greatest number of people, the promotion of economic opportunity, and the removal of the causes of social discontent and unrest. The act called for the improvement of transportation and communication facilities to open up markets for goods; irrigation and waterwork systems and artesian wells; credit and technical assistance to the peasantry; expansion of power resources and industries, social services, technical services, training and research facilities; re-

[28] *Congressional Record*, v. 102, pt. 16, April 19, 1956, p. A-3204; April 12, 1956, pp. A-2947-2948.
[29] Golay, *Public Policy*, cited, p. 303.

settlement and purchase of land for acquisition by peasants; financial stability; and general welfare.

One of the first acts of the Nacionalistas was to pass in May 1954 a Concurrent Resolution criticizing the existing economic aid program and setting up new priorities. It is an interesting document for the light it throws on Philippine objectives and for the frankness with which they are stated. It must be remembered that there had been a great deal of bitterness between the ICA and President Quirino over land reform. In addition, the country had so far recovered from the war that the Filipinos now felt a new confidence in themselves and their institutions, affirmed by the comparatively clean election of 1953 and the reduction of the military threat posed by the Hukbalahaps. As the fear of social revolution receded the need for social services, at least in the view of the Congress, was thought to be less pressing and the justification for land reform less urgent. The Concurrent Resolution, therefore, stated in part:

> . . . that undue emphasis had been placed on agricultural development . . . as well as on projects in the field of public administration and social development, the operation and maintenance of which have increasingly imposed financial burdens on the part of the Philippine government; . . . that the present administration is embarking on a continuing five-year economic development program . . . [with emphasis] on industrial development and that . . . there is need of promoting the growth and establishment of new and necessary industries. . . . [Therefore] there is need of shifting the direction of the aforementioned Agreement [of 1951] . . . to that segment of the economy requiring the promotion of industrial development so as to achieve a viable and balanced economy in the Philippines; . . . it is desirable that at least twenty per centum of such dollar promotion programmed and expanded each year should take the form of machinery and equipment for new and necessary industries in such manner that the peso proceeds realized from the sale of such machinery and equipment to private investors may be utilized to supplement the peso counterpart funds that are provided by direct appropriation by Congress.[30]

The United States adapted itself quickly to these priorities for economic aid. During the next three fiscal years (1955-57), as com-

[30] Same, p. 299.

pared with the three previous years, the investment of U.S. grant aid in industry and mining rose from $1.4 million to $37.6 million, that in agriculture went down from $25.5 million to $10.4 million, and there were steady decreases in the funds allotted to education and public health.[31] The total allocation of aid to the Philippines increased, partly because the economy could now absorb more aid, partly because of the vigorous Filipino propaganda comparing what the Philippines received with what other countries were allotted.

While the United States adjusted itself to the new policies of the Philippine government, it is well to remember that some institutions and programs would probably not be in existence had it not been for the influence of the United States. Land reform, as originally conceived, never came to pass, but ECA had quite a lot to do with the continuance of agencies for agricultural credit and cooperative financing in agriculture, as well as with the Farmer's Cooperative Marketing Associations, with community development, with research in crop improvement and land utilization, and with the building of roads to widen the market areas and help with land colonization. The United States has also used its influence to guide the process of industrialization in the Philippines along the same lines as those followed by the Colombo Plan countries. This is first to improve the production of food and raw materials and increase the social investment in education, technical training, and communications and then to invest in heavy industry.

To be sure, the United States has insisted on a degree of participation in Philippine affairs that has aroused Filipino senitivities, but it may have been more appropriate at the time than many of its critics would care to admit. Many Filipinos knew what should be done but were in no position to do it, and the moral and financial assistance of the U.S. Aid Mission, at its best, brought to life programs that otherwise might never have been started because of political opposition. Nor is there any way of measuring the considerable impact that the aid program had on

[31] Same, pp. 300-301. See also A. V. H. Hartendorp, *History of Industry and Trade of the Philippines* (Manila: McCullough Printing Company, 1958), pp. 383, 592-593.

the level of official discussion, the process of planning, and the degree of public participation in economic and political life. The reactions of Filipinos indicate, however, that the form in which economic assistance is administered is sometimes more important than the amount. Possibly the direct involvement of the United States in the domestic politics of the Philippines has reached the point of diminishing returns and there may be a strong case, not for stopping economic assistance, but for changing the forms by which it is carried out.

An alternative pattern is for the Philippines to arrange for capital investments through normal channels and to hire directly the technical help that is required. This was how Japan and the Soviet Union went about their industrialization. The method is successful if there is a strong and purposeful political group in power that is able to extract from the economy a high rate of capital investment, induce the people to make short-range sacrifices for long-range goals, and impose its will over a considerable period of time. Clearly the Republic of the Philippines was in no position to follow this pattern of development in the first postwar years. Whether it can do so now, while maintaining democracy, is one of the current issues.

What path does the Philippines intend to follow? President Macapagal, in January 1962, presented to the Congress what was in effect a small book on economic affairs, which included his proposed Five-Year Integrated Program for Socio-Economic Development (a document of 92 pages); a Three-Year Program of Economic and Social Development adopted by the National Economic Council in January 1959 (171 pages); and a report on Economic Growth in the Philippines, dated January 4, 1962, a document of 73 pages prepared by the staff of the International Bank of Reconstruction and Development. Summarizing his achievements in July 1962, six months after taking office, Macapagal claimed that he had laid the foundations for his socio-economic program. The dollar reserves, he said, had risen from $96.6 million to $141.9 million; increased revenues had turned an expected deficit into a 20 million peso surplus; expanding trade had resulted in a favorable balance of payments amounting to $27.51 million; there was an increased rate of growth in agriculture and mining; the peso was stabilized and there had been no flight of dollars.[32] Furthermore, graft and corruption, according to Macapagal, had been contained, and decontrol of the peso successfully launched.

The goals against which these achievements should be measured were described by the President as the immediate restoration of economic stability, alleviation of the plight of the common man, and establishment of a dynamic basis for future growth. The first was to be achieved by an orderly decontrol of the peso, which would liberate "the energies and imagination of our people and our entrepreneurs for economic projects of lasting value to the country." [33] The United States immediately supported decontrol with the promise of financial backing in the amount of $300 million. At the same time the Philippine government raised tariffs on nearly 700 articles produced by domestic industries in order to continue the protection they had under exchange control. As foreign capital is essential to economic development, conditions favorable to foreign investments must be created by the passage of appropriate legislation (which, however, did not happen in the first six months). In this connection, Macapagal said that Filipinos should be cautious of radical nationalism and nationalization measures that would frighten away foreign capital.

The lot of the common man in the Philippines, said the President, does not compare favorably with other countries and stands in sharp contrast to that of the wealthier elements in his own. Therefore, production capacity must grow faster than population. It is planned to achieve self-sufficiency in rice and corn and to improve crops, credit, marketing, transportation, irrigation, and water control. It is expected that an over-all increase in domestic production of about 6 per cent per annum would provide about 350,000 new jobs yearly, mainly in industry. The government is to invest heavily in public services such as education (₱.656.6 million), low cost housing (₱.15 million), and public health (₱.470 million).

In all this the aim of the government is to provide the con-

[32] *Manila Chronicle,* July 24, 1962, p. 1.
[33] "Five-Year Integrated Socio-Economic Program," cited, p. 17.

ditions under which private enterprise can do the job and to induce the private sector to risk idle capital for development purposes. But government will retain the economic leadership and "its exercise must be all the more firm as it is all the more just, imaginative, and skillful." [34] The government therefore will invest an annual average of P.562 million in establishing basic facilities such as communications, hydroelectric power, harbor facilities, and in developing land, forest, and mineral resources. Out of a total gross national income of P.78,200 million over the five years from 1963 to 1967, P.11,500 million in the form of domestic savings must be put into effective use to sustain the over-all investment requirements of the economic development program. This will involve a revision of the tax structure and the popularization of savings and loan associations. The capitalistic virtue of thrift is to be encouraged. All of these new policies will bring adjustments that the government must measure and anticipate in order to distribute the burden in an equitable manner, a not very capitalistic concept. "The goal of the program is essentially to ensure that domestic production, augmented by imports, shall be adequate to supply the needs of our people." [35]

In short, the specific target is an annual growth rate of around 6 per cent for gross domestic product. This can be achieved, according to the plan, if 16.1 per cent of gross domestic product is channelled into gross domestic investments during the five years and if savings reach 16.0 per cent of gross domestic product by 1967, if there is a net inflow of $860 million new foreign capital, and if export earnings average $740 million annually. It is expected that the total program can be financed from noninflationary sources such as domestic savings and foreign loans and investments. The International Bank of Reconstruction and Development proposes the doubling of capital formation in the agricultural as well as in the industrial sector, whereas Macapagal calls for a percentage increase of 6.71 in agriculture and 32.57 in manufacturing. The IBRD report points out that the failure of agriculture to show increased productivity of food crops is

[34] Same, p. 26.
[35] Same, p. 28.

related directly to the land tenure system.[36] Agriculture, including forestry and fishing, still accounts for about 34 per cent of the national product, some 60 per cent of exports, and 61 per cent of total employment. Agriculture's great potential must be used effectively, the report goes on, if the chronic social and economic problems of the country are to be mitigated. Such increase in agricultural production as there has been since the war is due entirely to the increase in acreage under cultivation. The spectacular increase in the output of forest products is due to a reckless and irresponsible slaughter of the forests, bringing in its train erosion and deteriorating climatic conditions.

The need for land tenure reform remains urgent, since it is estimated that 80 per cent of agricultural land holdings have not been officially titled or surveyed. Agriculture is also a "haven for tax evasion." [37] Real estate taxes in 1960 amounted to less than 6 per cent of direct tax revenues, and agricultural income provided only a little more than 3 per cent of all personal income taxes. Nor can much be done about this until there is a cadastral survey and title registration. The U.S. air force in the Philippines could help in aerial surveying of the land without much additional cost to the taxpayers of either country. As it is possible that changing the tax structure for agriculture might lower the resistance to land reform, such a survey would be an excellent investment.

According to the IBRD, the plans for the development of industry have to allow for the fact that it will take up to three pesos of investment to get one peso of growth. In the 1950s this ratio was 1.36 pesos to one peso. The big item in the industrial program is two iron and steel mills under construction with an annual capacity of 360,000 tons, which is about the present consumption rate. Plans are set for the building of copper smelting and refining plants, and of smelters for aluminum, nickel, and zinc. Chemicals, fertilizers, textiles, pulp and paper, plastics, food processing, and mining are all on the list. The plan calls for an increase in installed power capacity of over half a million kilo-

[36] *Report of the International Bank for Reconstruction and Development* (Manila), January 1962, p. 14.
[37] Same, p. 19.

watts, an increase in the irrigated area of 238,000 hectares, and the improvement of communications by sea, rail, road, and air. Some of these ambitious plans can achieve success without improvement in agriculture, but not many.

The problems are compounded by the Philippine population increase; its annual rate of around 3.25 per cent is one of the highest in the world. The IBRD report estimates the yearly increment in elementary school-age population will be around 150,000 in 1960-66 and 250,000 in 1966-70; the rate of increase of the labor force will naturally go up correspondingly. At present, the fully unemployed amount to about 670,000 or 6.3 per cent of the labor force, and the underemployed number an additional 12 per cent or probably more. It is expected that industry will absorb much of the surplus labor. The Five-Year Plan calls for a drop in the agricultural labor force from 61.7 per cent to 48.5 per cent in 1967, whereas in industry it will increase from 12.0 per cent to 20.2 per cent in the same period. Although the IBRD plan calls for a substantial rise in the percentage of the labor force engaged in manufacturing, it does not anticipate any change in agricultural employment as a percentage of total employment. These figures are probably the more realistic.

We can expect that a vigorous effort to implement the economic program will bring to the surface social and economic conflicts of serious proportions. Changes of the sort proposed will certainly arouse the opposition of various interest groups both in the Philippines and in the United States. What, then, are the chances of success for the Five-Year Plan? One minimum condition for success is that the middle class close ranks, which it certainly did not do in the election of 1961 when Senator Gil Puyat, an industrialist, ran for the vice-presidency. Another condition is that the middle class have the support of the intellectuals in the inevitable struggle for control of labor and peasant unions, for it is here that the decisive battles will be fought, since it can be assumed that an intelligent program to improve the economy will be violently opposed by the left-wing activists in the Philippines. Quite possibly the alliance of the extreme right and the extreme left, which existed for a time before the 1961 election, will reappear under new guise in this conflict.

The middle class cannot avoid the conflict by withdrawing from the field. An essential feature of the problem is that a massive effort is required by both government and people merely to maintain the present levels of consumption. The government must run fast merely to stand still. But very real changes are required to make the structural alterations necessary in the economy for an increase in per capita production and consumption. Inability to make some sort of headway would lead, within a few years, to serious political and economic instability. Firmly rooted as the democratic institutions of the Philippines may be, they may not be strong enough to withstand the burden of additional unemployment and the frustrated hopes of the intellectual proletariat. Unless there is strong political support of an administration that has the ability and determination to press the Five-Year Plan, or something similar, it is difficult to see how the Philippines will avoid a dictatorship of the left or of the right.

Success depends also on the economic and political role of the military. The Macapagal plan says nothing about national defense and the general expenses of government, whereas the IBRD report frankly admits that these expenses could drop from the present 29 per cent to 24 per cent of total public expenditures. This might mean a drop in the relative rather than the absolute amount as the total expenditures will be greater; in any case, there seems to be no question but that the burden of economic development will have as one consequence a continued reliance upon the United States for most of the real costs of defense, a political fact that can lead to considerable tension. A price has to be paid for cheap security. In addition to the practical price of surrendering some measure of independence in foreign policy, there is the much more serious psychological price, very difficult to measure, of limited responsibility for national defense. The Philippines is not alone in this. In fact, most of the powers of the Western world have had to accept, in some degree, limitations on their sovereignty in matters of defense, for the world trend is toward supra-national organizations for economic as well as for security reasons. But the problem is different for a country that has yet to establish its national identity and enjoy the feel of independence than it is for the old, established European countries.

On this issue the Filipinos may be vulnerable, as they are understandably ambivalent toward their military dependence. Pressure for higher military expenditure might come in answer to increased Communist guerrilla activity, but there also may be demands from extreme nationalists and others masquerading as nationalists who want to push the United States and the Philippines as far apart as possible. There seems every reason to believe that the Liberal administration is willing to accept a continuation of present security arrangements between the two countries. In this case, the United States can make a considerable indirect contribution to economic growth by helping to keep down military expenditure. As for the army, its political role in the program for economic growth is difficult to predict. If things go well, there is no reason to expect anything more from the armed forces than a passive role. Since one of Macapagal's first acts was to raise the pay of members of the armed forces,[38] it is reasonable to expect their good will towards the administration. But if things were to go badly—if the left wing secured control over labor and peasant unions and could boast of impressive student support—the armed forces might take matters into their own hands.

One of the most important of the steps toward the success of the Five-Year Plan was the passage by Congress of a Land Reform Act, July 1963, after six months of acrimonious debate. President Macapagal had broached the proposal for land reform legislation in January at the opening of the Fifth Congress and before a vast radio and television audience. Pointing out that the basic cause of agrarian poverty was the land tenure system, he insisted that the structure of agriculture must be recast before there could be any appreciable growth in productivity and incomes. The approach followed by the administration drew some of its inspiration from the experience of Taiwan whose Vice-President Ch'en Ch'eng, the man to whom much of the credit for

[38] *Manila Bulletin,* July 14, 1962. Law signed June 16th; appropriations totalling ₱.34 million for increased pay in the armed services implemented a month after.

Taiwan's successful land reform was usually given, visited the Philippines at the invitation of President Macapagal. It was very much in the mood of the Philippines to accept advice from another Asian country rather than from the United States. The introduction of the legislation was all the more surprising because the original Five-Year Plan had not indicated any sense of urgency about the agrarian situation. It is possible that the land reform question had been deliberately underplayed in that plan in order to secure its approval. It is also possible that the reform bill was pressed at this time in order to prepare the way for an appeal to the people in the next election. As the debates indicated, no politician could risk open rejection. The opposition therefore adopted the device of "improving" the legislation to death, and when that failed, of relying upon the Supreme Court to declare it unconstitutional. Full warning was given that the battle to subvert the act would continue.

The Land Reform Act, as passed, was an improvement over any previous legislation in this field. It abolished share tenancy as being contrary to public policy, and the lessee was guaranteed security of tenure. The act fixed lease rental of agricultural land at a minimum of 25 per cent of the average normal produce for the three previous years before the establishment of leasehold, minus cost of seeds, harvesting, and processing. Owners of expropriated lands were to be compensated 10 per cent in cash and the rest in bonds or shares of stocks of the Land Bank. "Just compensation" was to be determined on the basis of the rental value fixed by law. In other words, it was hoped that lower land values, combined with steady income from stocks or shares, would be more profitable than renting of land on the old share-cropping basis. The owners of land bonds could buy public agricultural lands at their appraised value to the extent of 144 hectares for individuals and 1,024 hectares for corporations. The Act authorized the establishment of an Agricultural Credit Administration to extend credit at 12 per cent to small farmers and farmer's cooperatives. A proposal to reduce interest to 8 per cent was pushed through by the enemies of the bill in a cynical demonstration of their love for the peasant and because this action involved a subsidy of several million pesos to keep the Agricultural

Credit Administration in the black. Subsidies can always be withheld by Congress.

Landholders were entitled to retain 75 hectares of their expropriated lands. The former tenancy law continued to apply to fishponds, saltbeds, and lands planted to coconuts and citrus fruits. An Agricultural Productivity Commission was to be formed to provide technical assistance and management services to farmers. A minimum wage of ₱3.50 was set for agricultural workers. The Land Authority was directed to appropriate first idle or abandoned lands, then those in excess of 1,024 hectares, and so on down to lands of more than 75 but less than 144 hectares. By giving priority to the expropriation of public lands the administration gave time to landowners to think about going into large-scale farming or converting their capital into industrial capital. Provided he could make it productive by using modern farming methods, it was still possible for a landowner to own thousands of hectares. It was hoped that the Land Reform Act's provisions were such that they would release the social and productive energies of the landowner as well as of the tenant. But, as Vice-President Ch'en Ch'eng reminded the Filipinos, even a modest land reform program cannot be achieved without the highest technical competence and the highest qualities of character of those who are in charge of its administration.

Another condition of the Five-Year Plan's success is a large flow of foreign investments; hence, President Macapagal's efforts to have Congress pass a new foreign investment law. Not all of the capital will come from the United States; in fact, the administration has made a point of enlisting support from other countries and from international agencies. But the bulk will undoubtedly have to come, if it comes at all, from the United States. The efforts of Macapagal's administration to provide attractive conditions for private investors may prove fruitful if the desired legislation can be passed, but American capital has not been eager to invest in the Philippines even under unusually favorable conditions. If private investors fail to meet the challenge, the question will arise as to what the U.S. government can and should do to fill the breach. Considering the issues at stake, it is clearly to the interest of the United States to do everything appropriate to assure the success of the Five-Year Program.

What the United States should do depends very largely on what the Filipinos do for themselves. The Macapagal administration has defined its objectives, described the means that will be employed, and taken several important steps toward implementing the program. The vigor of the Philippine effort should be matched by an equally brisk American approach. The fact that the Filipinos are determined to act independently and will not stand for old colonial attitudes does not mean that the United States must stand aside and speak only when spoken to. On the contrary, this is a time for participation in their economic and social program and for shrewd assistance in those places where it will do the most good for U.S. national interest. These are years in which the creative potential of the Filipino people may well be released, for good or for ill, and our relations with the Philippines are likely to be difficult and tempestuous whether or not they are productive.

What should be U.S. policy? The Filipino planners emphasize industrial development in iron, steel, chemicals, mining, and petroleum, and the importance of transportation, power, and dairy production. They feel that there is less urgency about putting capital into education, public health, and general public services, and most of them are not persuaded that much can be done about agriculture. So many things have to be done that the United States can safely support almost anything actually under way, but it is also important to maintain a sense of balance. If nothing effective is done about the agrarian situation, for example, then after a certain point it will be a waste of money to support industrialization; in fact, we might find ourselves financing a drive toward dictatorship. Economic growth depends on the coming together at the right time of so many different forces, some of them noneconomic in character, that those who are doing the day-to-day job may not be able to see the process in its entirety as easily as the participant-observer. This imposes on the United States both an opportunity and a responsibility.

Certain measures of a strictly economic nature that the United States can undertake are obvious, and some have already been pursued. Support of the decontrol measures was a case in point.

The Philippines will require considerable amounts of capital at various stages of their program as the pace of economic development increases. Since, hitherto, the lack of feasibility studies and soundly drawn-up projects has limited the use of external loans, the United States might give technical assistance in this sphere, so long as the Filipinos decide on the objectives.

For sound development projects a sizable amount of external capital is available. The IBRD, which has been modestly involved up to now, is a well-informed source since its survey was made. Japanese reparations should provide $25 million a year in capital goods, and Japanese commercial houses have agreed to put up development loans to the amount of $250 million. The OECD countries, especially West Germany, have already made short-term loans and are now turning to long-term ones. The Export-Import Bank has extended loans to the private sector for almost every sort of industry, and a few to the public sector for such projects as Ambuklao Dam, Manila Airport, and Manila Port. In 1961 it approved the loan of $62.5 million for a 250,000-ton integrated steel plant at Iligan in Mindanao. The Bank is one of the most versatile and experienced sources of funds for the Philippines.

There will be no shortage of foreign capital provided the Filipinos carry out the objectives they set for themselves, such as increasing internal revenue and domestic savings, promoting exports, reducing imports, and raising the general level of public morality and administration. They began with an adequate resource base, a modest national debt, and a reasonable chance of increasing exports. In spite of the availability of external financing, however, there will be an important role for AID loans when the debt service becomes burdensome and for AID investment guarantees for U.S. private investors. There is also every reason why technical and financial help should be given to the Philippines for the essential banking institutions, such as the Development Loan Bank. These matters present no great problems, they submit to competent expert judgment.

The manner in which the United States cooperates with the Philippines is a more political and delicate matter. It seems clear that whether or not the Filipinos are capable of planning and guiding their economic growth, they are determined to do it themselves. In some measure this is a tribute to the work of the U.S. economic missions in the past. At the same time it is important for the United States to have an AID Mission in the Philippines, although its function should probably be to give advice to the U.S. Ambassador rather than to the Philippine government. The task is one of understanding what is happening and of deciding where to use our influence rather than of telling and showing. For such a task the mission will require men who combine technical competence with a high degree of political insight and who are able to work as a team with each other, with the embassy, and with the military mission in order to achieve certain political objectives. The new situation calls for two changes of emphasis. The mission will operate best if it has a much higher degree of autonomy from Washington than it has had in the past, and greater identification as a member of the American country team. This is another way of saying that the economic mission should be considered an arm of the political representative—the ambassador—rather than an independent enterprise responsible to AID headquarters in Washington. The purposes of economic assistance are meaningless apart from the political objectives of the United States. These can be stated in the broadest terms in Washington, but in the field they have to be calibrated with care and skill under the political direction of one man if they are going to achieve our purposes.

The second change of emphasis should be in the direction of exploring new techniques of cooperation between the two countries, both in the private and the public sector. It has been proposed that a Philippine-American Joint Development Commission be established on the pattern of the Joint Commission on Rural Reconstruction in Formosa to undertake such special tasks as rural electrification, community development, and renovation of the educational system. There is much to be said for the establishment of commissions or authorities on the pattern of TVA or the Rural Electrification Administration strictly under Philippine control, especially on a regional basis. But there is some danger in our urging the setting up of joint commissions if they are intended to promote the things that the United States wishes to have done rather than those that the Philippines wishes to undertake. The JCRR in Formosa owes the measure of success it can claim to the fact that it was an adjunct to a land reform program, which the government had already decided to undertake and for which the JCRR provided invaluable supplementary support. If the Filipinos really want to use this sort of device we should cooperate, but only if they are first committed to the objectives it is expected to serve. Under these conditions the joint commission technique has great value because of by-products such as the demonstration of good administration, responsible use of public funds, and politically acceptable, constructive cooperation on an international basis.

In the private sector there are many techniques of cooperation that can be made to work if the proper attitudes prevail on both sides. The main way in which the U.S. government can help here is in making available as many opportunities as possible for the training of Filipinos in management and public administration. The AID and its predecessors have done something along these lines, assisting especially in public administration courses at the University of the Philippines and holding seminars for senior executives with the aid of the Harvard Business School. Much more can be done. The success of the economic and social program depends in the end not only on the amount of capital, resources, or trade, but on the quality of men who are behind it. These men belong to what we loosely call the middle class, our natural allies. Those engaged in the difficult task of changing a society need moral support—training, experience, association with those who have already succeeded or are engaged in the same struggle, assurance that they are on the winning side—in short, they need much more than material support. They need to know that when they are fighting for the things that will make a sound and possibly more democratic Philippines, they can count on the selective backing of the United States. Our allies are not necessarily our friends, but their enemies are our enemies. We should most certainly not support those who stand in the way of Philippine development. Nor should we proceed on the naive assumption that because we do not blatantly interfere in the internal affairs of other countries we have no influence on them. We cannot choose to have no influence; we can choose, however, whether or not to use it to support U.S. policy.

Chapter 11

U.S. Security and Philippine Defense

An aggressive strategy in Southeast Asia, such as the United States is pursuing in Viet-Nam, is strengthened immeasurably by the political and military support of the Philippines. In an area where the only effective answer to Communist guerrilla warfare is social revolution we have not only a base for operations but also an ally which is capable of revolutionary leadership. Whether or not that leadership is to be forthcoming in full and adequate measure depends mainly on the Filipinos and only partly on the United States. In this connection it is fortunate that the long relationship of the U.S. army to the Philippines has been marked by more than a purely military tradition. From the very beginning the U.S. army has been a force making for social, political, and economic change. Even during the years of conquest and pacification the army began the building of roads, the construction of schools, the enforcement of public health measures, and the holding of elections. It was the army that brought over the first group of several hundred American teachers in the troopship *Thomas,* which gave the name Thomasites to the men and women who taught in the first public schools in the barrios. The tradition of the U.S. army as a social force is even more important today than it was before independence because of the key role that it is playing in mobilizing Southeast Asian countries in the struggle to cope with the Communist pattern of insurrection.

It is not generally realized that the United States needs from the Filipinos something more than the loan of military bases; it requires their political support in promoting social reform, the only kind of social revolution that will contribute to the long-term stability of Southeast Asia, including the Philippines. This is really the issue that lies behind the complex problems of cooperation between powers of such contrasting military might. We have first to agree on the character of our mutual political-military objectives before we can decide such questions as the role of each partner or the degree of consultation about matters that involve great risks or might lead to war. Otherwise how can we determine who will decide what action shall be taken for what purpose and against whom? Both countries have been feeling their way toward the solution of these problems over a long period of time. While the Filipinos wish to secure a binding U.S. agreement to defend the Philippines, they also want to exercise as much influence as possible over the course of U.S. Asian policy and have therefore pressed for prior consultation on regional security questions. As a result of the Bohlen-Serrano agreement of 1959, the two countries set up a Mutual Defense Board that has been working reasonably well. In fact, the Filipinos have been successful in securing a special relationship to the United States and a leading role in arrangements for regional security, but only after a long and acrimonious dispute centering around the question of the status of American bases and armed forces in the Philippines, which has always been at the heart of the problem of U.S.-Philippine relationships.

The Bases Issue

The issue of the status of American bases had its beginnings in the first Independence Act (the Hare-Hawes-Cutting Act of 1933), which authorized the United States to keep such of its military bases in the Philippines as it wished. President Quezon held this provision to be the most objectionable part of the law at the time when he engineered its rejection by the Philippine legislature. The Tydings-McDuffie Act of 1934, the substitute law that was subsequently agreed upon, provided in Section 10 for the surrender by the United States of all rights over "all military and other reservations of the Government of the United States in the Philippines (except such naval reservations and fueling stations as are reserved under section 5)." The final disposition of these naval bases would be negotiated between the two countries within two years after the proclamation of independence. During World War II the American Congress in 1944 approved a resolution reversing the policy on bases embodied in the Tydings-McDuffie Act. President Quezon accepted this Joint Resolution 93, Section 2 of which stated:

After negotiation with the President of the Commonwealth of the Philippines or the President of the Filipino Republic, the President of the United States is hereby authorized by such means as he finds appropriate, to withhold or to acquire and to retain such bases, necessary appurtenances to such bases, and the rights incident thereto, in addition to any provided for by the Act of March 24, 1934 [Tydings-McDuffie Law], as he may deem necessary for the mutual protection of the Philippine Islands and of the United States.

On the basis of this resolution the two countries negotiated for the lease of bases in the Philippines. The result was the assignment to the United States of some twenty-three bases for a 99-year period.

There is little material to explain President Quezon's rationalization of his about-face on the question of bases, for no pertinent documents have been discovered among those turned over to the National Library. According to former President Sergio Osmeña, writing some sixteen years after the event, Quezon changed his mind in the early days of the war. While the Commonwealth government was on Corregidor, President Roosevelt's message came, assuring the Philippines that its freedom would be redeemed and its independence established and protected. Osmeña pointed out to Quezon that the message implied the existence of American bases in the Philippines. "Do you favor them now?" "With the lesson of this war," Quezon replied, "we cannot escape from the necessity of accepting it." Right there, in his quarters, says Osmeña, they agreed to support the establishment of military bases. "Hence, the provision on American bases that was eliminated during our domestic controversy on the Hare-

Hawes-Cutting Act was fully restored under the impact of the war, with the sanction of the United States Congress and the united support of the Filipino leaders. These bases, built on Filipino soil, stand—in the words of the resolution [Joint Resolution 93]—'for the mutual protection of the Philippine Islands and the United States.' " These bases, concluded Osmeña, provide for the security of the Philippines.[1]

The motives that led to the establishment of the bases are questioned less today than their role and status. After independence the United States continued to administer the base areas as if they were American territory. On its base at Subic Bay, for example, the United States navy directly administered the town of Olangapo and its 20,000 inhabitants. Such anomalies were not troublesome until the coming to power of the Nacionalistas in 1953, when the changed temper of the Filipinos led to disputes over incidents that would earlier have passed without public comment. Now they were being brought forcefully to the attention of the press and the legislature. One such incident occurred in 1956 at the town of Capas, Tarlac, when the American authorities at Clark Air Force Base challenged the right of Filipino miners to quarry and transport manganese ore in what was claimed to be part of the military reservation. To get at the mines the Filipinos had to pass a checkpoint. To bring the ore out they had to contend with what Filipinos argued were obsolescent American claims dating back to the administration of Theodore Roosevelt. Senator Claro Recto, counsel for the miners, brought the issue of sovereignty into sharp focus. The Philippine press gave much attention to this case, as it had also done to disputes the previous year over conflicts of jurisdiction in the city of Olangapo.

Feelings likewise ran high over the case of George Roe, a United States seaman, who was accused in January 1956 of causing physical injuries through reckless driving. Under the terms of the 1947 military bases agreement Filipino authorities released him to the custody of Sangley Point naval officials. Seaman Roe, however, was transferred to the United States and dis-

---

[1] Sergio Osmeña, "Quezon and the American Military Bases in the Philippines," *Philippines Free Press*, August 20, 1960, p. 57. Hereafter cited as *Free Press*.

charged. The Philippine Foreign Office sent a formal protest to the United States Embassy in language both pointed and explicit: "It has been noted that this is not the first time that members of the armed forces of the United States who have been accused before the Philippine courts for one crime or another have been able to avoid trial and thereby defeat the ends of justice by seeking transfers from the United States military authorities to other places beyond the reach of the jurisdiction of the Philippine courts." [2] At the same time the press took up the case of pilferers at Clark Air Force Base. Over a period of ten years, some 20 persons had been killed while scavenging for bombs dropped by U.S. planes on their gunnery range. It was in this atmosphere that negotiations began in August 1956 for the revision of the 1947 U.S.-P.I. Military Bases Agreement.

The Philippine panel of negotiators, led by Vice-President Garcia, put forward a series of demands ranging from return of unused base areas, creation of a Philippine-United States Defense Council, and full application of Philippine laws within the bases, to more definite assurance of automatic United States retaliation in the event of an attack on the Philippines. The experience of World War II meant to many Filipinos both that the presence of American bases invited attack and that this was intolerable unless there was the fullest assurance the United States was willing and able to prevent it. Being now independent, the Philippines felt that it should have something to say about the purposes for which the bases were to be used. The Filipinos stuck to their original demand for broadening the civil and criminal jurisdiction of Philippine courts to cover certain categories of on-base offenses committed by personnel of the U.S. armed forces. The United States panel, led by Ambassador Albert Nufer, stood by the original status-of-forces provisions in the 1947 agreement, although it was willing to be flexible about other matters. On these issues the negotiations became deadlocked.

Several reasons account for the failure of negotiations. The two panels contrasted sharply in membership: except for the Am-

[2] O. D. Corpuz, "U.S. Military Bases and Philippine-American Relations," *Progress Magazine 1957* (Published annually by the Manila Times Publishing Co., Inc.), p. 30.

bassador, the U.S. panel was composed entirely of military representatives; the Philippine panel was political in its make-up and included three members of the legislature. Recto and the other legislators also made it clear that they would not necessarily accept the terms agreed upon by the delegates, a move that made it dangerous for the Filipino negotiators to be associated with very much less than an extreme position. The negotiations were carried on more through press releases than by secret diplomacy. The result was that, once positions had been taken by either side, the possibility of compromise was seriously diminished. In this atmosphere reasonableness could easily be interpreted as weakness, and neither side was willing to make the first concessions. It seems clear now that the Filipinos welcomed an occasion to express not so much an anti-American feeling as their need to be accepted as an independent people. They drew attention to American agreements on bases with the United Kingdom, Spain, and Greenland, comparing their own unfavorably with them, particularly in the matter of jurisdiction. The United States had entered on the discussion with nothing more complicated in mind, apparently, than to negotiate an amendment of the bases agreement so as to bring about the return of superfluous areas in exchange for new bases; its delegation was not prepared to encounter, as it did, demands for a complete overhauling of the entire agreement. When negotiations were broken off in December 1956 (after having considerably worsened the relations between the two countries), it was by the unilateral decision of the American panel.[3]

Negotiations were eventually taken up again in conferences between Ambassador Charles Bohlen and Secretary of Foreign Affairs Felixberto Serrano in 1959. As a result of their talks they reached agreement on several points, the most important being the delimitation of American base areas and relinquishment by the United States of approximatly 117,962 hectares, reduction of the term of the lease from 99 to 25 years, the definition of

[3] R. F. Soriano, "U.S.-P.I. Relations," *Progress Magazine 1956*, pp. 42-48; 216. Emilio Aguillar Cruz, "Year of Nationalism," same, pp. 18-25; Vicente Albano Pacis, "Politics of Our Time," same, pp. 26-35.

metes and bounds on all military areas and surrender of the Manila port area reservation to the jurisdiction and control of the Philippines, and the transfer of the Olangapo community to the Philippine government. In addition, the United States agreed to set up a Mutual Defense Board and install Filipino liaison officers in the bases, consult with the Philippine government before installing missile sites or using the bases for any purpose other than mutual defense, and elevate to a treaty commitment U.S. responsibility to repel instantly any attack on the Philippines. Although the criminal jurisdiction question remained to be resolved, the atmosphere had improved considerably, largely because the Filipinos felt, as President Garcia put it, that the United States had recognized the legitimacy of nationalism in the Philippines.[4] At the conclusion of the talks Ambassador Bohlen issued a statement that indicated American appreciation of the new temper in Philippine politics:

Any nation or any individual who would dare say that the government of the Philippines would be subject to pressure or any form of influence by other nations or individuals, particularly by the United States or any of its officials, has only to sit across from Secretary Serrano at a conference table, to realize that such pressure and influence are absolutely impossible.[5]

Secretary Serrano's comments at this stage of the negotiations emphatically expressed the official position of Filipino nationalism:

Philippine-American relations have been brought through a crucial period without impairment of the means of negotiating and thrashing out mutual problems. The department has taken a tough stand on some issues and an accommodating stand on others. The aim has been to establish a respected independence, and to help the nation find the root and soul of the national spirit. . . . The direction of foreign affairs will remain oriented as it is now, as befits the continuity of an administration posture. "Filipino First" will continue to be the watchword

[4] Felixberto M. Serrano, "The Conduct of Our Foreign Affairs," *Progress Magazine 1959*, pp. 70-72. Teodoro M. Locsin, "Nationalism So Far," *Free Press*, February 27, 1960, pp. 2-3; 74.

[5] Teodoro M. Locsin, "Respectable Independence," *Free Press*, December 12, 1959, p. 160.

and assertion of nationalism, the means of bringing the Philippines to a new place in the sun.[6]

Clearly the Filipinos were thinking of their national pride, and of their relative standing among the friends and allies of the United States.

The United States could adjust itself to what Serrano called "respected independence," but the controversy also brought out extremist views that injected a new note into Philippine-American relations. The view that the Philippines should break all political, military, and cultural ties with the United States is not new, especially when used as a bargaining weapon, but it is seriously advocated today in some quarters as a practical policy. The editorials and commentators of the *Manila Chronicle,* owned by sugar interests, expressed this view with relentless eloquence. In commenting on the Serrano-Bohlen talks and achievements, the *Chronicle* damned them with faint praise. Many Filipinos, it pointed out, think that identification with America is an end in itself, sufficient to elevate the economic and cultural status of the Filipino, but the "unabashedly pro-American orientation of previous administrations failed to yield the expected results. On the contrary, Filipinos continued to be mired in poverty and continued to be the laughing stock of other Asians for their brazen insistence that they were 'Oriental-Americans.' "[7] The Garcia administration was credited, in a somewhat patronizing manner, with making the monumental discovery that to regain the respect of other peoples and to put an end to the baneful habit of depending too much on the United States for economic and strategic security it was necessary to establish a respectable independence. Not that the Foreign Secretary had succeeded in discharging his task of "re-affirming the affinity of the Philippines with Asia, for the ties with the United States cannot be brushed aside that easily, but at least he is moving in the right direction."[8] In the context of such editorials the policy of "affinity with Asia" is meant to indicate a complete break with

[6] Department of Foreign Affairs, *Editorial Trends,* no. 1, January 4, 1960 (Manila: Division of International Information), pp. 1-2.

[7] Same.

[8] Same.

the United States rather than the policy of the Garcia administration to build up honorable relations with both the United
States and Asia. The first step of the "affinity with Asia" school
would be to establish neutralism as the policy of the Philippine
government; the second, presumably, would be to forge alliances
with "Asia," a term left deliberately vague because it is meant to
include mainland China rather than Japan.

The Great Debate

The long-drawn-out negotiations over the bases have provided
the Filipinos with a ready-made platform for the discussion of
every problem, real and imaginary, that concerns the two countries. As a result, more Filipinos are aware today of the case for
neutralism than ever before. Secretary Serrano found it necessary to reply directly to those who advocated breaking ties with
the United States by pointing out that this would be a hasty
decision which no "sensible Filipino" would approve.[9]

The "great debate" over the bases is obviously a debate about
the identity of the Filipino, his nationalism, and his posture in
the world. Years of intense argument in the press and the legislature have helped to clarify the policy of the Garcia administration and to identify the opposition. In setting forth the administration policy clearly and succinctly in a statement of April 20,
1960, Secretary Serrano said that the Philippines recognizes the
realities of the world situation and has forged a mutual defense
pact with the United States and a regional defense arrangement
with other countries of the free world community. These two
agreements constitute the cornerstone of Philippine defense policy. With the United States, there are a military assistance agreement and a military bases agreement under which both countries
seek to strengthen their mutual undertakings to make common
defense effective. "It is towards this goal that we have succeeded
to elevate to the category of a treaty obligation the American announced policy of instantly repelling any attack upon the Philippines. It is likewise towards the same goal that we are endeavoring to secure from the U.S. a more effective program of military

[9] *Manila Chronicle*, June 13, 1961.

assistance. It is the context of these efforts that the President has openly urged for modern weapons for the protection of our national security." [10] Thus, in the administration's view, disputes with the United States take place within the context of a close alliance and firm commitments.

The rival view holds that the Philippines should sever its connections with the United States and seek its future in an Asia including Communist China. Those who argue the neutralist position do not necessarily favor it for the same reasons. Apart from motives of emotional anti-Americanism, some want neutralism as a first step toward an alignment with the Soviet bloc; others want it as a bargaining weapon to secure better terms for a policy of commitment; and yet others, as an affirmation of a truly independent Philippines. Among the latter was the late Senator Recto, who protested President Garcia's willingness to have nuclear missiles in the Philippines, not because he wanted to help the Soviet bloc (he recommended the increase of sea-based Polaris weapons), but because he thought missiles would serve as magnets in a nuclear war and would deprive the Philippines of the chance to choose the alternative of surrender. An aggressive, self-reliant nationalism was the basis of Senator Recto's neutralism and, however self-contradictory some of the positions he took, there was no doubt that his motivation was to assure the independence of the Filipino people. Much of the rationale for neutralism today, however, comes from sources that do not necessarily have the national interest of the Filipinos at heart—sources that may well misrepresent the late Senator while exploiting his popularity with the intellectuals. Recto was not peddling as neutralism either the sterility of escapism or a concealed betrayal to the Communist bloc. Neutralism for Recto was a policy that could bring no greater dangers to the Philippines than the alliance with the United States, and might, if properly pursued, avoid the greatest danger of all, nuclear destruction. But Recto said so many things that it would not be difficult, through judicious selection, to make him appear to have been in favor of a break with the United States and the Western powers in order

[10] *Manila Bulletin*, April 20, 1960, p. 1; see also Felixberto M. Serrano, "The Philippines in World Affairs," *Progress Magazine 1960*, p. 28.

to pursue an "Asian" orientation, a course that he certainly did not advocate. Now that he is gone, the leadership of the neutralist groups is most likely to fall to the left-wing intellectuals and professionals, whose interest it is to impose their own definition of neutralism as the only alternative to the dominant middle-of-the-road policies of the Macapagal administration. In this they have made some progress by skillfull use of the tremendous interest aroused during the protracted base negotiations, and they have been particularly helped by the death of Recto.

Tension and misunderstanding will continue until the issue of jurisdiction over crimes committed in the base areas is settled to the satisfaction of both sides. On July 4, 1956, Vice-President Nixon stated in Manila that the United States recognized Philippine sovereignty over all Philippine territory, thus reversing the interpretation Attorney General Herbert Brownell made three years earlier. Brownell had stated, "On the basis of the Tydings-McDuffie Law, title to the American bases in the Philippines was retained by the United States. And, therefore, all issues pertaining to jurisdiction shall be under the determination of the United States for the right to exercise U.S. sovereignty over the bases covers both procedural and substantive law." [11] Nixon's statement settled the matter of principle but not the matter of procedure. Negotiations still proceeded on the issue of *de facto* jurisdiction.

The bases agreement of 1947, still under attack, divided jurisdiction over offenses into two general classifications: those committed inside and those outside the bases. The United States exercises primary jurisdiction over all offenses committed within the bases, except when the offender and the offended are both Filipinos, unless the offense is against the security of the United States. The Philippines has primary jurisdiction over all offenses committed outside the bases, except in cases where both parties are members of the American armed forces, or the offense is committed by a member of the American armed forces while engaged in the actual performance of a specific military duty.

The main difference between the U.S. agreement with the Phil-

[11] Lorenzo Tañada, Jr., "A Question of Sovereignty," *The Manila Sunday Times Magazine,* November 2, 1958, pp. 10-14.

ippines and those with NATO powers and Japan is that Filipinos can come under the jurisdiction of the U.S. military authorities. This is all the more irksome because many Filipinos live on the bases, and in one case, a whole town, Olangapo, had been under the jurisdiction of American naval authorities. The agreements with the NATO powers make no distinction between crimes committed on or off base and expressly exclude the United States from jurisdiction over nationals of the host state. All these arrangements are reciprocal, whereas the U.S.-Philippine agreement is not.

In 1959 the revised agreements between the two countries conceded to the Philippines jurisdiction inside U.S. bases over crimes committed against Filipinos by American servicemen off duty, while American military authorities retained jurisdiction if the servicemen were on duty. But who is to say whether the crime is committed on duty or off duty? According to the United States, it is the American authorities; according to the Filipinos, it should be the Philippine courts on the ground that jurisdiction is inherent in sovereignty.

The problem of how to arrange for jurisdiction over American troops abroad is not an easy one to settle, although in practice the arrangements have worked reasonably well.[12] Reluctance to agree to Philippine demands is due partly to the tradition of American rule, with all the habits of command that the military authorities on the bases find hard to forget and the Filipinos find equally hard to forgive. This condition does not apply in Europe and was true for only a short period in Japan, where the decision in the Girard case to turn an American soldier over to Japanese authorities betokened an acceptance of Japanese sovereignty that was of great interest to the Filipinos. In the Philippines, American authorities have for some time been avoiding the bringing of Filipinos to trial. But in matters of sovereignty the acceptance of a right is sometimes more important than the deed. Experience in other countries has shown that where the

[12] Figures compiled by the Judge Advocate General of the U.S. army show that out of 21,708 cases of American citizens subject to foreign jurisdiction from December 1952 to November 1956, only 4,620 were actually tried, and of 490 sentenced to prison terms, 264 were suspended. Same, p. 13.

sovereignty of the host country is accepted and arrangements about jurisdiction are reciprocal, there is a reasonably satisfactory situation. Where national pride is honored, the host country can afford to be lenient, as the Girard case demonstrated.

Would this be true in the Philippines? The Philippine legal system was set up by Americans, but there is seemingly some reluctance to believe that it operates with fairness and justice to all. The most extreme statement to this effect was made in December 1959 by an American congressman, Phil Weaver, after a short visit to the Philippines. Congressman Weaver called for moving U.S. bases to Thailand on the ground that American troops were subject to false arrest by Philippine authorities, and that they were the victims of condoned thievery, looting, blackmail, extortion, and assault ". . . all winked at or openly approved by perhaps the most corrupt governmental organization in the world . . . The situation is the result of a graft-ridden government composed of venal men whose sole aim in life is to make a fast buck at the expense of the Americans." [13] Statements such as these reveal attitudes rather than facts, the morbid, arrogant, and insensitive attitudes of some of the military officials on the bases. The men who hold or transmit these views see nothing wrong in sending out of the country an American sailor who stabbed a Filipino to death in a bar on the American naval base in Olongapo. Foreign bases always create problems for the host country, but the problems are almost qualitatively different in Asia because of the violent contrast in standards of living, habits, and values between the Americans stationed at the base and the host population. "Any amateur sociologist would be able to foresee the result," according to one Filipino columnist, Carmen Guerrero Nakpil.[14]

Most of the Americans on the bases have little contact with Filipinos other than those in the lower social strata, including those with whom many American servicemen collaborate in smuggling and illegal traffic in dollars. Small wonder, then, that many of them take such a jaundiced view of the Filipino, or

[13] Teodoro M. Locsin, "Should the U.S. Pull Out of the Philippines?" *Free Press,* December 5, 1959, p. 3.
[14] Same, p. 58.

that the Filipinos often think of the American as arrogant. In any other country the situation would have come to a head long before it did in the Philippines. Sooner or later the United States will have to accept in the Philippines the same sort of status-of-forces agreement that it has elsewhere, and it will be in the American interest to do so. There is no logical ground on which to stand in refusing to grant to the Philippines what we give to other allies. It is extremely poor policy to extract every ounce of resentment, tension, and misunderstanding from protracted negotiations over an issue to which there can be only one conclusion.

Future Problems and Opportunities

Military cooperation with another power must be founded on a clear understanding of the purposes that each has in mind. At present it is apparent that U.S. bases in the Philippines are there to protect the United States; they are an essential part of a defense system against Communist expansion, and it would be very difficult to do without them. The overseas bases make it possible to deploy the means available to deter Communist power and, when necessary, to mount limited warfare operations.

For the present Filipino leaders the bases are an investment in collective security and a guarantee that the United States will defend the Philippines in case of attack. The price, especially if nuclear missiles are to be included in the weapons allotted to the Philippines, is the danger of being a direct target for the enemy. If they adopted the alternative, a neutralist foreign policy, the Filipinos would still be an object of Communist aggression, the difference being that they would be able to choose surrender.

U.S. defense policy in the Philippines must take into consideration the future trends of Philippine policies. If preoccupation with the economic affairs of the country dominates domestic policies for the next five to ten years, as it should, it is not likely that the Filipinos can afford any radical changes in the present division of labor between the two countries. The Philippines stands to gain economically if the United States continues to be responsible for the over-all defense of the country. Economic advantage, however, is not the only determinant of policy. The very nationalism that stimulates economic growth may also stimulate irrational and costly moves in matters of national defense. Those who oppose the government's plans for economic growth will insist on such moves in the name of nationalism as one means of embarrassing the administration. Under pressures from the extreme right and left President Macapagal may find it difficult to maintain the moderate position in economic and military affairs that he has tried to establish.

These pressures may take several forms. One might be a skilfully manipulated effort to commit the Philippines to small-power imperialism in the remaining colonial territories, such as Borneo. A worsening of relations between the Philippines and her neighbors would suit the Communists very well, and they can hardly be expected to neglect any opportunity to bring it about. President Macapagal would find such a movement hard to handle. Again in the name of nationalism we can expect a drive to reduce or eliminate American military power in the Philippines on the ground that it antagonizes Asian friends and neighbors and keeps the Philippines in a colonial status. We can expect the charge that an imperialist United States is using the Philippines as a base from which to destroy the independence of Asian peoples and to undermine the growing friendship between the Filipinos and their neighbors. Propaganda appeals along these lines will have some effect because there are many Filipinos of moderate political persuasion who are genuinely interested in improving the relations between their country and their Asian neighbors, who would much prefer to have the Philippines fully responsible for its own defense, who resent being taken for granted, who would have no objection to acquiring a little territory in Borneo, and who would like their country to play a leading role, if not in Southeast Asia, then at least in a Malaysian federation. Filipinos with these views may be vulnerable to extremist appeals presented in terms of nationalism.

In Southeast Asia the Communist powers can be expected to increase their efforts to establish governments friendly to their interests or subservient to their will. At present the United States is using the Philippines as an important and convenient base for the application of American military power on the mainland of Asia in support of U.S. and Philippine commitments to SEATO. As the situation in Southeast Asia grows increasingly serious there is no doubt but that the United States will need its bases in the Philippines more than ever before. If this were purely a military struggle, it would be quite possible, though not desirable, to fight without bases in the Philippines. But it is not that sort of war. The struggle for Southeast Asia will vary from country to country, but it is certain to be limited war, and in most instances, there will be guerrilla warfare. As in South Viet-Nam, it will take the form of a contest over the attitudes and loyalties of the peasantry, the type of warfare that led to the development of "counterinsurgency" doctrine and methods to oppose enemy use of infiltration and guerrilla warfare tactics. Guerrilla warfare of the Mao Tse-tung variety is the most important event in Asia since the coming of the West and may, in fact, be as great a catalyst of social change. Where it has produced a positive and successful reaction, as in the struggle with Communist terrorists in Malaya and the Huks in the Philippines, it led to political and social changes that would otherwise not have occurred for decades, if at all. Mao Tse-tung has indirectly helped to bring about a dynamic relationship between the strong and the weak as well as between different classes and races. Under the impact of his type of warfare many old American concepts have also changed.

At long last the U.S. army is now training significant numbers of officers and men in the doctrines of counterinsurrectionary warfare, and officers from several Southeast Asian countries are taking part in this training at U.S. staff colleges. The doctrine of the subordination of military to civil power no longer prevents the U.S. armed forces in Asia from being blind to their political potential. It is now accepted that the task of the U.S. armed forces in certain parts of Southeast Asia is to persuade the local government that Communist guerrilla activities cannot be stopped unless the peasants are on its side and cooperate with the government and army in taking the steps necessary to win over the peasants. Armies therefore become instruments of social change because they have to change peasant attitudes and village organization. For most Asian armies it is a novelty to treat the peasant as a human being, to pay him for his food and services, and to make an effort to secure his confidence and cooperation. The social revolution in the villages and the political revolution in the government are essential elements in military strategy in Southeast Asia. The only successful answers to Communist insurrection are inspired by the positive, humanitarian, and cooperative aspects of the Western tradition.

The revolutionary potential of counterinsurrection is of particular importance to U.S. relations with the Philippines. This is an area in which the Filipinos can make a unique contribution for which they have been prepared by the peculiar circumstances of their history. They can help themselves while they are helping the common cause, by raising the political consciousness and dedication of their educated classes. As the officers in the army come from the middle class they will perform best if they have the backing of that class in the difficult task, at home as well as abroad, of dealing with Communist-type insurrection. If they do not have the sort of political support that they require, the sort that Magsaysay once gave them, then they might prove inadequate in the field when opposed to Communist guerrilla operations, or they might come to despise politicians and business men and turn to the tactics of the radical right. The task of statesmanship in the Philippines is to galvanize Filipinos of all classes to the realization of their potential role as leaders in social and political revolution in Southeast Asia.

Chapter 12

Emergence of
a Foreign Policy

The Philippines has two related aims in foreign affairs: to clarify its relations with the United States, and to establish a new relationship with other countries, particularly its neighbors in Asia. In order to achieve these objectives, as former Foreign Secretary Felixberto Serrano often pointed out, the Filipino had first to establish the spirit of independence, to become aware of his own nationalism, to acquire the self-respect that is the first condition of the respect of others, to overcome the feelings of dependence, servility, and acquiescence to the wishes of the stronger partner. Serrano himself is partly responsible for the fact that during the Garcia administration there was a qualitative change in the attitude of Filipinos toward the United States, and indeed toward their own role in international affairs in the direction of greater nationalism and independence. As President Macapagal has shown, Filipinos will no longer be taken for granted.

The Affirmation of Independence

Long before the cold war began, the Philippines committed itself to binding alliances with the United States and aligned itself with the free world. It is not neutral. By choice it has given up the bargaining position that the uncommitted nations enjoy as they play off one side against the other in the world-wide power struggle. But this does not mean that the Filipinos are unaware of the opportunities open to the weaker member of an alliance for influencing the policies of the stronger by appealing, for example, to the declared good intentions of the stronger and making much of the proven loyalty of the weaker member. During the last few years, the Philippine government has sought to establish the posture that it can stand up to the United States in bilateral negotiations and even force the revision of agreements, a strategy whereby it hoped to build up respect for the Philippines as an independent country, especially in Southeast Asia. Hence its insistence on the settlement of issues relating to sovereignty and status—such as jurisdiction over American troops, the parity clause giving American businessmen unilateral advantages over other foreigners, and the participation of the Philippines in making policy about mutual security. It has come to terms with Japan and cultivated economic relations with other countries with a view to diversifying its economy in anticipation of the ending of the special economic arrangements with the United States in 1974.

The bid to establish a new relationship to the United States began with President Magsaysay. His strategy was to maintain pressure on the issues that were best calculated to put the United States on the defensive, such as the omnibus claims, the amount of economic assistance, and the sugar quota. On all these issues the Filipinos could plead their case in terms of promises unfulfilled, the rights of a loyal ally, or just plain equity.

On January 14, 1955, the Philippines officially presented claims for a total of around one billion dollars, including additional war damage payments, the gold devaluation losses of 1933, and various veterans' claims.[1] It has been pointed out in debate in the

[1] *Congressional Record,* v. 105, pt. 2, February 24, 1959, p. 2854. Omnibus Claims:

$24 million in gold devaluation funds.
$130 million in additional war damage payments.
$173 million in coconut oil processing tax.
$1 million in claims of Philippine customs duties of imports of the U.S. army and navy.
$75 million in sugar excise tax.
$600 in various military (war damage) claims, known as the bulk claims.
See *The New York Times,* April 17, 18, 1963, for comments on lobbying in the U.S. Congress for various claims.

U.S. House of Representatives that the total bill for the so-called "omnibus claims" is too high and that the nonmeritorious claims discredit the more reasonable ones. As far as war damages are concerned, the larger approved claims (those above $500) were paid up to about 52 per cent of the balance over $500 by pro-rating the amount of money available from the 1946 appropria-tion of $500 million, a figure picked out of the air and subject to revision. Congressman Miller referred to the moral obligation to pay the war damage awards "which we have left unpaid," to which Congressman Judd added that ". . . we have a moral commitment to carry through what we said in 1946 we would do and which we have not done fully." [2] Stalwart supporters of the Philippines, such as Congressman Zablocki, introduced bills to meet some of the omnibus claims year after year before achiev-ing some success.

Some of the anti-American feeling that developed in the Phil-ippines was probably deliberately whipped up by a small group, and it was given extensive coverage in the press; but unquestion-ably the failure to pay the war damage claims in particular cre-ated a good deal of general resentment. It is reinforced by the political consideration that there is something in the omnibus claims for practically every important group to be resentful about—the church, the veterans, the business community, and the government. As Philippine Ambassador to the United States, General Romulo often referred to these various claims in his speeches. "The general impression that we have been beneficiar-ies of extra-lavish American assistance," Romulo said on one oc-casion, "must be corrected for, aside from war damage payments which were certainly due us who suffered incredible destruc-tion from an enemy attack aimed at the United States—the Phil-ippines was American territory at the time—the actual receipts of economic help are much less than those given to other coun-tries in Asia, some of them former enemy countries, others neu-tral or uncommitted, certainly none linked by political, military, and economic ties as closely as the Philippines." [3] Filipino friend-ship, he said on this and many another occasion, is being taken

2 Same, pp. 2851-2853.
3 Same, v. 105, pt. 18, January 26, 1959, p. A-487.

for granted. Such is the informality of American-Filipino relations that the Ambassador felt free to call on Americans to write
to their congressmen urging favorable action on legislation of
interest to the Philippines. No other ambassador would be permitted this liberty. In the spring of 1962, when the Congress again
refused payment of the $73 million war damage claims, President
Macapagal cancelled a goodwill trip to the United States. Very
soon after this, Congress approved the payment.

The main explanation why the omnibus claims have not been
met in full (apart from the fact that some of them are exaggerated) is the feeling that the Filipinos cannot use such large sums
of money efficiently and that payment would undermine the
efforts of the economic aid mission. Many members of Congress
hold that the Filipinos mismanage their fiscal and monetary policies and take it for granted that the United States will help them
out. On the other hand, there are those who argue that the
shortage of foreign exchange is due to heavy investment in industries and that the Filipinos must be trusted to go their own
way toward economic independence, and that in any case a moral
obligation exists and must be met. Filipinos feel that the United
States would rather exert its influence over the Philippine economy through aid than simply give them their due, to do with
as they wish.

The Filipinos have strong opinions about these claims and
interpret U.S. reluctance to come to a settlement as an indication
of ingratitude for their loyalty during World War II. American
officials and legislators tend to avoid and underrate the issue
because some of the omnibus claims are preposterous and others
exaggerated for bargaining purposes. This is short-sighted, especially when dealing with a people of long memories who still insisted in 1961 on receiving payment of the relatively small sum
still owed them as a result of the gold devaluation in 1933. To
leave these claims unsettled is dangerous, for they are a matter
of national pride, and the bad feelings associated with them can
easily provide fuel for the extreme nationalists and their Communist fellow-travellers. It would most certainly be to the advantage of the United States to continue to examine the omnibus

claims very carefully, perhaps through a joint American-Filipino commission, and settle the matter once and for all.

The recurring theme that the United States gives more aid to former enemies and unaligned neutrals than to the Philippines is an oversimplification of a very difficult problem. When the figures are given in totals, the Philippines is lower on the list than when the amounts are stated on a per capita basis. The aid given to a country also depends on the amount that can be usefully absorbed and on military and strategic considerations, particularly the military role of each country in the cold war. Filipinos do not conduct the arguments on this basis so much as on the moral plane of comparative loyalty to the United States and to the cause of the free world. To be sure, the Filipinos have aligned themselves in no uncertain manner with the United States, and they see international relations in terms far more personal than do Americans. They feel that the very special relationship they have to the United States should be expressed in concrete ways that everyone can understand. The settlement of the war damage portion of the omnibus claims may go far to neutralize this particular theme.

Every time the U.S. Congress has discussed the sugar quota, the Filipinos have presented long and often brilliant memoranda urging an increase in the quota for the Philippines. As to the general facts there cannot be much dispute: the larger quotas resulting from the increase in American consumption have usually been shared by American beet sugar interests and the "full duty" countries, such as Cuba, but there was no increase for the Philippines. The powerful sugar bloc in Philippine politics, which has no wish to see an end to the guaranteed American market in which sugar is sold above the world price, is responsible for a great deal of the anti-American propaganda in the Philippines aimed at compelling the U.S. Congress to raise the sugar quota rather than to risk losing Philippine friendship. Those American businessmen who have an interest in seeing a larger quota allotted to the Philippines echo the Filipino arguments of equity with other sugar-producing countries, reward for loyalty, and the immediate economic necessity. The sugar quota question reverberates through both American and Philippine politics, and there are few subjects on which Filipino representatives in the United States show better preparation, more persistence, and greater experience. Despite this long-sustained pressure to raise the sugar quota, there was no reaction from the American Congress and public until Castro came to power in Cuba and an embargo was placed on Cuban sugar. Only then did the Philippines receive an increased quota for the sales of its sugar to the United States.

While the battles over sugar, aid, and claims are not likely to undermine the alliance, they generate a great deal of propaganda on both sides, and this reflects the much more important problem of mutual respect. From the United States the Filipinos want respect and equality of status much more than money or favors. They want the American government and people to accept their nationalism, whatever its strengths and weaknesses, as naturally as they accept that of other countries. That is why they have felt it necessary to demonstrate, in negotiations with the United States as well as through their role in the United Nations, that the Philippines arrives at its policies independently, even when they coincide with those of its partner.

What Bonds with Asia?

Contact with the rest of Asia was a traumatic experience for the Filipinos, partly because of their ignorance of its peoples, partly because of their own feelings of superiority to their neighbors, and partly because they found themselves regarded as "stooges" of the United States. They had thought of themselves as more advanced politically and economically than other Southeast Asian countries and as potential leaders of the new nations in that part of the world. They were surprised to find that other Asians thought of them as more Western than Asian, as puppets of the United States. In fact, Nehru refused to accept their independence as complete. Putting the matter rather bluntly Ambassador Romulo said, "We do not want to be a pariah in Asia and no self-respecting nation wants a pariah for an ally." [4] To turn toward Asia for friends and allies is a natural impulse,

[4] Same, p. 2853.

in the view of Filipino nationalists, and the more success the Philippines has in building up its relations with Asian countries, the more valuable it will be, so it claims, both as a friend of the United States and as a potential bridge to Asia. It must therefore make its own contacts and arrangements with its neighbors.

The cultivation of relations with Asian countries is one of the most important new directions of Philippine policy since independence. One exception to this policy is Communist China, toward which the Filipinos take a stand similar to that of the United States; in fact, they have stated that even if the United States were to recognize Peking, they would not do so. President Garcia even went out of his way to make it clear that so long as he was president he would not open diplomatic relations with the Soviet Union. President Macapagal apparently agrees. Some Filipinos, however, have traveled in Communist China, and a few journalists have visited Moscow on the invitation of the Union of Soviet Journalists. In 1957 Congressman Roces and several newspapermen made a conducted tour of Communist China and published their not unsympathetic impressions in the Manila press. The subject of trading with Communist China has occasionally been raised in business circles.

The late Senator Recto definitely favored recognizing Communist China on the ground that this was the most realistic way of fighting communism, as contrasted with what he called a policy of evasion, indifference, retreat, and "brinkmanship." Communist China cannot be ignored, he argued, and if it were admitted to the United Nations, its misdeeds could be challenged on legal and moral grounds. That Recto held these views carries weight with the intellectuals.

Relations with Japan have been restored practically to normal. For some years after the war, anger and resentment against the Japanese occupation forces made it difficult to resume any sort of relations, though a bilateral financial agreement signed in 1950 made trade possible on the open account barter system. The Philippines refused to ratify the 1951 peace treaty with Japan, although Article 14 gave the Philippines the right to claim reparations from Japan. The reparations settlement took several years and a great deal of bargaining. Under the terms of the reparations agreement, Japan promised to pay to the Philippines $800 million in capital goods, services, and loans over a twenty-year period. In 1958 the two countries signed a bilateral trade agreement, and in February 1960 they started negotiations for a treaty of amity, commerce, and navigation.

In the Philippines the administration of the reparations agreement puts a great deal of patronage at the disposal of the president, and Garcia was not reluctant to use it. As might be expected, Japanese and Filipino businessmen collaborated in overpricing goods and sharing the profit, to the detriment of the Philippine government. The Philippines is getting some benefit by way of capital goods and services on public projects, such as the Marikina dam and the telephone service, but the main effect may well be to assist in the accumulation of private capital by those in positions of power and influence, including the so-called "farmers," or large landed interests.

In foreign affairs the chief result of the reparations agreement has been to break the ice between the Philippines and Japan. Japan is back in Philippine trade and is strongly influencing the growth of the Philippine economy. Trade with Japan in 1949 amounted to ₱.22,700,000 in exports and ₱.32,100,000 in imports; in 1959 the figures were ₱.233,300,000 for exports and ₱.179,900,000 for imports.[5] There is a growing tendency to think of this trade as a natural exchange of Philippine raw materials for Japanese manufactures, and the Philippines is now willing to allow Japan to share in its economic development; yet the old fears have not disappeared, particularly the fear of aggressive Japanese economic penetration. Upon starting negotiations for a treaty of amity, commerce, and navigation in February 1960 the Philippine panel was instructed to protect the domestic program of industrialization, to keep within constitutional limitations on the exploitation of natural resources and operation of public utilities, and to extend parity rights and preferential treatment to U.S. citizens only, however tempting the reciprocal advantages

[5] Naotoshi Tsuchiya, "Trade Possibilities Between the Philippines and Japan," *Fookien Times Yearbook, 1960* (Manila: The Fookien Times Co., Inc.), p. 115.

might be. The Filipinos do not even wish to give to the Japanese the most favored nation treatment that they demand. It will be a long time before the memories of the Japanese occupation recede, but the trade with Japan is so profitable that, other things being equal, economic relations between the two countries are likely to become more and more intimate. The Japanese trade may, indeed, become a means of undermining the special privileges enjoyed by the United States.

Only when the Filipinos turn to Southeast Asia do they feel they can assume a position of leadership. Indonesia, Malaya, Viet-Nam, Cambodia, Laos, Thailand, and Burma are much closer to the Philippines than are China or Japan in standards of living, cultural traditions, and military power. Within this region is the group of Malay-speaking nations that has long been thought of as a natural unit—Malaya, Indonesia, and the Philippines would be its core. With these countries the Filipinos feel the bonds of language, custom, and geographical proximity. For some years after independence the Filipinos also believed that they were the foremost power in the Malay group in view of their political institutions and adjustment to the modern world, and on occasion they affected the pose of leadership but the offer of leadership was not accepted. According to former Secretary of State Felixberto Serrano, "We were like the son of a big politician. No matter how much the son tried to impress the people in the community, he was treated as nothing but the image of his father, and the constituents would rather deal directly with the father until the son could prove his own worth." [6] The Filipinos must slowly win the respect of their fellow Asians, according to Serrano, and that can be achieved only when the democratic institutions of the Philippines bear the "mark of our own national soul and native genius."

After taking much of the initiative in setting up the Southeast Asia Treaty Organization (SEATO) and in formulating the Declaration of Manila, the Filipinos followed these moves with negotiations in 1962 for the establishment of an Association of Southeast Asia (ASA), in which they were joined by Malaya

[6] Felixberto M. Serrano, "The Philippines in World Affairs," *Progress Magazine 1960* (Manila Times Publishing Co., Inc.), p. 28.

and Thailand, but not by Indonesia. President Garcia himself carried on most of the diplomatic negotiations for the Association during his own state visits to the prospective members and the return visits of Asian leaders such as Prime Minister Abdul Rahman Putra of Malaya and President Diem of Viet-Nam.

According to its official statement, the Association of Southeast Asia was founded for friendly consultations, collaboration, and mutual assistance in the economic, social, cultural, scientific, and administrative fields. Its creation was greeted with caustic comment from the Soviet *New Times* which did not believe that it was a regional economic bloc but rather an auxiliary of SEATO, "inspired by outsiders," and designed to bring neutral Asian countries into the stream of American policy. SEATO, according to Soviet propaganda, is an aggressive military bloc set up to combat the Asian national liberation movement, and ASA was expected to compensate for the shortcomings of SEATO by bringing in Indonesia, Burma, and Cambodia—but they have refused to join. Only a beginning had been made in achieving the larger dream of Philippine diplomacy.

Efforts were made to cultivate close cultural relations with Indonesia, but relations between the two countries soon cooled when the Indonesian government felt that the Philippines had given aid and comfort to the insurgents in the rebellion of 1958. Two good will missions went to Indonesia, one led by Senator Pelaez and the other by Senator Recto. A cultural agreement of May 1958 arranged for an exchange of students and professors, and in October of the same year Foreign Minister Subandrio made an official visit to Manila. But the Filipinos themselves admit that whatever good was achieved by these efforts was undermined by President Garcia's failure to recall the much criticized Philippine Ambassador, José Fuentebella, who was described by the Indonesian *Times* as being as welcome as the bubonic plague. Fuentebella, among other things, declared his independence of his own foreign office and returned to Djakarta without Manila's permission. His continued presence as ambassador, said the *Manila Bulletin* of May 2, 1958, would slow down, possibly to a standstill, Philippine efforts to win back the respect and goodwill of the Indonesian people. The efforts, however, were continued by President Macapagal.

To establish a reputation for independence, Filipinos think they must act in such a way as to convince Asian and other nations that their country is not a satellite of the United States. This has had its dangers. Nationalism, even "respectable nationalism," cannot grow on hollow victories, it must have substantial successes. Filipinos realize that in order to face the world with confidence in 1974 they must be able to maintain themselves economically without the present degree of dependence on the American market, but it is difficult and costly for them to take the necessary measures to diversify their industry and commerce.

While it was seeking to improve its standing in Southeast Asia, the Philippines began a drive to increase trade outlets in Europe. The most receptive of the European countries, West Germany, sent a twelve-man trade mission to appraise the potentialities of trade with the Philippines and offered to donate a complete chemical pilot plant to train Filipino engineers and technicians in basic chemical industries. West Germany also offered to finance a proposed steel mill at Iligan. The Department of Commerce, under the firm leadership of former Secretary Manuel Lim, increased both the quality and the number of its representatives abroad, and President Macapagal visited Western Europe during his first six months of office to solicit, among other things, trade and investments. Macapagal seemed to realize that the degree to which Filipinos succeed in preparing themselves for 1974 will indicate the quality and resolution of their national purpose far more than any single factor other than their military capacity.

Efforts to establish economic and cultural bonds with Asian countries make more obvious the special privileges, such as parity, that must be reserved for Americans, and the temptation to yield to pressures to abolish them is all the greater. It is difficult to move away from economic dependence without seeming to be anti-American because the United States is responsible historically for the economic colonialism that warps the economy, for the isolation of the Philippines from the rest of Asia, and for the reluctant yielding of concessions to Philippine sovereignty and self-respect even after the coming of independence. To date the Filipino brand of nationalism has been free from the one-sided interpretation of colonialism as a strictly capitalist phenomenon that holds sway among so many Asians. But if Filipinos feel that the United States is standing in the way of real independence, the blame for all the ills of the country will fall on the former imperial power. Strong, well-organized forces in the Philippines are carrying on a day-by-day campaign to popularize this view.

The issue is: can the Philippines build up economic and cultural ties with Asian nations outside the regional security pacts without giving up the alliance with the United States? The experience they have had with ASA would seem to indicate that this effort will be a very difficult one. Although Japan has shown that it is possible to trade with Asia, Africa, and Europe while being allied to the United States, it is also true that the American-Japanese security pact is a divisive issue in Japanese domestic politics. The Philippine search for diversification of trade outlets and for political prestige and position among Asian and African countries may also lead to serious domestic disputes over the wisdom of the American alliance. Discussion of the advantages of breaking with the United States may not be, for many of its sponsors, an expression of neutralism, but it is sure to generate pressures that would assist those who want neutralism for reasons of their own. The failure of Indonesia and Burma to join ASA gives some point to the jibes of left-wing commentators that to President Garcia the slogan "Asia for the Asians" meant Asia for the "Asian nations who are indebted economically and tied up militarily and committed politically to the United States." [7] The price for greater Philippine participation in Asia is higher than many had supposed. This objective of Philippine policy, we have to remember, was born out of hurt pride and national humiliation, and economic resentments during the next decade might well be allied with national prestige to bring into question the value of the American connection.

[7] *Manila Chronicle*, June 19, 1961.

What Role for the Philippines?

The Filipinos often justify their interest in their neighbors as the desire to serve as a bridge between East and West. Both the Nacionalistas and the Liberals hold that the Philippines can be a bridge between the United States and Asian countries within the framework of the security treaties because the Filipinos are at the same time Asians and good friends of the West by virtue of their long acquaintance; they can interpret the one to the other. Obvious difficulties beset this policy, not the least being the ambivalent attitudes of many Asian countries toward the Filipinos, and the inexperience of Filipinos in Asian affairs. Nevertheless, the Filipinos have been acting in accordance with this view of their role in ways that are not always fully appreciated. Their unabashed, if not uncritical, approval of the United States is a political asset that rises in value as the Filipinos establish their credentials as a new nation with an independent policy. They have also taken it upon themselves to give to the United States advice about its policies in Asia in forthright but acceptable terms, some of which is well worth listening to. Few statements of the Asian position are clearer than that made by former Ambassador Carlos P. Romulo in the following ten points:

1. The Asian peoples will no longer tolerate the shackles of colonialism. What they want is a status of equal partnership and voluntary cooperation with other peoples.
2. The Asian peoples are fired with an aspiration to human dignity and economic well-being which can no longer be held in abeyance.
3. The Asian peoples will not fight for the vague concept of a free world; they will fight on the side of the free world only if they have a stake in freedom themselves.
4. The West must work with and through the responsible nationalist movements in Asia rather than through puppet regimes that have no popular support. By denouncing and opposing genuine freedom movements in Asia as Communist-inspired, the West, in fact, exposes such movements to Communist infiltration and control. The objective must be to isolate Communist agitation from the legitimate nationalist aspirations of the Asian peoples.

5. Military measures are at best a short-term device for staving off an immediate threat of Communist aggression. The long-term struggle against communism, however, requires economic and financial assistance that will enable the Asian peoples to raise their standards of living.

6. Assistance should be offered on a basis of equality and mutual respect, and not as a special favor with political strings or as a disguised survival of colonialism.

7. As there can be no world peace without Asia, so there can be no economic stability in the world without Asia. You cannot neglect Asia and, by continuing to pour dollars into Europe, expect to stabilize the world economy, including the European economy itself.

8. Asian political, economic and social organization is predominantly on an authoritarian pattern. Therefore, it should not be assumed that the Asian peoples will automatically adopt democracy of the Western type; rather, they will adopt it with necessary modifications and only as it demonstrates its superiority in the actual experience of daily life.

9. Asian neutralism must be recognized partly as the result of a genuine desire for peace, partly as dictated by the serious internal problems of many countries in the region, and partly as inspired by a lingering distrust of the motives of the colonial powers.

10. The Asian peoples will not give their support to any program, policy or course of action affecting Asia that is taken without consulting them.[8]

In short, the Ambassador was arguing that most of the problems of Asian countries arise from the denial of the legitimate aspirations of responsible Asian nationalism, and that if the United States will adjust its attitudes and policies to these aspirations, most of the problems will be manageable.

There is a great deal of truth in these assumptions, and the United States has gone a long way toward accepting them. During the last ten years it has agreed to a revision of trade agreements in favor of the Philippines; to a modification of the bases agreements; to a larger share for the Filipinos in the making of mutual defense policies; to a partial settlement of the omnibus claims; and to some important shifts in Philippine foreign

[8] Carlos P. Romulo, *Congressional Record*, v. 100, pt. 6, June 9, 1954, pp. 7972-7973 (83rd Cong., 2d sess.).

policy. A few months after the Kennedy administration came into power, one of the most relentless critics of the United States wrote that the United States had broken from the past by modifying the policy on aid so that "stability and adherence to democratic principles, not subservience, became the conditions for the granting of aid." By abandoning the John Foster Dulles notion that independence and noninvolvement are immoral, the United States, he wrote, has shown that it "is no longer interested in puppets," and it has come to believe that a self-respecting ally is more dependable in the end than a subservient one.[9]

In the United Nations the Filipinos have supported the United States on all important issues. But they have also frequently asserted their independence and have courted the Afro-Asian bloc, especially on the issue of colonialism. The Filipinos, however, have consistently rendered a great service by insisting, at Bandung and in the United Nations, that colonialism behind the iron and bamboo curtains is just as bad as, if not worse than, the rapidly retreating colonialism of the West. On a famous occasion in the United Nations in October 1960 when Khrushchev himself denounced Senator Sumulong, a member of the Philippine delegation, as a "jerk and stooge of American imperialism," apparently because of his references to Soviet imperialism, the Philippine Senator replied effectively in defense of his country's honor. (Ironically, the Philippine delegation was actually preparing to vote for the Soviet proposal to discuss a declaration on the granting of independence to colonial countries in a plenary session rather than in the Political Committee, as preferred by the Western powers.)

The impact of emergent Asia and Africa has brought to the fore another concept of the "bridge," a concept directly opposed to the one that characterizes policy at present. This is the view that the Philippines should break the alliance with the United States and join the ranks of the uncommitted nations in order to help form a bridge of understanding not between the United States and Asia, but between the United States and the Soviet Union. Dr. Gumersindo Garcia, one of the first pensionados and a regent of the University of the Philippines, stated at the time

9 *Manila Chronicle*, January 31, 1959.

of Senator Recto's death that the small and weak nations of Asia and Africa must detach themselves from alliances with the great powers and serve as "bridges of understanding." [10] Such a position is identical in form with that which was supposed to unite the conference of so-called uncommitted nations at Belgrade in September 1961. It is part of this concept that all nations should be included in the world organization of states. There are important Filipinos who detest communism but are persuaded that the United States should recognize Communist China. They feel that such a course would reduce fear and suspicion and would permit the other members of the United Nations to begin the process of controlling Chinese behavior through the force of world opinion.

The view that small countries should be free to secede from alliances if they so wish has serious implications for the free world. It is necessary to realize, however, that while such views may serve the interests of the Communists, they are held by Filipino nationalists who think of themselves as being strongly anti-Communist. If Filipinos come to feel that the rewards in terms of recognition, leadership, and national pride are potentially greater through close association with the Afro-Asian countries, then it is always possible that more and more Filipino nationalists might see the future of their country as one of leadership among the smaller Asian and African powers, uncommitted to either bloc, though "positively neutral" in favor of the free world. It will be highly important to distinguish between those who hold these views on the basis of their convictions as Filipino nationalists and those who adopt them as a tactical device to bring the Philippines one step nearer to the Communist world.

Closer relations with Asian countries will not necessarily create bridges of peace, they may even lead to conflict. Southeast Asia encompasses a wide variety of countries with different social and political systems, different and often competing economic interests, and in some cases, strong drives for expansionism. Several factors may make for conflict. One is the trend toward regional groupings for economic purposes in order to bargain more effectively with the Common Market countries. Another is the paral-

[10] *Manila Chronicle,* August 22, 1960.

lel trend towards supranational associations for political protection, which may or may not coincide with the optimum boundaries of the economic groups. Such trends naturally raise the question as to who will lead? Another factor making for possible conflict is the liquidation of the remaining colonial territories, especially those in Borneo and New Guinea. The decision of the Dutch to give up West Irian relieved them of a costly and unprofitable colony and made of the Indonesian Republic an imperialist power that may well have ambitions to "liberate" more neighboring territories. For the time being, however, the Dutch decision avoided a head-on collision. According to Indonesia's Foreign Minister, Subandrio, the Philippines gave consistent support to Indonesia's claims in the West Irian affair. Vice-President Palaez had much to do with the decision to support Indonesia and with the actual negotiations. In conjunction with an Asian country and with the United States the Philippines achieved a quiet diplomatic victory, but it did not lay the foundations for future cooperation with Indonesia in regional affairs.

The trend toward the liquidation of colonial territories in Southeast Asia may raise more than Indonesian ambitions for territorial expansion. The Philippines has made claims to North Borneo that it attempts to justify on legal grounds as well as cultural and geographical affinity.[11] The Philippine claim to North Borneo was first made after World War II on behalf of the descendants of the Sultan of Sulu. In a note of June 22, 1962, to the British government, the Philippines claimed sovereignty over this area of 29,388 square miles and 454,000 people. One-quarter of the people are Chinese, Malay, Indian, and European, and the rest are indigenous people related to the Malay. The issue was important because the proposed new political community was to combine the eleven states of the present Federation of Malaya, the self-governing state of Singapore, the British Crown Colonies of North Borneo and Sarawak, and the British-protected State of Brunei. A federal association, this new state was a close neighbor

[11] For discussion and documentation see *The Philippine International Law Journal*, v. 2, January-June 1963, *passim;* also *Free Press*, especially February 17, 1962, March 3, 1962, and March 10, 1962.

of the Philippines. In the Philippine view the Federation of Malaysia would still be very much under British influence, especially as it would most likely have military arrangements with the United Kingdom and be a member of the Commonwealth.

A concern of a different order would be the danger to Philippine national security from the easier access of Singapore's Chinese left-wing activists to Borneo. Malaysia would be a neighbor with 3,780,000 Chinese as against 3,500,000 Malays, all under one roof. If there were communal disputes between Malay and Chinese, the latter might appeal to Peking for support and this would have repercussions in the Philippines.[12]

The Philippine action opens up the possibility of claims to British Borneo coming from Indonesia, which actually has a more plausible case here than it had in West Irian. The temptation to grab contiguous pieces of territory from a retreating colonial power is very great and very dangerous, especially when it takes place in an area well infiltrated by Communists.[13]

The Filipinos have often been accused of having only a pecuniary interest in North Borneo, but, even if true, this is not necessarily the whole picture. The government probably never expected to have its claims taken too seriously; but they were useful as a means to having a voice in the future of the Malay area and essential if Malaysia failed to materialize, for then the claims could be used in opposing an Indonesian effort to take over the whole of Borneo. No one can deny that the Philippines utilized its claims to North Borneo to its own diplomatic advantage. In June 1963 the Philippine government brought the foreign ministers of Malaya, Indonesia, and the Philippines together in Manila to lay the foundations for a "summit" conference, held in July, of Abdul Rahman, Sukarno, and Macapagal at which it was agreed that the birth of Malaysia should be delayed until September 15, 1963, in order to give the United Nations time to conduct a survey of opinion in North Borneo to find out

[12] Alejandro M. Fernandez, "Threat from Malaysia?" *Free Press*, February 24, 1962, p. 7, 54, 56-59. Napoleon J. Rama, "A Matter of Security," *Free Press*, February 23, 1963.

[13] William A. Hanna, "Malaysia, A Federation in Prospect," *American University Field Staff Reports*, Southeast Asia Series, v. X, no. 1-5, January-March 1962.

whether or not the people wished to join Malaysia. The United Nations team reported that the public sentiment was in favor of Malaysia and the new state formally came into being. Indonesia and the Philippines immediately severed diplomatic relations, and the power struggle for leadership in the Malay world entered on a new phase. The Philippines and Indonesia both wanted a larger federation of Malay states because both hoped to lead it, but there was little else on which they agreed. In the long run, the interests of the Philippines were likely to have more in common with those of Malaysia than with those of an ambitious and expanding Indonesia.

President Macapagal claimed that the main achievement of his administration in foreign affairs was indeed the establishment of *Maphilindo*, a composite name given to a loose understanding between Malaya, the Philippines, and Indonesia. Addressing the Manila Overseas Press Club on August 21, 1963, Macapagal compared this to the passage of the Land Reform Act. "The establishment of Maphilindo will remove the barriers that have been built artificially to divide the peoples of the Malay race." The President indicated some of the aspirations of Philippine diplomacy by comparing Maphilindo to the empires of Sri-Visaya and Madjapahit, with the difference that this was a voluntary association of sovereign states. The precursors of Maphilindo, said Macapagal, include the Asian Relations Conference of 1955, the Afro-Asian group in the United Nations, and the Association of Southeast Asia. In other words it was nonwestern and anticolonial. In this significant address President Macapagal made much of the Baguio Conference of 1950, called by President Quirino and attended by India, Pakistan, Ceylon, Indonesia, Thailand, Australia, and the Philippines. This conference agreed on the principle of joint action for the region and on making the interests of the peoples of the region the primary consideration in solving their problems. Maphilindo expresses these ideas without, however, being racially exclusive. "While developing new strength in cooperation with our neighbors, we shall continue to welcome the assistance of friends we already have."

But there is more to it than that. Filipinos also see the idea of Malay unity going back to Mabini and their own revolution, for Mabini saw Philippine independence from the Spaniards as the means to the liberation of Oceanea. There was talk of *Malaya Irredenta* in the 1930s among Filipino students, one of whom is said to have been Macapagal. There is something exciting about the idea of the Malay peoples, divided for so long among three imperial powers, now coming together again. History may even be rewritten a little in order to exaggerate the degree to which they were once one people. But there is no denying the sympathy of the Filipinos for those who rejoice in the withdrawal of the British, even if their anticolonialism does not carry with it the antiwestern flavor of some of their new-found friends. Perhaps the concept of Maphilindo can be made to be more significant than that of Malaysia. The Filipinos see the common bond as the threat of Red China, for they argue that Indonesians fear the Chinese and can see that a union of 140 million Malays would make of the Overseas Chinese a small minority and present Communist China with a stronger bulwark against expansion than would Malaysia.

Philippine diplomacy had never been more active. Sukarno met with Macapagal in Manila in May, followed a few days later by Tunku Abdul Rahman. Then, after the Tunku and Sukarno met in Tokyo, the three foreign ministers met for five days in Manila and accepted the idea of a Malay federation. They even agreed that all three countries shared the responsibility of preventing subversion in this area. More than that, they agreed that there should be consultative organs set up to handle their joint affairs, particularly economic matters, and that the method of discussion should be through *musjawarah,* which means arriving at decisions through consensus. The Under-Secretary Lopez, soon to be Secretary, claimed that Philippine foreign policy was now dynamic, not static, and that Manila was becoming a center of diplomatic activity. For good or for ill, the Philippines was at last expressing its nationalism as an independent power among its Southeast Asian neighbors.

Thus, the struggle for control of Borneo, an island of great strategic importance, has already begun. If the Federation of Malaysia concept can work and achieve its objectives of containing the Singapore Chinese and developing the area economically, it would be a pity to endanger its success in any way. But if it should not work and political chaos ensues, then the United

States might find itself involved in counterinsurrectionary activities on this island of extraordinary contrasts, difficult terrain, and very backward peoples. If it came to fighting neither the Philippines nor the United States could do very much in Borneo without the help of the other.

There is bound to be tension between the needs of Philippine nationalists to express themselves in foreign affairs and the limitations imposed by the American alliance. If the greatest powers of the world find it difficult to adjust their policies to the facts of collective security, how much more difficult and frustrating is it for small powers to do the same, especially when they cannot look back on years of successful life as an independent nation. As there is no way of solving this problem once and for all, we have to live with it. Most of the difficulties are plain to see. The Philippines must act as a loyal ally of the United States and other members of SEATO when dealing with the Asian members of that organization. But the Republic's standing with the uncommitted countries, it feels, can be established only by disproving the charge that the Philippines is a puppet of the United States. It is easy to fail in both. The Filipinos have ambitions to be bridge builders between the United States and the peoples of Asia and possibly Africa, yet they have not been able to bring the uncommitted countries, such as Indonesia and Burma, into free world alliances. Nor was the first Malay republic included in the plans for the State of Malaysia.

The United States has the problem of supporting, as carefully as possible, the need of the Filipinos for a dignified and honorable role in foreign affairs while keeping the major objectives of both countries to the fore. The extremes of left and right will probably combine to encourage the Philippine government in nationalistic adventures and small-power imperialism, and it is not going to be easy to handle these moves. The debates in the Philippine Congress over the Borneo claims showed how difficult it is for moderate voices to be heard. The Philippines and the United States have a joint interest in seeing that Communist subversion does not succeed in Borneo, the area nearest home for the Filipinos. Yet by the spring of 1963 the United States and the Philippines had publicly committed themselves to opposing positions on Malaysia. Problems of this gravity can lead to disaster if not handled in close cooperation, for the Communists are experienced in using such affairs to achieve the maximum of division among their enemies. Such cooperation is possible only if the Filipinos feel that they are being treated as an independent ally whose own needs and interests are at stake. The other side of the coin is a willingness on the part of the Filipinos to consult with the United States on moves that may lead to serious involvements affecting the national interest of their powerful ally.

The active role that the Philippines played in the West Irian affair temporarily improved its relations with Indonesia at no cost to its relations with the United States, which worked quietly with Manila toward a common goal. But there are many difficult problems in store for the free world in Southeast Asia, and there will be many temptations to lure the Filipino nationalist off course. While Filipinos must have the opportunity to satisfy their legitimate and inevitable nationalism in foreign affairs, it is to our interest that it be satisfied within the framework of the alliance. There is every reason, therefore, why there should be much more consultation between the two countries on foreign affairs than has previously been the rule. In handling the problems of Southeast Asia the United States and the Philippines must be partners if either is to serve its own national interest.

Chapter 13

The Communist Bloc
and the Philippines

One of the long-range objectives of the Communist bloc is to take over the Philippines, a particularly rich prize because of its special relationship with the United States. This relationship involves the prestige of American political institutions and of the Christian religion. On the face of it, the prospect for the Communists might appear to be discouraging. The Filipinos have proclaimed their adherence to democratic institutions, and since 1946 their country has supported, in the main, all the major developments in U.S. policy in Asia. They accepted both economic and military aid, agreed to the establishment of American bases on Philippine soil, joined in regional security arrangements such as SEATO, sponsored the Manila Charter, denounced Communist imperialism at Bandung, refused to recognize Communist China, and assisted the United Nations in the struggle in Korea. Thus far, the Philippines has rejected neutralism. It would appear, indeed, as though there were no serious tensions between the Philippines and the United States, no clashes so fundamental that there is no hope of adjustment. Few former colonies have identified themselves so closely with the former metropolitan power. Yet only a few years ago the Communists came close to capturing power in the Philippines, and they are preparing for another serious bid for power when the occasion permits.

The Philippines, China, and the Overseas Chinese

The Philippines today is a society in transition. Even though the parallel is far from being an exact one, the rapid transforma-

272

tion of China between 1946 and 1949 provides a warning of what can happen in the briefest span of years. It can be said of the Chinese during these years, as of the Filipinos today, that the United States had many friends among them and a strong sentimental interest in their future. There was apparent agreement on fundamental goals. In the case of China then, as of the Philippines today, the United States made charges of corruption in government, bureaucratic inefficiency, neglect of agrarian reforms, state direction of industry, poor opportunities for foreign capital, lack of management skills, and a weak national spirit. Although the military power of the Huks, unlike that of the Chinese Communists, has been broken, the Communists in the Philippines are relentlessly carrying on the war by methods that are potentially just as dangerous, such as the manipulation of political symbols and the creation of a new intellectual climate. As in China in 1946, there is little to indicate today that events could move so rapidly and so disastrously for the government in power.

In 1954 the Communist bloc adopted new tactics in its efforts to take over the independent Asian governments that it had failed to destroy. Since neutralism was now seen as a step on the way to communism, persuasion and parliamentary methods of change-over became the order of the day. It was at this time that the "Five Principles of Peaceful Coexistence" were written into the Sino-Indian Treaty on Tibet.[1] In those countries with which Communist China and the Soviet Union had diplomatic relations it was possible to make openings for cultural exchange, barter agreements, granting of long-range credits, and arrangements for technical assistance. While the para-military units in neutral countries were not given up, the armed conflict was played down in favor of pressure for recognition of a legal Communist party, but always on Communist terms. As Deputy Premier Mikoyan made clear at the Twentieth Congress of the Soviet Communist Party in 1956, the smaller, neighboring countries can be peacefully manipulated into "Socialism," but armed force will be used if necessary.

[1] The Five Principles are: mutual respect for one another's territorial integrity and sovereignty; nonaggression; noninterference in one another's internal affairs; equality and mutual benefit; and peaceful coexistence.

What does this mean for the Philippines? Not being a contiguous neighbor of one of the big Communist powers, the Philippines cannot be subjected to the same sort of military blackmail as India and Laos, or Burma and Thailand. On the other hand, the Philippines can be assured that the price of alignment with the United States is the enmity of the Soviet bloc, which will use every means available to get rid of American bases and encourage neutralism.

Thus far, the Communist bloc has not succeeded in securing Philippine acceptance of its offers of trade and aid, although the offers are discussed and some degree of division of opinion within the Philippines has been achieved. There are many ways in which the propaganda themes of anti-Americanism, anti-imperialism, and neutralism can be spread in a country whose press enjoys such an extraordinary degree of freedom as it does in the Philippines. There is also in the Philippines an important Chinese minority which contributed to the Huks during the war and is obviously a target for infiltration and subversion. In spite of the fact that the Philippine government is thoroughly alerted to the dangers of Communist subversion, especially among overseas Chinese, there is no doubt that well-trained Chinese agents are coming into the Philippines from the mainland and that the traffic cannot be stopped. The Nationalist government still enjoys considerable prestige among the Chinese in the Philippines, but in the long run their reaction to Communist pressures will depend in great measure on the way in which the Filipinos treat them. In this matter the record is not always as encouraging as it should be.

By the end of the Spanish period there were probably thirty to forty thousand Chinese in the Philippines.[2] Today, as the result of the application of American immigration laws during the colonial period, there are half a million or more; and because Chinese women were also admitted, the Chinese have tended to maintain their cultural identity. There were some ugly anti-

[2] Joseph R. Hayden, *The Philippines: A Study in National Development* (New York: Macmillan, 1942), p. 692. These Chinese were mostly laborers, not the highly organized businessmen of today—according to Benito Legarda, "Our Growing Entrepreneurial Class," *Manila Sunday Times Magazine,* v. 16, no. 13, November 6, 1960, p. 15.

Chinese riots during the American period, somewhat fewer under the Commonwealth, and one instance of an attempt by China to protect the interests of her nationals in the Philippines by the threat of reprisals against American interests on the mainland. Not until 1954 did the Philippines pass a law to Filipinize the retail trade. There have been no large-scale riots against the Chinese since independence.

The Filipinos, however, are concerned about the same old problems of the overwhelming economic influence of the Chinese and their potential threat to the national security. The two problems are closely related; in fact, some Filipinos make a good living by charging the Chinese with Communist activities in order to extort money from them.[3] Officials of Nationalist China and of the Philippines have been negotiating for many years about the so-called "overstaying Chinese." The figures vary as to their number. It is estimated that of the Chinese residents in the Philippines, 200,000 are registered with the government and 400,000 are illegal unregistered entrants, many of them political agents.[4] The Nationalist government regards these refugees from Communist China as a Philippine problem, while Manila wishes to send them to Taiwan. A former Secretary of Foreign Affairs, Raul S. Manglapus, stated that it was the strong economic position of the Chinese that prompted the Philippines to continue recognizing Nationalist China rather than ". . . give a Red Embassy in Manila a chance to coerce a ready-made economic empire into subversive action." [5] Communists have tried to direct attention away from the Chinese to American imperialism, which they insist is the real enemy, for the very good reason that they have other uses for the Chinese. Peking, as Liu Shao-chi has pointed out, intends to use the overseas Chinese for its own purposes: "We must continue to unite with patriotic Chinese living in various places abroad; they are a component part of the united front."

The Filipinos know that the Chinese problem can be solved

[3] *Manila Times,* April 5, 1960.
[4] Same, August 26, 1958.
[5] Raul S. Manglapus, "The State of Philippine Democracy," *Comment,* no. 14, First Quarter, 1962 (Manila: Regal Printing Co., Inc.), p. 74.

only by a combination of two processes—the absorption of the Chinese into Philippine society both culturally and racially, and the assumption by the Filipinos of economic leadership and control. If the Chinese are absorbed, if there are no questions as to their loyalty and identification, then as Filipinos they can add their wealth and talents to the development of the country. But if they are not absorbed, the tension between Filipino and Chinese will grow, with disastrous results.

The present relationships cannot be permitted to continue. At present too many Filipinos use political influence to exploit the Chinese. It is true that the Chinese are unwilling to give up their traditional culture (there are nearly 200 Chinese schools in the country), and that the Chinese look with ill-concealed contempt on Philippine culture. But at the same time the Filipinos make it very expensive and difficult for Chinese to acquire citizenship. It takes several years and several thousand pesos in bribes to acquire citizenship. The difficulties of working out a statesmanlike solution to the problem of having so many economically powerful and culture-bound aliens in their midst are increased a thousand times by the policies of the Communists. The Chinese are a real security problem. One foreign diplomat put it vividly, perhaps too vividly, when he said that if 200 Red Chinese officers were landed in Luzon they could immediately commandeer an army of 200,000 Chinese.[6] General Vargas testified that about 10 per cent of the overstaying Chinese were suspected Communists.[7] Many Chinese seem to have dual citizenship, and considerable sums of money still are transferred to the mainland every year.

The Communist parliamentary struggle requires money. So long as the Filipinos cannot guarantee protection of the individual from blackmail, it is reasonable to assume that much of the fund comes from the rich Chinese, either as a result of blackmail or of the old custom of supporting both sides.

The Philippines desperately needs a clear and well-administered policy toward the Chinese. It should be humane, positive, and decisive. There are not many alternatives. The one most likely to be successful would be to make citizenship easy to ac-

[6] *Manila Times,* August 26, 1958.
[7] Same, March 19, 1958.

quire and force an immediate declaration of intent from the Chinese. There would have to be rewards for those who choose citizenship and penalties for those who do not, and this would involve considerable self-discipline on the part of those Filipinos who now look upon the Chinese, citizens or not, as a source of easy money. The Filipinos would do well, perhaps, to realize that only the Chinese can control the Chinese in the Philippines. The path of wisdom, therefore, would be to treat extremely well those Chinese who wish to commit themselves to the Philippines and to cultivate them as political allies in the struggle with those who are there for other purposes. Present practices tend to force all Chinese together into an undifferentiated mass, an extremely dangerous thing for the Filipinos.

Communist Strategy and Tactics

The various pressures that the Soviet bloc has at its disposal are being used to swing the Philippines to a neutral position and to prepare a climate of opinion among the intellectuals favorable to Communist objectives. The current objectives and strategy of the Communist party in the Philippines are described in several political transmissions, most of which were captured in the field from Communist units. As might be expected, in this period of the "parliamentary approach" the Communist party of the Philippines is instructed to revitalize the party, to recruit and train new cadres; it is to infiltrate into existing organizations, particularly those of workers and peasants; above all, it must secure ideological leadership rather than formal or nominal leadership. There are detailed instructions to underground workers on how to recruit members to the party, from which classes to select them, how to go about propaganda work, how to take advantage of the electoral process to secure the election of councilors, mayors, governors, and congressmen who are party members or sympathizers, and how to proceed without frequent contact with higher organs of the party.

The main ideological weapon is nationalism, which is defined in Communist directives as anti-Americanism. "To be pro-Filipino one must necessarily be anti-American imperialist. To split hairs or to make 'subtle' semantic distinctions is merely to confuse and relegate the real issues to the background." [8] It is estimated that about 400,000 of the half million who voted for Senator Claro M. Recto can be claimed as true nationalists, many of whom belong to the intellectuals. There are not now, nor are there soon likely to be, enough votes to elect a pro-Communist government, but they provide a significant beginning for manipulating the main political parties.

Philippine Communists and their sympathizers have infiltrated many of the leading newspapers, they run many of the popular columns in the press, and they have secured important positions in certain political organizations. It already is possible to identify several ways in which the Philippine Communists are implementing the tactics laid down in the political transmissions. One of the most important Manila newspapers, the *Manila Chronicle,* is a forum for left-wing writers. Known Communists are extremely influential in the Philippine League for Economic and Cultural Nationalism (formerly the Social Science Association), an important business group that backs candidates for organizations such as the Philippine Chamber of Commerce. They are influential in the Federation of Labor Unions, organized in April 1959, which claimed to have a total of 300,000 members and to be the most important organization in the labor world. They have infiltrated student organizations; Philippine government documents draw attention to the degree to which student groups are already under their control. During the last few years students have been called to demonstrate in front of foreign embassies and in rallies for or against congressional legislation. They are used to break up the meetings of groups that are not under the control of the Communists.

The legal and parliamentary strategy calls for the full use of front organizations, which are more effective if they are not identified as being Communist inspired or dominated. One of the most ambitious front organizations that showed certain signs

[8] Editors, "Political Transmission No. 15," *Philippine Studies,* v. 8, no. 1, January 1960 (Published quarterly by the School of Law, Ateneo de Manila), pp. 3-50. These transmissions are not available in published form, although some of them have been quoted and discussed in the press.

of being at least inspired by Communists was the Kilusang Makabansa (KMB). The KMB claimed to be the first organized mass movement for Philippine nationalism since the uprisings of the late nineteenth century. Over half of its leaders belonged to the extreme left wing. The founding convention of the KMB, attended by nearly 200 delegates, adopted a constitution and by-laws, formulated the Nationalist Manifesto, and appointed a host of provincial and city directors of the organization (who were sworn into office by Associate Justice Jesus G. Berrera of the Supreme Court). The KMB was obviously to be used both as a training ground for activists and a platform from which to dominate political discussion.

Published in the Manila newspapers in May 1959, the Manifesto of the KMB attempts to link Philippine nationalism with what it calls the Asian Revolution, by which is meant the "rebirth of Asia" after four centuries of Western bondage. After a perfunctory bow to Rizal, the emphasis is put on Bonifacio, who "presaged the Asian dawn" and has long been played up by certain Filipinos as the real hero in the revolt against Spain because he led the "masses." The imperialist expansion of Europe is explained in Leninist terms without the jargon about monopoly capital, but the thesis is there. It continues with the revised view of history that in the Philippines Bonifacio's Katipunan fought for a social revolution, thus showing a more "progressive" approach than the *ilustrado* class, which petitioned Spain for reforms and called for unity among the Filipinos. Then American aggression "served to reduce a social revolution into a mere political compromise ending seasonably but uneventfully with the restoration of independence on July 4, 1946." [9]

The century of Asian nationalism, according to the Nationalist Manifesto, has only passed through its first stage, that of political independence; there remains the second stage of social revolution, economic emancipation, and social regeneration. An essential part of the argument is that the whole fabric of Philippine society is "colonial, subject to foreign influence, secular and

[9] Teodoro A. Agoncillo, *Revolt of the Masses: The Story of Bonifacio and the Katipunan* (Quezon City: University of the Philippines, 1956), pp. 126-129.

otherwise." [10] Corruption and graft in government do not stem from the character of the Filipino so much as from the efforts of the aliens, American and Chinese, to maintain their economic power. Those Filipinos who represent, protect, or advance foreign interests, as well as the "misguided few who cry for reforms conducted in comfort and without real sacrifice," are to be isolated and attacked. There follows the direct appeal to the Filipino—"What Filipino at one time or another has not felt a stranger, an outcast, in his own land" because of the domination of foreign (i.e., American) mores, taste, wealth, and power. Thus, nationalism emerges as a response to the challenge of history, as rewritten, and to the clamor of the "broad mass of the people" for a decisive change in existing society. But the "broad mass" is not to be confused with the electorate, which represents the interests of the Filipino people to only a limited degree. The nationalist must answer to the "invisible community," an abstraction meant to indicate the "free wish of the people."

The Manifesto recommends the abrogation of the parity amendment to the constitution, calls for the Philippinization of the educational system, and demands an independent—meaning neutralist—foreign policy and closer ties with Asian neighbors, presumably including mainland China. The Manifesto anticipates the opposition of the so-called antinationalists and spells out their argument. They will say that nationalism and communism resemble each other, they will support piecemeal reforms, not "transformation of society on the general level," they will oppose the planned industrialization of the country in favor of retaining colonial agriculture, they will not accept support from all and every nationalist movement (including Communists calling themselves Nationalists), and they do not believe in the people. Admittedly great though the odds are, "no foreign ruling class, however powerful and established, can long sustain itself against a militant and organized mass movement ably and conscientiously directed." The KMB Manifesto is obviously Marxist and Leninist in concept if not in jargon, and the hands that wrote it were probably the same as those that wrote the political

[10] KMB Manifesto, *Manila Chronicle,* May 1, 1959.

directives. The writers of the Manifesto dissected the weaknesses in Philippine society and by using a mixture of fact and fiction presented their analysis in such a way as to implement the political objectives of the KMB. The KMB, eventually unmasked by the Roman Catholic clergy, ceased to be an effective organization by the time Macapagal came to power.

The ideas contained in the political directives and the KMB Manifesto have also found an outlet in the pages of the *Manila Chronicle,* an important English language daily owned by members of the sugar bloc. This is not surprising, for the politics of the sugar bloc are opportunistic. They are designed to preserve the financial status of the sugar interests, which is natural, but on a basis of special privilege, which is expensive for the rest of the country. The sugar bloc (which should be distinguished from the sugar industry) has exercised its influence on politics by contributing to the campaign funds of both parties and by buying votes in the sugar districts. As recent revelations have shown, it has also used its political influence in the government to its own financial advantage. Before 1946 the sugar bloc opposed independence; but even when independence came, it managed to secure an extension of the sugar quota until 1974. Many think that the sugar bloc is trying to prepare the Philippines for trade with Communist China by advocating, through its controlled press, a neutralist foreign policy. There are reports that one high ranking member of the sugar bloc has already been to Peking. This explains why the *Manila Chronicle* has opened its columns to writers who maintain a heavy drumfire of criticism of the United States. There are other financially important Filipinos, owners of mass media and members of Congress, who have enlisted the help of left-wing intellectuals in achieving short-range goals, such as the expropriation of foreign-owned business under the cloak of nationalism or the slogans of the Filipino First movement. Each side in this alliance presumably assumes that it will control the other when the immediate task of expropriating foreign business is accomplished. The financial oligarchy, however, may find itself faced with a group of men who control labor and peasant unions and can call out thousands of students at will.

The Intellectual Climate

Difficult as it is to measure changes in the intellectual climate or to estimate exactly the degree of control that the underground Communist movement has established over mass organizations, there is no doubt, however, that the Communists have made progress on some fronts. In contrast with a few years back, certain leading Filipino writers today take it for granted that the Soviet Union has scientific leadership in the world, that Soviet achievements in education provide a working model for the Philippines, and that Europe may have more to offer than America as a cultural exemplar. While it cannot be given full credit, the left-wing has certainly helped to bring about a change in the image of America among the elite. Important politicians and publicists are questioning American motives in a way that was not common several years ago. The idea that to be pro-Filipino one must necessarily be anti-American and anti-imperialist came to be more and more acceptable under the Garcia administration. Student and labor organizations have gone on record with numberless resolutions condemning Western imperialism and colonialism, nuclear tests, and U.S. bases overseas. Demands for repeal of the parity amendment to the constitution and of the Laurel-Langley agreement, for revision of the Bell Trade Act, for disarmament and neutralism, are constantly kept before the public.

Some years ago, for example, it would have been unlikely that the question of Filipino student participation in the Vienna Youth Festival, sponsored by the World Federation of Democratic Youth, would become a national issue. The Department of Foreign Affairs had decided to ban participation by Filipino students in the Festival, and efforts were made to prevent the students from leaving the country under false pretenses. Whether this actually was wise is not the point. The reaction to the government's decision however, had all the earmarks of an organized campaign. The *Manila Chronicle* raised the hue and cry about a witch hunt and denounced the evidence of Communist subversion of schools and student organizations collected by the House Committee on Anti-Filipino Activities. The Council of

Elders, an informal group of highly respected citizens whose Action Committee was dominated by left-wing intellectuals, denounced the ban on travel to the Festival as "an insult to the intelligence of the country's youth." Several organizations dominated by the same men actually denied that the Festival was Communist sponsored. The systematic exploitation of opportunities of this sort has been very apparent.

An important aspect of the campaign to change the climate of opinion is the effort to establish an image of the United States as the jealous guardian of economic privileges in the Philippines, the enemy of any attempts made by Filipinos to break away from a colonial economy. In Political Transmission 15 much space was given to providing facts and figures about the Philippine economy in support of the contention that the United States has been drawing off the wealth of the islands for fifty years and is continuing to do so. There is no such thing as national communism, says Transmission 15, but Communists may be nationalists during the period of national liberation when the foreigner must be hated. When independence is secured, then nationalism ceases to be a progressive force. What the Communists are trying to do, as H. de la Costa points out, is to capture the elemental force of nationalism, bottle it up under pressure, and concentrate a thin but deadly stream of it upon a highly specialized and almost entirely negative object—United States imperialism.[11]

The various political transmissions are designed for the educated person, not the illiterate peasant. Most of the 87 tightly packed pages of Transmission 15 are devoted to a detailed, apparently scholarly effort to substantiate the thesis that foreigners, mainly Americans, are responsible for all the economic and other ills of the Philippines. The so-called facts and figures are exaggerated and the relationship between the two countries is misrepresented, but for those who want to believe that the ills of the Philippines are due entirely to the previous colonial relationship, the presentation is convincing. The case is so persuasively set forth that even those who do not have any emotional need to believe in this proposition join in the discussion of the figures

[11] Horatio de la Costa, "The Transmission on National Politics," *Philippine Studies,* cited, p. 42.

without realizing that they are accepting the basic assumption of colonial-type exploitation. "Even if the figures are cut by half, the story is still impressive" is a typical comment from an anti-Communist Filipino commentator. If the theme is accepted, figures can be sacrificed.

Although the Communists have not yet captured the ideological leadership in the Philippines, they have made some headway. It is now more difficult than it was before to maintain a moderate position, as the trend toward the polarization of politics makes itself felt. In the election of 1961 there was much more emphasis on the idea that those who were not in favor of Filipino First were antinationalist. If the Communists should succeed in imposing their own definition of nationalism on those groups and parties that claim a monopoly on that sentiment, the tide will turn very much in their favor. Much depends on how seriously the Macapagal administration tackles the problem of graft and corruption, accepting it as a Philippine responsibility rather than a legacy of imperialism. If real progress is made on this front, it would still be possible for a moderate rather than an extreme nationalism to survive. If no real progress is made in curbing corruption, then the polarization of politics will continue. In the meantime the Communists continue with every effort to control the mass organizations with which they can make their influence felt through strikes and violence.

The existence of a well-organized subversive group does not necessarily mean that it will bring communism to the Philippines through parliamentary means during the next few years. The Philippine Communists are facing some obstacles today that they did not have to face twenty-five years ago. The main one is that the Philippine government is thoroughly alerted to the danger of communism and has the great advantage of already having crushed one serious and widespread effort to seize power. Communists are better understood now as a local and an international phenomenon, and powerful domestic forces are aligned against them. The chances of the party being given legal recognition are not very high at present although it is possible to imagine changes in the climate of opinion resulting from supposed easing of cold-war tensions. For the time being the Philippine Communists have to operate without a legal branch, but this is not a crippling handicap for a movement that normally keeps the main part of its work underground. In many ways it is much more difficult to fight an illegal than a legal Communist party if only because the organizations it infiltrates and the ideas it promotes are harder to identify.

The Philippine army is certainly anti-Communist at present, and much of its prestige derives from the successful military campaigns against the Hukbalahaps. But the political training of the army is not necessarily proof against the spread of the Communist concept of the social content of nationalism. The Roman Catholic Church, the only other institution that is nationwide in organization, is certainly anti-Communist, but it has long since ceased to have an ideological monopoly. The secularization of the state under the American regime, the rise of a business and professional class, and the institutions of public education have tended to neutralize the influence of the church in politics. At the same time the decision of the Roman Catholic Church early in 1960 to denounce publicly the KMB from all its pulpits made it impossible for President Garcia to continue supporting the KMB and helped to bring the organization to an end. The organized church is still a formidable obstacle.

From the Communist point of view conditions today are in some ways actually more favorable than they were a quarter of a century ago. Since the war the Filipinos have established a large number of private colleges and universities run on commercial lines, which provide a shoddy education for thousands of students who cannot get into the University of the Philippines and the few other institutions with high standards. Many of the graduates of these diploma mills are unemployed and dissatisfied with their lot, a sort of intellectual proletariat, ripe for the picking by the Communists. From them come many of the active members of the party and the participants in front organizations. Nor do we need any Communist propaganda to emphasize the miserable condition of much of the peasantry and the large numbers of partially or totally unemployed peasants and workers. It would take only a slight depression in the economic condition of the people to destroy hope and multiply impoverishment beyond endurance. At the other end of the social scale, among the elite now in power or near the center of power, there are those who feel that Philippine nationalism can only be expressed by taking a course different from that of the United States and who therefore toy with anti-Americanism and neutralism.

The adjustment of the new Asian nations to each other, after the long isolation under imperial controls, is one of the revolutionary political facts of our time. Out of this have come mutual criticisms such as the differences over neutralism, cooperation such as the Colombo Plan, and alliances such as SEATO. There has also come a watchful competition between the new nations to find a workable solution to the problems of national development. The result is ideological confusion. Countries that are politically committed to the free world may be ideologically uncommitted, and vice versa. It is difficult to find our bearings; but it is quite clear that the Communists have engaged us on the most crucial issue of all, that of the Filipino view of the world, the place of the Filipino in it, and the shape of the future for the Filipino nationalist. Whoever captures Philippine nationalism, captures the Philippines. That is why the real struggle is about the attitudes of the elite and about the models of national development that will attract them. This is no abstract academic affair to which the United States need pay only lip service and then get on with military and economic aid.

The Macapagal Program and the Left Wing

The election of President Macapagal has given the Philippines a breathing space on the Communist issue. One big move in the parliamentary struggle, the effort to garner votes for the Nacionalistas with the help of front organizations appealing to nationalism (anti-American imperialism) and to Filipino First, did not succeed. Macapagal campaigned on a strong anti-Communist plank, accusing Garcia and the Nacionalista party of flirting with fellow-travelers and helping communism by neglecting the people. The Nacionalistas accused the Liberals of having perpetuated a colonial economy, the sole cause of corruption, by the arrangements they made with the United States in their previous administration. The Liberals accused the Nacionalistas of using nationalism as a smokescreen behind which to hide their corruption. Of the corruption there was no question.

The Macapagal administration is harder for the strategists of the parliamentary struggle to handle than was the Garcia administration because Macapagal gives the appearance of being genuinely nationalistic by such devices as shifting the date for the celebration of independence, canceling a trip to the United States, and deporting an American businessman. More important, he devalued the peso, thus eliminating a great deal of corruption, began to force the pace of economic growth with the help of foreign investments, and included in his plans some measure of improvement in agriculture. In many ways he is the most formidable sort of enemy the Communists could have because he promulgated a vigorous, moderate, reform program. If his program meets with any measure of success, it will be that much more difficult to bring about the polarization of political life that the Communists want.

The Communists, however, have something to work with. They can be expected to make the most gains where the administration is weakest, which is in its ideology. They will press the battle of ideas in the labor unions, the front organizations, the schools and colleges, the press and magazines, the literary and artistic world, and in foreign affairs. Political Transmission 17, captured in 1961, repeated the earlier directives to infiltrate labor unions, suggested forming organizations using the names of national heroes, and urged, for the first time in many years, resumption of the armed struggle. Assuming that the paramilitary organization has been carefully rebuilt since the defeat of the Huks, it would be quite logical for the Communists to start enough guerrilla warfare to increase the military budget and to distract attention from Viet-Nam.

According to one of the transmissions, the revolution in the Philippines is in the national-democratic stage, not the bourgeois-democratic. By national is meant national liberation, by democratic is meant control of capitalism and radical agrarian changes. The correct policy for the Communist party, therefore, is not to form a united front with the middle class in a struggle against foreign imperialism and native feudal elements but to prepare, by legal and parliamentary means, for the violent seizure of power. While the careful preparations for guerrilla warfare proceed in secrecy, the task of psychological warfare during this period is to create the appropriate conditions in society. Communist objectives have been described as involving a long-range effort to create in the ruling, upper, and intellectual classes of non-Communist societies, frustration, confusion, pessimism, guilt, fear, defeatism, hopelessness, and neurosis—in essence, the psychological destruction of anti-Communist leadership. Communists try to split a society into many competing and mutually hostile groups and to sap the spirit of loyalty, community, mutual helpfulness, positive expectation, and willingness to take risks and to act. They seek to create an all-pervading sense of fear and anxiety and to secure semantic domination of intellectual, emotional, and socio-political life as well as the semantic control of all political arguments.[12]

The Communists made substantial progress during the 1950s in the semantic domination of public discussion by taking advantage of the very natural and necessary interest of the Filipino in re-examining his relation to the United States and to the countries of Asia, as well as of his search for national identity. One result of some political importance is the tendency to leave the intellectual skirmishing with Communists to the writers and journals of the Roman Catholic Church. The non-Communist intellectuals, who should be disposing of Communist nonsense in their books, articles, and classrooms, are usually anticlerical, and because many of them think that clericalism and the church, which the Communists denounce, are the greater danger, they are neutral and unaggressive. The Catholic hierarchy still carries great weight, but it is inclined to be associated with the traditional order of things in spite of such exceptional leadership as that of Father Hogan among the dockworkers and Father Mauri among the farmers in the promotion of unionism. It is not likely to become the modernizing intellectual elite. Another very signi-

[12] FERREUS, "The Menace of Communist Psychological Warfare," *ORBIS*, A quarterly journal of world affairs, v. 1, no. 1, April 1957, pp. 118-119.

ficant trend, especially among politicians, is to denounce all suggestions of social reform, especially anything connected with the land, as Communist inspired. Nothing could please the Communists more, for those hardy spirits who want to do something about widespread unemployment, extremes of poverty and wealth, social injustice, and limited educational opportunities are potential recruits to the underground organization since they are going to be labelled as Communists in any case.

The level of political discussion in the Philippines is as high as that in any other Asian country. But some feel it would be much higher if there were a political party with a social ideology distinct from that of the two major parties, a party that would campaign for a total overhaul of the Philippine socio-political structure. The editor of *Comment,* a lively journal of opinion, suggests that there should be a socialist party, a workers' or farmers' party which, though it might never get into power, would stimulate the other parties to carry out part of its program.[13] The labor unions and the peasant unions are already politically inclined and have discussed socialist ideas for many years. In dealing with the parliamentary struggle, the middle class would do well not to denounce a new socialist party, if one arises on the British model, as it might well be better qualified than any other to do the front-line fighting with the Communists in the factories and in the fields. When we recall that the Philippine Communist party opened its first congress in 1931 with only forty delegates, and that fifteen years later it challenged the government with a well-trained army and extensive mass support, and that it came close to being successful, it is well not to underestimate the power of ideas and the capacity of the Filipino for large-scale organization when strongly motivated and ably led.

The United States can hardly remain indifferent to the manner in which the battle of ideas is being fought. It should be clear that this is no time in Philippine history to press for nonpolitical unionism in theory or in practice. Some Filipino labor leaders have come to realize that they have more to learn from the British than from the American models of trade unionism with respect to

[13] F. Sionil Jose, "Commentary: Old Threats, New Tactics," *Comment,* no. 14, First Quarter, 1962 (Manila: Regal Printing Co., Inc.), pp. 3, 92-96.

participation in politics. There is much that trade union organizations in the United States and Britain can do to help these Filipino unionists who want to avoid domination by Communists.

In the realm of ideas, as expressed in books, journals, and the mass media, the United States is not seriously engaged. Despite the fact that most Filipinos who have been educated abroad have received that education in the United States, there is really remarkably little intellectual discourse between the two countries. There is more interest in the Philippines today among American social scientists than there was before the war, but it is still not very significant, and in the Philippines the universities have been eliminating courses on American history, literature, and politics. The two countries do not give the impression that they are talking with each other, and there is so very much to talk about. The combination of blandness and patronage that marks so much of the intellectual relationship between the two countries is very deceptive. Because of the past, Americans have to make a special effort to realize that Philippine political ideas, literature, and art are not all derivative. They may be in form, but not in substance. Beneath the surface there is going on in the Philippines an intellectual renascence, fed by nationalism, which can only partly be measured by the changing tone of the noisy press and the struggling journals. It is not easy, but it is very important for American citizens to be engaged in this intellectual life much more than they are today. Members of American government agencies in the Philippines are suspect, and American businessmen have never shown much interest in Philippine cultural and intellectual life. The establishment of a Philippine American Cultural Foundation, with a fine building and facilities, may do no harm, but it is likely to be too official and social to reflect the whole range of intellectual life among all classes of the people. Some of the responsibility for intellectual understanding and cooperation undoubtedly rests with the universities. It is the mark of a free society, however, that contact can take place on every level. For our own good as well as for the good of the Philippines it is high time that the United States showed as much interest in the intellectual and cultural life of its ally as it does in its strategic, economic, and political significance.

Chapter 14

Postlude:
Prospects and Problems

U.S. policy toward the Philippines assumes that the interest of the Philippines is to stay within the association of free nations and that there is no fundamental conflict between Philippine national interest and our own; the two are complementary. If this is true, the United States has everything to gain from the successful maturation of the Macapagal social and economic program and everything to lose from its failure.

While the cold war has created issues, such as the status of U.S. forces in the islands and the amount of economic and military aid, that would not otherwise have interposed themselves in the relations between the two countries as major problems, the pressures of the cold war have also induced us to meet other problems that owe nothing to the existence of the Soviet bloc with greater boldness and imagination than otherwise would have been called forth. The shabby treatment of the Philippines in 1946 illustrated the tepid condition of U.S. political and moral obligations to a former colony. It stands out in sharp contrast with the vigorous efforts to energize the Philippine economy that marked U.S. policy after the Korean conflict began. Because Filipinos realize that U.S. policy might change if the threat of communism to U.S. security should decline, they have, as it were, a vested interest in the continuation of the cold war. So long as present dangers persist, it is to be hoped that we can convince the Filipinos that what is good for the United States is good for the Philippines. We have to assume that the Filipinos understand that the United States has to do what is best for its own national interest and that there may be occasions in the future when policies might change, and for this the Philippines must be prepared.

A Special Relationship

Such considerations make it advisable to examine, from the point of view of U.S. policy, the "special" relations between the two countries. The very existence of this long relationship helps to perpetuate certain attitudes that took shape under the colonial period. Some of these are constructive: for example, the feeling that American pride is involved in the success or failure of the Philippine experiment, the powerful sentiment of kinship with an Asian people beside whom Americans have fought and suffered in a long war, the many personal friendships between Americans and Filipinos. Other attitudes can be disruptive, one being the persisting view that the Philippines should be a little America, a show window of democracy. There is also the benevolent paternalism, coupled with tough economic bargaining for U.S. advantage and the jealous tendency to resent other than American influences in the Philippines. These attitudes stem directly from the sentimental brutality that marked the conquest and occupation. Americans tend to take Filipino friendship so much for granted that signs of danger that should stimulate action are not taken seriously.

That a basic friendship between the two peoples can be assumed is borne out by the subjective evidence of individual relationships. Buttressing it is a remarkable degree of agreement on foreign policy matters between the two governments, including memories of cooperation in the anti-Japanese war and the Korean conflict. Americans share with Filipinos important values; they feel more at home in the Philippines than in any other Asian country. This is a privileged relationship, and not all Americans are aware of its quality.

The Filipino, as has been pointed out, does not think of friendship in the same way as the American unless he is emancipated from Philippine society to an unusual degree. He tends to think of the relationship within the framework of values that he knows best—those of the kinship system. He looks on the American as a compadre; he thinks of the relationship as being somehow a "special" one. The richer partner, like the richer relative, is expected to support the poorer and show his leadership by granting favors and gifts. In return for this the poorer relation can be called upon for such services as he is in a position to render. This does not match the American concept of friendly relationships. What looks to the American like mendicancy on the part of the Filipino is in his view the natural and rightful request of a relative. The issue of Philippine bases for American armed forces, for example, is to the American a cooperative participation in mutual defense, but the Filipino may think of the bases as an exchange for economic aid. The danger is that the Filipinos may have unrealistic expectations of the rewards and obligations involved which the United States cannot meet on such premises. Though the Philippines most certainly has a special and possibly unique place in U.S. relations with Asia, it would be dangerous to perpetuate by word or deed the Philippine view of what a "special relationship" involves. Such a relationship can be as fragile as it is intense, for according to Philippine values the man who does not fulfill his obligations within the kinship group is a social outcast, worthy of the utmost contempt and entitled to little mercy.

In this delicate balance between like and dislike it may be necessary gently but firmly to make it clear that the United States respects pride, independence, and nationalist spirit and will have no truck with less admirable traits, of which Filipinos have their share. It is even important to create an atmosphere in which open criticism of the United States by those who are friendly can be freely and naturally expressed, if only to deny a monopoly of the field to those who are not so friendly. This cannot be done if Americans play personal or party politics or adopt a paternalistic attitude. The American can help establish an appropriate relationship when he is an incorruptible, detached, but accessible mediator, adviser, and ally. If older Filipinos still speak with admiration of some of the governors-general, it is because they demonstrated these qualities. Today, it is the ambassador who can set the tone. If this is done successfully the old relationship can lead, not to difficulties and misunderstandings, but to a new partnership of great significance for the Philippines and for Asia. For if the minimum objective of U.S. policy is to prevent the Philippines from becoming a Communist state, the maximum is to develop to the full the enormous potential contribution that the Filipinos can make to the free world.

Where shall our sights be set? Judged by the copybook standards of American democracy, Philippine shortcomings are only too obvious and sometimes lead Americans to unnecessary despair. Judged by the standards of Eastern Asia, the Philippines has important elements of political strength and some of the essential characteristics of a democracy. Judged by historical perspectives, the Philippines is not unusual, for no nation has ever developed to maturity without violence, corruption, greed, and injustice.

What then can be expected? First, we can expect that the period of development on which the Filipinos have now embarked will be turbulent, for there is bound to be class struggle, social dislocation, and economic imbalance whether the Philippines is achieving economic growth or retreating in the face of insoluble problems. Second, we can expect these problems to be compounded by the efforts of the Communists to create conditions for the seizure of power not only in the Philippines, but also in other parts of Southeast Asia. Third, we can foresee that the world tendency toward the creation of supranational organizations for economic and political purposes will have far-reaching effects. The Philippines will have to make some difficult choices with respect to its Asian neighbors. Fourth, there is only one class in the Philippines that has the motivation, the knowledge, and the opportunity to force the pace of economic growth and take the leadership in social change. This is the middle class, broadly defined to include politicians and entrepreneurs, the professions, government servants, the managers, and the intellectuals.

The Objectives of Policy

In order to achieve both the minimum and maximum objectives, U.S. policy should concentrate every means at its disposal on supporting, guiding, and cooperating with those Filipinos who are capable of satisfying the aspirations of their people within the framework of democratic values and institutions. Reduced to its simplest and most concrete terms, U.S. policy is concerned with that group of middle-class Filipino men and women who are now the leaders in education, literature, research, science, labor, industry, commerce, law, and medicine, and who have a share in government and politics. The United States has a stake in their values, their courage, and their abilities. U.S. policy will best be served if the Filipinos are able to build a healthy society, a task that calls for considerable administrative reform, modernization of agriculture, a diversified economy, a rapid rate of economic growth, control of population, restoration of universal education, and above all, a self-respecting national spirit. The men and women who can do these things cannot be conjured forth, but the United States can choose between policies that further and those that obstruct the conditions under which such persons can emerge and succeed. The problem is how to assist these men and women in achieving power, and, once this is done, how to protect them from domestic and foreign enemies.

There is an amazing amount of agreement between American observers that the main problem in the Philippines is the need for honest, responsible, and dynamic leadership. This is the burden of confidential political surveys no less than of missionary journals; it is expressed in one way by the sophisticated political analyst and in another by the American who unfortunately still thinks of the Filipino as his little brown brother. They all mean the same thing, and they are quite correct.

Most of the responsible American businessmen in Manila feel that the Filipinos are now in control of their economy and are quite capable of running it if they are not interfered with by U.S. economic aid missions and their own government. The tendency in many large business concerns has been, for many years, to replace senior American management personnel with Filipinos as contracts expire, and for present needs there is a sufficient number of well-trained Filipino technicians and professional men to make it possible to reduce American technical assistance to a minimum. According to more objective evidence, the Filipinos already have control over their economy if we count as "alien" business only that which is in the hands of non-Filipino citizens. To some extent this begs the question, for many naturalized Filipinos behave as if they were members of a minority group, but whether or not they continue to behave this way depends in some measure on Filipino businessmen and politicians. Certainly Filipinos have increased their own investment in the economy. According to one study,

In 1946 Filipino capital accounted for about 50% of the ₱.45,000,000 total investments in new firms. Chinese accounted for one-third, and Americans one-ninth. Over the years, the amount of Filipino investment has increased by sevenfold, the Chinese has doubled, and the American remained negligible. By 1960, Filipino investment in newly registered businesses amounted to about 85% of the total.[1]

The increased entrepreneurial opportunities in the 1950s were exploited more by those who already had a start in manufacturing or commerce and were able to take advantage of the opportunities to make money during the 1950s, when political influence was almost a *sine qua non* for economic success. Although there are obviously successful entrepreneurs in the Philippines, it would still be dangerous to overestimate the extent and aggressiveness of the capitalistic spirit as distinguished from a natural acquisitiveness in exploiting opportunities created by political influence. Without going into Max Weber's views on the correlation of Protestantism and entrepreneurship or into the development of capitalism in modern Roman Catholic countries it seems quite certain that any middle class must have the outlook and the qualities necessary for entrepreneurial success, whatever accommodation it may have made with kinship or religious values.

[1] David Zenoff, "A New Look at Economic Nationalism," *Philippine Studies*, v. 10, no. 1, April 1962 (Published quarterly by the School of Law, Ateneo de Manila), p. 116.

To support the leadership of the Philippine middle class is to accept certain risks. The middle class is not very strong, nor will it necessarily show the qualities of leadership that are called for; but without the support of the United States its chances of success would be very slender indeed. As Reinhold Neibuhr has pointed out, two political conditions seem to be necessary if democratic institutions are to survive in a developing industrial society. One is that the middle classes be strong enough to break the mold of the traditional society dominated by landed wealth or to adjust the landed aristocracy to the requirements of a commercial and industrial economy. The second condition is that the grant of new liberties and rights to the industrial workers shall not be so long delayed as to invite rebellion against the standards of democracy. When these two conditions have not been met, democratic governments have not achieved health and maturity.[2] Germany had to lose two world wars before she could rid herself of a military aristocracy. Not until defeat and occupation did Japan shake off the military class that led her into war. Yet both countries had large, wealthy, and technically proficient middle classes. The Philippines does not have to shake off a military class of the German or Japanese variety, but it has a still powerful landed oligarchy which must be dealt with in some way.

In the Philippines, which suffered defeat and occupation half a century before Japan, the power of the landed oligarchy was not broken, but other changes occurred in politics and society that now make it possible for a vigorous middle class with strong leadership to bring about rapid economic growth without domestic violence. Possible, but not inevitable. When social forces are uneasily balanced, as they are in the Philippines, the quality of leadership may well be the decisive factor. President Macapagal is the first president of the Philippines who openly presented himself as the leader of the middle class and who shows signs of understanding the need for allies among the working class and the peasantry. Whether he succeeds or not in his stated objectives, revolutionary changes in the Philippines are now

[2] *The Wall Street Journal,* August 9, 1961, p. 10.

gathering momentum and are bound to come with even greater speed.

It is wiser for the U.S. to anticipate and encourage change and to influence and guide it than to support those elements that resist it on principle and are sure to be swept aside. Such a policy calls for considerable U.S. participation in the internal affairs of the Philippines, always a dangerous business. The risks must be taken unless we are willing to let our military and political alliance disintegrate and to accept either a neutralist or a Communist Philippines. A partnership as all-embracing as the one between the United States and the Philippines must either go forward to the development of its full potential or become an empty shell.

A general strategy of supporting the middle class calls for an understanding of its composition, outlook, and characteristics. We have seen that the Philippine middle class is not identical with the industrial and commercial strata of English society that came into power with the Reform Act of 1832, ready to put into practice the classical liberalism of nineteenth century England; nor is it like the bourgeoisie of Bismarckian Germany. It includes Roman Catholics, anticlerical intellectuals, Protestants, and members of the Aglipay and the Igglesia in Christo churches. Many have studied in the United States, and the majority are college educated. It includes the leaders of labor and peasant unions, most of whom are lawyers, some of the clergy, officers in the armed services, and many members of Congress. Its beliefs include the strong property concepts of classical liberalism, as well as the doctrines of natural law of the American revolution and a Hamiltonian view of the relation between government and business. There is very little Jeffersonian democracy and not much public spirit in them. Those who make up the middle class are concentrated rather heavily in the Manila area, and they are the main exponents of the spirit of nationalism.

There are several reasons why the United States has to take this nationalism very seriously. First, it is the only sentiment that can galvanize the middle class into effective leadership. Second, nationalism is essential to provide the political dynamism that is

necessary to bring about important social changes. Third, nationalism is the most effective weapon against the Communist
movement. Fourth, nationalism can help provide that sense of
community which the Philippines must acquire if it is to become a mature, self-reliant nation, proud and conscious of its
own heritage. Last, courses of action based on resisting or discouraging nationalism are demonstrably self-defeating. If there
were some other sentiment that could produce an adequate sense
of community in the Philippines, it would be preferable to nationalism, but there is no alternative. Philippine nationalism has
several unusual features when compared with nationalism in
other Asian countries. It came to terms with American imperialism some years ago in a peaceful manner, and it is remarkably
free from vulgar Marxism. While it is not inflamed by xenophobia, there is always the possibility that it could quite easily
turn against the Chinese in the Philippines.

During the administration of President Garcia the Filipino
First movement seemed, on the surface, to provide a mature approach to nationalism. President Garcia claimed that it was designed to give to Filipinos every advantage in trade and commerce and to make the Philippines a self-reliant, dignified, united,
and proudly independent nation. This was to be achieved by
steadily reducing control of the economy by alien interests,
mainly Chinese, but also American. Taken at face value, there
was nothing wrong with the Filipino First movement, but the
crude efforts of the left-wing intellectuals to use it to arouse anti-
American feeling on the basis of "colonialism" discredited the
movement and helped lead to its defeat in the election of 1961.

The Filipino First movement was defeated in the rural areas
where few votes are won by anti-American appeals. Why is this
so? Why is it difficult to persuade the peasant that his miseries
stem from colonialism? It is not because the peasant loves the
United States even if he may like individual Americans. He
has difficulty in comprehending the idea of a Philippines, let
alone of a United States of America. Nor is it because he is
concerned mainly with immediate economic issues. It is more
likely that the peasant did not understand what the Filipino

First propagandists were talking about because they were presenting him with two interrelated concepts, nationalism and anticolonialism, neither of which he understood or cared about. But the miseries of the peasant will persist, and nationalism is bound to reach him sooner or later. What form that nationalism will take when the peasant finally feels that it has meaning for him is very important for U.S. policy. Will he acquire his sense of belonging to the Philippine community by cooperating in the building of a new society, or will his involvement come through class war, xenophobia, and sloganized ignorance? When the right appeals are made, the fact that the peasant, like most other Filipinos, puts economic questions ahead of nationalism will be no protection against the Filipino First type of appeal. On the contrary, the drives for economic betterment, or just plain survival, are potentially of tremendous explosive power. The middle class, therefore, must have both the practical solutions to the main economic problems of the Philippines and the gift to present its program in terms that can release the social energies of the people. Part of the problem for U.S. policy is that the middle class does not speak with one voice or fully understand how urgent it is to reach the peasant and the worker before the Communists capture them. These are matters in which a friendly ally can be helpful.

The targets of U.S. information and cultural activities should be those men and women who are formulating, in words and in actions, the social and political policies of the middle class, especially those directed toward workers and peasants. The open participation of the U.S. embassy in such matters is probably not the best way to go about it, but the embassy can do much by indirect means to engage American universities, labor unions, foundations, and leading public men in an intellectual discourse with key Filipinos. To take an example of private initiative in these matters, a small American foundation is concentrating its efforts on finding or providing opportunities for the training of specialists in agricultural economics and community development. This is being done quietly, unhurriedly, and with the essential element of continuity and personal attention.

Transforming Philippine Society

Too few Americans realize how important it is to give moral and intellectual support to the leaders of an underdeveloped country, for leadership inevitably involves some degree of alienation from the traditional social values. Societies do not change easily, and those who undertake to force the process of change need a conceptual framework in which they have confidence and which is relevant to their problems. It is very much to our interest, as it is to that of the Philippines, that we bring about an increase both in the quality and the quantity of intellectual discourse between the two countries. There is actually very little discourse at present. One reason is the persistence, on our side, of the teacher-student relationship; another is the fact that there are very few Americans in the Philippines other than officials, some businessmen, and a few tourists; a third reason is that some of the best Filipino minds are found on the left wing and are hard to engage. In spite of appearances to the contrary, far too much of the serious discussion of social and political issues goes on out of range of Americans in the Philippines. It should be a matter of policy to devise ways and means of increasing our intellectual communication and cooperation with the Filipinos.

Some sort of judgment about the relationship between technological advancement, which can be easily imposed on a society, and the growth of a sense of community is always necessary, for they can get dangerously out of balance. It is probably impossible to guarantee harmony between cultural growth and economic advancement, but it is still the course of wisdom to avoid obvious pitfalls. One of the pitfalls, which U.S. policy is often accused of stumbling into, is to develop the means of intellectual and physical communication in an underdeveloped country without first having a political program with which to exploit them. There have been occasions when Communists have successfully taken advantage of technical improvements for which the United States advanced the credit and provided the know-how. Hence the importance of improving our intellectual communication with the leaders of the middle class and of enabling them to draw upon the moral and spiritual resources of the free world in order to clarify their own sense of direction and improve their strategy and tactics.

Another pitfall is the temptation to undertake vast material improvements, such as rural electrification or building and staffing technical schools, both of which have been suggested, in the expectation that environmental changes will bring about desired cultural and moral changes. Such undertakings may do more harm than good if they are not high on the list of Philippine priorities and unless the Filipinos contribute substantially to their achievement. For example, the artesian wells that the government drilled and gave to the barrios are neglected, but those that the peasants in the barrios helped to construct are well taken care of.

With these warnings in mind, it is clearly possible, by making changes in the environment, to hasten changes in values. High on the list is improvement in the quality and quantity of public education, a matter in which we are now helping and can help much more if the Filipinos want us to. Education certainly needs attention if the Filipinos really wish to speed up economic growth. Population increase alone demands 300,000 new jobs every year, yet present vocational schools can fill only one-quarter of these, and the training is of poor quality. When 75 per cent of all children at the secondary level are not attending school, democracy is not on a very firm foundation. The United States can encourage the Filipinos to improve their educational system, perhaps, by decentralizing administrative and financial responsibility, or by introducing rigorous measures for accreditation and for certification of instructors in order to raise the standards of schools and colleges, particularly in the "diploma mills"; but it cannot compel them to adopt such measures. Only through education, in the long run, can the Philippines build up a national sense of community, and only then if the education is basically the same for all and available for all. Public education is the main hope for bringing minority groups, such as the Moslems and the unassimilated Chinese, into the larger community.

U.S. policy is very much concerned with the problem of the unassimilated Chinese, potentially the most explosive minority group of all. There is no assurance that the leaders of the middle class will have the wisdom to handle the Chinese problem through public education, as there is a strong temptation to take short-range advantage of the Chinese. Powerful monopolies that want to get their money out of the enterprises that will suffer when full tariff restrictions come into effect in 1974 will keep up the pressure to take over the profitable businesses of the Chinese, and this will make a statesmanlike approach all the more difficult. There is every reason, therefore, for U.S. policy to encourage the Filipinos to make it attractive for Chinese to become citizens and to strengthen their Philippine educational system enough to facilitate the absorption of the new citizens. The explosiveness of anti-Chinese sentiment among Filipinos is very serious because most of the resident Chinese support Taiwan, and we can expect Communist agents in the Philippines to encourage anti-Chinese feelings in order to make it difficult for the government to uphold a sane and sensible policy toward the Chinese.

Support of economic growth along the lines of the social and economic program of the Macapagal administration is a high priority for U.S. policy. The willingness to help has been there from the beginning. In the words of A. D. Calhoun, president of the Philippine-American Chamber of Commerce,

President Macapagal demonstrated political courage in departing radically from former nationalistic excesses, and he expected all the encouragement, morally and financially, that the United States could give to his nation. The American Government, the International Monetary Fund, and private banking interests as well, did indeed respond with generous credits to shore up the financial condition of the country. . . .[3]

The Philippines has always had available, on the same terms as other countries, the resources of the free world as well as the special concern of the United States. But it has not always been ready to use them. The problem is still one of getting the middle class to support the Macapagal program and then pushing the necessary measures through the Congress.

The most delicate problem, in view of the importance of

[3] *Hearings,* Committee on Foreign Relations, U.S. Senate, S.2380 and S.3329, 87th Cong., June 12, 21, 1962, pp. 31-32.

agrarian reform to the development of industry, is that of bringing about improvements in agriculture. If the will is there, the technical problems are not serious. Not only is there much sound legislation on the books in the Philippines, but the Filipinos also know well how to go about making investment in industry more attractive than the purchase of land merely for rent, security, and status. Filipinos know, moreover, what can be done to improve production by the application of science and capital to agriculture for profit. Some land has produced 287 cavans per hectare instead of the average 25 cavans. If measures are taken in time, there is every reason to think that it is possible to remove the obstacles to agricultural improvement in a way that makes it profitable for both landlord and tenant and at the same time avoids the drastic solutions that have been tried before. Taiwan has been quite successful in establishing a tax structure that facilitates the movement of capital from land to industry, as well as in applying science and capital to the land. All that is required in the Philippines is the will and the power. The legislation limiting landholdings and regulating sharecropping, to take only two examples, is not enforced because there is too much opposition in Congress and too little authority in the hands of local units of government where only the pork barrel allotments from Manila can provide the funds to solve the most modest problems of local livelihood.[4]

In March 1963 President Macapagal presented to the Congress an "Act to Institute Land Reforms in the Philippines, including the Abolition of Tenancy and the Channeling of Capital into Industry, Provide for the Necessary Implementary Agencies, Appropriate Funds Therefor and for Other Purposes." In his message to Congress the President made it clear that he did not favor expropriation, that the landlord must receive assets which are more attractive than land, and that farmers will eventually become owners of the land they till. The landlords will be paid in government land bonds and stocks. The government will acquire, either through direct purchase or expropriation, private land now idle or abandoned, land owned by absentee landlords and

[4] Albert Ravenholt, "Why Cardona Wants Electricity," *American University Field Staff Reports,* Southeast Asia Series, v. IX, no. 3, July 1961.

operated by leaseholders, and land in excess of the statutory retention limits. The objective is a country of owner-operated fam-
ily-size farms and an agricultural leasehold system instead of
share-tenancy. A Land Authority will handle the sale or expropriation of land and a Land Bank will finance its acquisition by
paying the landowner 70 per cent in the form of land bonds and
30 per cent in stocks. The government proposed setting up agencies to provide cheap credit to farmers, to assist in the improvement of agricultural techniques and to help with legal problems.
This bold program, if sufficiently well advertised in the countryside, can bring in a rich harvest of peasant votes at election time,
sufficient, perhaps, to force it through a reluctant Congress and
to give some hope of its implementation.[5]

The middle class will need the cooperation of the workers and
the peasants in order to achieve its objectives, and the United
States can use its influence in helping the middle class secure
their cooperation. This means, in effect, working with the leaders of the peasant and labor unions. The less the U.S. government and its official representatives are directly involved in such
contacts the better, but they can do a great deal behind the scenes.
Some small foundations, such as The Asia Foundation, have long
been active in the field of labor, and so, to some extent, has the
Roman Catholic Church. But the international labor organizations and the U.S. unions are best equipped to bring the thinking
of the Filipino union leaders into line with that of their counter-
parts in the free world. In this general strategy the AID mission
has given substantial financial help to the office of Presidential
Assistant on Community Development (PACD), which has
nearly 2,000 workers in the field and is doing something, although far from enough, to develop democracy at the grass roots.
If this work could be increased considerably, it might well help
the peasant in planning for his own economic welfare.

The union leaders have a lot to learn about democratic practices within the union and about the laws of economic growth.
By following unenlightened policies, the unions can do much to
obstruct the very economic developments which will be beneficial

[5] See the excellent discussion by Teodoro M. Locsin, "Land for the Land-
less, Capital for Industry, Social Stability," *Free Press*, March 23, 1963.

to them in the long run however painful they may be in the short run. The union leaders have two choices. They can follow the road established by the American unions in the 1930s—the greater the production, the greater the benefits for all; or they can use as a model some of the European unions, which means class war. Mr. Harry Bridges, of the International Longshoremen's and Warehousemen's Union, who understands these matters very well, has had his agents working among the labor unions in the Philippines for several years. There is some difference of opinion as to the extent to which the Filipino union leaders are politically inclined to the left, but there is no doubt that many of them are following policies indistinguishable from those of the Communist party. On this battleground the fate of the economic plans might well be settled.

There is the possibility that in alliance with middle class intellectuals the labor and peasant unions might be successful in establishing a Socialist party in the Philippines. Philippine political parties may come to resemble more the Western German or Italian models than the American as the social and economic struggle gets more and more intense, as it is bound to become, and one might see Philippine Social-Democrats or Christian Socialists. Such a development would change the character of Philippine politics and present the United States with opportunities that should not be missed. If such a party should emerge, the United States should use every means at its disposal to make sure that the socialism is democratic in theory and practice. The advice and assistance of some of our European allies would be of use, for the United States has had little experience with a successful anti-Communist Socialist party. It would be a great mistake, even if such a party were strongly infiltrated by Communists, to surrender the organization to them. From the point of view of U.S. policy the course of wisdom will be to keep communications open to any party, however socialistic, so long as it is anti-Communist. The policy of the United States must be directed toward keeping in the driver's seat a combination of men and parties that might be called the political "middle," and toward preventing the Communists from bringing about the polarization of Philippine politics. As the Filipinos are usually undiscriminating in charging political foes with Communist leanings, thus making it more difficult to distinguish between Communist and non-Communist, the implementation of such a policy will require of Americans in Manila and Washington considerable courage and high political skill.

The policy of giving moral, political, and material support to the middle class involves more than the complex coordination of U.S. political and economic measures. It must also be integrated with U.S. policy toward the Philippine military establishment. There are two reasons for this: one is that the Philippine military can do a great deal to help in the development of the country; and the other is that if the middle class fails, the military will take over either with or in opposition to the Communists. It is very important, therefore, that the Philippine military should continue to be democratic in outlook, support the constitution, and back the right kind of nationalism.

There is a widespread disposition among Americans and Filipinos to take the loyalty and competence of the armed forces for granted. The army played a decisive role in the elimination of the Huks and at no time threatened a *coup d'état* on the Burmese or Korean model. The important aspect of the army's achievement against the Huks was not strictly military, it was the enforcement by Magsaysay of a social and political plan. If conditions in the Philippines should deteriorate, and if the politicians again are unable to handle the situation, then it will make a great deal of difference whether the armed forces are still able to fight Communist guerrillas as they did before. For this reason the United States should do everything possible to keep alive in the Philippine armed forces a concept of their mission that is more than strictly military. The armed forces of the Philippines should be a strong ally of a revolutionary middle class, a source of the political dynamism that can provide the only military security in the sort of struggle that is now taking place in so many parts of Southeast Asia and from which the Philippines may not be any freer in the future than it has been in the past.

The course for U.S. policy to pursue is fortunately clear. It is to emphasize the contribution that the Filipinos have made in the past to both the theory and practice of counterinsurrection and which they now are making in the operations in Southeast Asia. It is to de-emphasize the concept of a conventional defense establishment with prestige weapons in pale imitation of our own. To the extent that this policy already is being implemented it is easier for counterinsurgency to be accepted by the Philippine armed forces as something in which they can specialize without loss of prestige. It is as a leader in the art of counterinsurrection that the Filipino might well bridge the gap between the United States and Asia, an idea that some Filipino politicians have often advanced in propagandistic and superficial political terms. In the villages of Southeast Asia the Filipinos have already shown what they can do as military technicians and as doctors and nurses in Operation Brotherhood. Their unashamed friendship for the Americans with whom they worked, as well as the quality of their contribution to the most arduous kind of warfare, are tremendous assets for the free world.

In counterinsurrectionary activities the Filipinos are getting daily experience in the task of bringing government and people together in joint undertakings, in creating confidence, and in changing social and political relationships. They become experts in what the army calls "Civic Action." But there is irony in the situation, for there is need in the Philippines itself for the skills of the Filipino men and women who are giving so much to the people of other countries where the struggle with Communist insurrection is now urgent. The more the armed forces of the Philippines specialize in counterguerrilla warfare, the more the Magsaysay tradition will persist and the more competent the armed forces will be to assist the middle class to succeed or to save the situation if it does not. The social revolution in the Philippines may well be won in the jungles of Viet-Nam.

A Rationale for American Partnership

Certain assumptions about the way in which change occurs in underveloped countries have now eroded and must be definitely discarded. Among them is the commonly held philosophy that, given capital and technical assistance, social change and modernization will take care of themselves. If the door is opened to the future, it is assumed that all will rush in. Americans naturally tend to project on to other societies the values and experiences of their own. Americans never had to fight feudalism, and they began the battle against nature with weapons that had already been forged. Seeing the world in optimistic terms, they expect that social forces in Asia will behave as they do in the United States, where social mobility is high, social change is expected and welcomed, increasing production is considered a supreme good, and the rule of law is a fact of life. Few of these things are true of Asia, but aid is often given on the assumption that they are. All societies that are not industrial democracies are labeled as traditional or transitional, terms that define nothing but imply that all pre-industrial democracies are similar, which is nonsense except to the Communists, who still believe in the unilinear theory of societal development. The problem at the heart of economic growth is the value system and our main objective is therefore to provide incentive, will, and leadership.

To focus our efforts on the leaders of the middle class and the armed forces is not to imitate the approach of the Soviet Union. The Soviet approach, which is political in a very special way, is to use any and every device, including massive doses of foreign aid, to secure for the local Communist party complete control over the social process. The revolution begins after, not before, the seizure of power. Whereas the Soviets will pervert and exploit existing values in order to gain power, the U.S. approach is to promote conditions in which the new values will come to dominate. The revolution takes place before, and leads up to, the acquisition of power. If the middle class should come to lead the Philippine revolution successfully, it would do what it had promised and would not suddenly reveal a hidden set of values and objectives as would the Communists. It is neither possible nor desirable to equate U.S. methods and objectives with those of the Communists, for the ultimate political objectives differ and the means are not subordinate to the ends.[6]

[6] Lucian W. Pye, "Soviet and American Styles in Foreign Aid," *ORBIS*, A Quarterly Journal of World Affairs, v. 14, no. 2, July 1960, pp. 159-173. See also, Morton Kaplan, *United States Foreign Policy in a Revolutionary Age* (Princeton University: Center of International Studies, 1961).

It is the genius of a pluralistic society that relations with a foreign people are conducted simultaneously on both the official and private levels with the minimum of restrictive coordination and the maximum of autonomous and spontaneous initiative. Such an approach works well with mature, open societies, but it has unanticipated consequences in underdeveloped countries, whose social and political structure is not strong enough to absorb the powerful impact of American influence.

Since the war the U.S. government has on several occasions found it necessary to intervene in Philippine affairs in a manner that would not have been acceptable to European allies and may no longer be possible in the Philippines. But it will be necessary for some time to come for government to establish a firm sense of direction. That this is sometimes difficult to do stems from the growth of great administrative divisions—the military and economic missions, for example, which operate on their own premises and create their own policies in almost splendid isolation. There must be more integration of the efforts of these various missions so that the full weight of our influence can be brought to bear in the pursuit of one over-riding objective.

The problem is conceptual, not administrative. It cannot be solved by administrative centralization, for the lack of integration arises from the fact that each mission has its own almost water-tight body of theory or platitudes about the task with which it is entrusted, and it tends to see the rest of the American effort in a supporting role. Put in simple terms, the economic mission sees the role of the military as that of holding back Communist aggression while economic growth takes place, and this in turn will produce political stability. The military mission sees economic aid as a supporting activity which will provide the financial sinews for defense against Communist subversion, and defense contributes to the maintenance of political stability. The cultural mission tries to project an image of America the beautiful by securing a favorable local press and, in effect, discouraging open discussion of U.S. policies, thus supposedly contributing to political stability. Political stability is desirable and attainable if it is understood as the cultivation of attitudes and institutions that further the growth of the Philippines toward national independence and constructive partnership in the free world. If dynamic growth with all its accompanying changes is thought of as the objective, then political stability may well be the by-product. At a time in history when the Philippine Republic is in a stage of acute and rapid social change, sorely testing the social cohesion of Philippine society, our participation in Philippine affairs calls for more than a formal reaffirmation of democratic principles. It demands a shrewd, imaginative, and forthright association with those Filipinos who are most likely to value our partnership and to understand the mutuality of our separate national interests. In spite of our many shortcomings, the record shows that we are more than equal to the task.

Index

Publications of the

FOREIGN AFFAIRS (quarterly), edited by Hamilton Fish Armstrong.

THE UNITED STATES IN WORLD AFFAIRS (annual). Volumes for 1931, 1932 and 1933, by Walter Lippmann and William O. Scroggs; for 1934-1935, 1936, 1937, 1938, 1939 and 1940, by Whitney H. Shepardson and William O. Scroggs; for 1945-1947, 1947-1948 and 1948-1949, by John C. Campbell; for 1949, 1950, 1951, 1952, 1953 and 1954, by Richard P. Stebbins; for 1955, by Hollis W. Barber; for 1956, 1958, 1959, 1960, 1961 and 1962, by Richard P. Stebbins.

DOCUMENTS ON AMERICAN FOREIGN RELATIONS (annual). Volume for 1952 edited by Clarence W. Baier and Richard P. Stebbins; for 1953 and 1954, edited by Peter V. Curl; for 1955, 1956, 1957, 1958 and 1959, edited by Paul E. Zinner; for 1960, 1961 and 1962, edited by Richard P. Stebbins.

POLITICAL HANDBOOK AND ATLAS OF THE WORLD (annual), edited by Walter H. Mallory.

AFRICA: A FOREIGN AFFAIRS READER, edited by Philip W. Quigg.

SOUTHEAST ASIA IN UNITED STATES POLICY, by Russell H. Fifield.

UNESCO: ASSESSMENT AND PROMISE, by George N. Shuster.

THE PEACEFUL ATOM IN FOREIGN POLICY, by Arnold Kramish.

THE ARABS AND THE WORLD: Nasser's Arab Nationalist Policy, by Charles D. Cremeans.

TOWARD AN ATLANTIC COMMUNITY, by Christian A. Herter.

THE SOVIET UNION, 1922-1962: A Foreign Affairs Reader, edited by Philip E. Mosely.

THE POLITICS OF FOREIGN AID: American Experience in Southeast Asia, by John D. Montgomery.

SPEARHEADS OF DEMOCRACY: Labor in the Developing Countries, by George C. Lodge.

LATIN AMERICA: Diplomacy and Reality, by Adolf A. Berle.

THE ORGANIZATION OF AMERICAN STATES AND THE HEMISPHERE CRISIS, by John C. Dreier.

THE UNITED NATIONS: Structure for Peace, by Ernest A. Gross.

THE LONG POLAR WATCH: Canada and the Defense of North America, by Melvin Conant.

ARMS AND POLITICS IN LATIN AMERICA (Revised Edition), by Edwin Lieuwen.

THE FUTURE OF UNDERDEVELOPED COUNTRIES: Political Implications of Economic Development (Revised Edition), by Eugene Staley.

SPAIN AND DEFENSE OF THE WEST: Ally and Liability, by Arthur P. Whitaker.

SOCIAL CHANGE IN LATIN AMERICA TODAY: Its Implications for United States Policy, by Richard N. Adams, John P. Gillin, Allan R. Holmberg, Oscar Lewis, Richard W. Patch, and Charles W. Wagley.

FOREIGN POLICY: THE NEXT PHASE: The 1960s (Revised Edition), by Thomas K. Finletter.

DEFENSE OF THE MIDDLE EAST: Problems of American Policy (Revised Edition), by John C. Campbell.

COMMUNIST CHINA AND ASIA: Challenge to American Policy, by A. Doak Barnett.

FRANCE, TROUBLED ALLY: De Gaulle's Heritage and Prospects, by Edgar S. Furniss, Jr.

THE SCHUMAN PLAN: A Study in Economic Cooperation, 1950-1959, by William Diebold, Jr.

SOVIET ECONOMIC AID: The New Aid and Trade Policy in Underdeveloped Countries, by Joseph S. Berliner.

RAW MATERIALS: A Study of American Policy, by Percy W. Bidwell.

NATO AND THE FUTURE OF EUROPE, by Ben T. Moore.

AFRICAN ECONOMIC DEVELOPMENT, by William Hame.

INDIA AND AMERICA: A Study of Their Relations, by Phillips Talbot and S. L. Poplai.

JAPAN BETWEEN EAST AND WEST, by Hugh Borton, Jerome B. Cohen, William J. Jorden, Donald Keene, Paul F. Langer and C. Martin Wilbur.

NUCLEAR WEAPONS AND FOREIGN POLICY, by Henry A. Kissinger.

MOSCOW-PEKING AXIS: Strengths and Strains, by Howard L. Boorman, Alexander Eckstein, Philip E. Mosely and Benjamin Schwartz.

RUSSIA AND AMERICA: Dangers and Prospects, by Henry L. Roberts.

FOREIGN AFFAIRS BIBLIOGRAPHY, 1942-1952, by Henry L. Roberts.

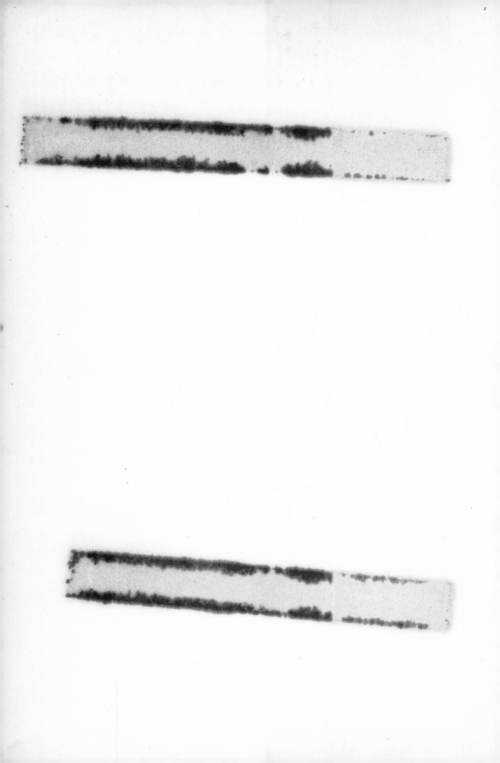